WITHDRAWN
UTSA Libraries

RENEWALS 458-4574

Lyric Poetry

Lyric Poetry

THE PAIN AND THE PLEASURE
OF WORDS

Mutlu Konuk Blasing

PRINCETON UNIVERSITY PRESS

PRINCETON AND OXFORD

Library
University of Texas
at San Antonio

Copyright © 2007 by Princeton University Press
Published by Princeton University Press, 41 William Street,
Princeton, New Jersey 08540
In the United Kingdom: Princeton University Press, 3 Market Place,
Woodstock, Oxfordshire OX20 1SY
Requests for permission to reproduce material from this work should be sent to Permissions,
Princeton University Press.

All Rights Reserved

LIBRARY OF CONGRESS CATALOGING-IN-PUBLICATION DATA

Blasing, Mutlu Konuk, 1944–
Lyric poetry : the pain and the pleasure of words / Mutlu Konuk Blasing.
p.   cm.
Includes bibliographical references and index.
ISBN-13: 978-0-691-12682-1 (cl : acid-free paper)
ISBN-10: 0-691-12682-8 (cl : acid-free paper)
1. Lyric poetry—History and criticism. I. Title.
PN1356.B63   2006
809.1′04—dc22   2005056497

British Library Cataloging-in-Publication Data is available

Permission to reprint the following material is gratefully acknowledged:
Excerpts from "Burnt Norton," from *Four Quartets* by T. S. Eliot, copyright © 1936
by Harcourt, Inc. and renewed 1964 by T. S. Eliot. Reprinted by permission of the publisher.

"The Tree" by Ezra Pound, from *Personae*, copyright © 1926 by Ezra Pound. Reprinted
by permission of New Directions Publishing Corporation.

Excerpt from "Said the Poet to the Analyst," from *To Bedlam and Part Way Back*
by Anne Sexton. Copyright © 1960 by Anne Sexton, renewed 1988 by Linda G. Sexton.
Reprinted by permission of Houghton Mifflin Company. All rights reserved.

This book has been composed in Adobe Caslon

Printed on acid-free paper. ∞

pup.princeton.edu

Printed in the United States of America

1 3 5 7 9 10 8 6 4 2

Library
University of Texas
at San Antonio

For John

CONTENTS

ACKNOWLEDGMENTS

I AM GRATEFUL TO Randy Blasing for his encouragement and many useful suggestions through the years; to Nancy Armstrong, for her support and helpful comments; to Hanne Winarsky, whose interest in this book made it possible; to Ellen Foos and Kathleen Cioffi, for seeing it into print; and, finally, to both readers for Princeton University Press, whose responses were invaluable to me as I made my final revisions.

Lyric Poetry

Introduction

❖

"MAKING CHOICE OF A HUMAN SELF"

It is the human that is the alien.
—*Wallace Stevens*

POETRY HAS PRESENTED a problem for disciplinary discourse from the beginning. "There is an ancient quarrel between philosophy and poetry," Plato declares; he gives no evidence and makes no argument as to why poetry would have a quarrel with philosophy, but his own discourse offers clear evidence of philosophy's issue with poetry. Poets are banned from the Republic, ostensibly on the grounds that mimetic fictions are imitations of imitations and thus twice removed from Truth. This threat to the discourse of Truth would not in itself pose a practical danger if it didn't also appeal to something "within us" that does: these "productions which are far removed from truth . . . are also the companions and friends and associates of a principle within us which is equally removed from reason" (1974, 77, 73). If "epic or lyric verse" is allowed into the state, "not law and the reason of mankind . . . but pleasure and pain will be the rulers in our state" (76). For along with the "manly" principle of reason, is a "womanly," "other principle, which inclines us to recollection of our troubles and to lamentation, and can never have enough of them, [which] we may call irrational, useless, and cowardly" (75, 74).[1] The real threat, then, is not mimesis but a language use that mobilizes emotions, the variability and inconstancy of which pose a further problem (75). While "reason" would standardize a citizenry of coherent, self-determining subjects in charge of the "city" within their souls, the "other principle" is subject to variations, both within and among individuals. Poetry plays to the volatile part of our "nature" and thus has the power to create "bad" cities: it can move the "promiscuous crowd" at "public festivals," for it is a "sort of rhetoric which is addressed to a crowd of men, women, and children, freemen and slaves" (75, 37).

On the social level, poetry threatens the project of establishing order in the "city" within the citizen as well as in the city of discourse;[2] it stirs unruly emotions, which are subject to different kinds of persuasions, and it has mass appeal.[3] But at the discursive level, the threat of poetry is not a threat of anarchy, for the autonomous, stringent orders of the linguistic and formal codes are evident. Rather, it is the threat of a different system underwriting—and, therefore, in effect overruling—the order of reason. What imperils rational language is what enables it: a nonrational linguistic system that is logically and genetically prior to its rational deployment. The mimetic theory of poetry is a disciplinary suppression of the emotional and nonrational public power of the linguistic code itself for the philosophical agenda, and it paves the way for banning poetry for the political agenda. Representations must be politically controlled, but before that, the power of the linguistic code itself must be discursively controlled, which is precisely what a mimetic theory of poetry ensures.[4]

Thus one is tempted to say that the attack on mimesis is something of a red herring. And it keeps on working. Even defenses of poetry remain within the framework of mimesis, representation, and "Truth"—although, of course, "Truth" keeps changing and Representation, for instance, can come to be the truth that poems represent. More important, the philosophical ban on linguistic emotion—a ban on the emotional power of language itself, which poetry focuses and intensifies—is also still at work. It has succeeded in keeping linguistic emotion out of the critical discourse on poetry by limiting our conception of poetic emotion to imitations, representations, or presentations of real-life emotions. Remarkably, there is no established critical vocabulary, theory, or methodology to engage the nature of specifically poetic emotion that draws on the rhetorical power of the affectively charged materials of language.

Such linguistic emotion and the relation it bears to the systematic formality of poetic language are among the questions that concern me in this study. Although I begin with Plato's ban on poetry, my project does not belong to the genre of "pittiful defence[s] of poore Poetry."[5] I invoke Plato only because I attempt to think of poetic language outside a Platonic framework and account for poetic emotion without swerving to the grounds of mimesis, representation, and truth. I focus on lyric poetry, where an "I" talks to itself or to nobody in particular and is not primarily concerned with narrating a story or dramatizing an action. Without these other ends in view, the lyric presents us with poetic language per se, which is my subject.

Lyric poetry is not mimesis. Above everything else, it is a formal practice that keeps in view the linguistic code and the otherness of the material medium of language to all that humans do with it—refer, represent, express, narrate, imitate, communicate, think, reason, theorize, philosophize. It offers an experience of another kind of order, a system that operates independently of the production of the meaningful discourse that it enables. This is a mechanical system with its own rules, procedures, and history. It works with a kind of logic that is oblivious to discursive logic.

The nonrational order that the formality of poetic language keeps audible is distinct from any cultivated, induced, pathological, or "deviant" irrationality, or the irrationality of dreams and other comparable experiences, which certain poetic practices may invoke. Nor is it to be understood as some "primal" irrationality. Such "irrationals" implicitly affirm logical language as the norm, but precisely that norm is in question in the formality of poetic language per se, which is not oriented in relation to reference and rational discourse. It is simply another "language," another system of communication,[6] and it commands power, for every speaker of a language emotionally responds to the language itself, even though complex ideas and figures may not be any more accessible to everyone than philosophical thought would be. The formal materiality of poetic language makes for its radically *popular* basis. And the more regular the patterns of the verse are, the more popular the verse. As Robert Frost puts it, the "spirit" of poetry is "safest in the keeping of the none too literate—people who know it by heart" (1968, 55).

Poetic language cannot be understood as deviating from or opposing a norm of rational language,[7] because poetic forms clearly accommodate referential use of language and rational discourse. But they position most complex thought processes and rigorous figurative logic as figures on the ground of processes that are in no way rational. When poetry construes the symbolic function and logical operations as kinds of games one can play with language—right along-side wordplays and rhymes—all superstructures, all claims to extralinguistic "truths," are in jeopardy. Poetry is a cultural institution dedicated to remembering and displaying the emotionally and historically charged materiality of language, on which logical discourse would establish its hold.[8] It poses an ever-present danger for rational discourse, which must, for example, vigilantly guard against such poetic encroachments as alliterations or rhymes in "serious" prose. By contrast, in poetry words that carry the most import are highlighted as such by rhyming with other important words, by carrying more than one sense, or by where the beat falls. Poetry "argues" by appealing to the authority of the linguistic system, and poetic forms can host rational discourse, but not the other way around. While poetry ensures a constant alternation or pulse of sense and nonsense, rational discourse cannot afford to flash glimpses of the nonsensical, absurd, material base of the superstructure that it is.[9] Reason needs to establish and maintain itself as what is "not nonrational."

Thus one must not—if one wants to think poetry as such—posit an "unconscious" or "instincts" or any bodily "drives" to account for the power of poetry and its threat to rational discourse. Even if we were to recognize such entities, their relevance to poetry is highly questionable. Indeed, all such extralinguistic "irrationals" are historically and culturally specific disciplinary constructions of the "others" of disciplinary discourse, and they work only to confirm the priority of rational language. But poetry foregrounds a linguistic nonrational that is not a byproduct of reason; rather, it is the ground on which rational language and disciplinary discourses carve their territories, draw their borders, and designate their "irrational" others.

Just as the disciplinary state in the service of Truth must rule out and/or censor poetry, so must any disciplinary discourse in pursuit of truth, for the status of language is always at stake: it must remain a neutral, stable instrument of thought. Certainly, the thinkers who shaped modern disciplinary thought register the threat of poetry. Marx, for example, started out with poetic ambitions but abandoned poetry for philosophy. Poetry was unsettling: "Everything real grew vague," he writes his father in 1837, "and all that is vague lacks *boundaries*." He decides to focus on "positive studies only"—"I burned all my poems"—and to demonstrate "our mental nature to be just as determined, concrete, and firmly established as our physical."[10] Freud started with hysteria and the dangerous contamination of language—the contagion of the body, affect, and the operations of the linguistic code—but he abandoned hysteria to establish his "science" of psychoanalysis. Saussure abandoned his fascinating early work on anagrammatically inscribed names in Saturnian funerary verse, which display the compulsions of language and jeopardize its status as an instrument of communication, in order to formulate a "science" of linguistics. In a sense, these disciplines implicitly draw the line at poetry as something that must be exorcised, displaced, or bracketed in order to establish their "territories," carve out their "nation-states." Disciplinary discourse inaugurates itself as "not poetry." This rough outline, which would require another project to fill in, is meant only to point to the special, extradisciplinary status of poetic language and its fundamental challenge to any rational discourse in pursuit of truth.

Today poetry is largely ignored by literary studies because it forces the question of the category of the poetic as such, for poetry does not respond very well to current constructions of the "discipline" of literary study, which emphasize the social, economic, or political determinants of literary production. Literary production may be so determined, but critical approaches to poetry from these angles cannot tell us much about the nature and function of poetic language, which may be said to be the marker of the literary, the presumed object of literary study.[11] The form that the disciplinary censoring of lyric poetry takes today is a determined evasion of the special status of poetic language as such. Under the mandate to "historicize," for example, the lyric reduces to a documentary of the inner experiences and private affairs of a bourgeois "individual." The lyric is a foundational genre, and its history spans millennia;[12] it comprises a wide variety of practices, ranging in the West from Sappho to rap. "Historicizing" the lyric as essentially a late-eighteenth- and nineteenth-century European invention in effect universalizes a historically and geographically specific model of a subject.[13] And the term "lyric," still used in this sense, has come to serve as an ideological weapon in the ongoing politicized poetry wars. Whether the lyric is read as oppositional or complicitous, it is still understood to be the self-expression of a prior, private, constitutive subject.

Lyric language is a radically public language,[14] but it will not submit to treatment as a social document—of a certain stage of capitalism, for example—because there is no "individual" in the lyric in any ordinary sense of the term. The lyric makes audible a virtual subjectivity in the shape of a given language, a mother tongue, and the historical permutations of the concept and status of an "individual" are not of help in understanding poetic subjectivity, which will elude methodologies that assume that concept as a given—itself a Western bourgeois assumption.[15] The emphasis on an extralinguistic "individual" is a historically specific form that the repression of the material and formal rhetoric of poetic language takes. For the subject represented *in* or *by* or *as* the poem's referential language, the subject that is its fiction, is absolutely distinct from the subject produced and heard in the voice, rhythm, and sound shape of the poem.

In the form of a poem the prescriptive shape of the language itself becomes audible, and the "voice"—an individuating emotional inflection and rhythm, a voiceprint of a speaker—is heard in and as its manner of submission to the constraints of a prescriptive code. While the sorrows of the bourgeois "individual" may be a historically specific resonance of the lyric subject's discourse of alienation, the alienation in poetic language is not specific to lyrics of bourgeois subjectivity: it is the enabling condition of subjectivity in language. The concept and status of an a priori "individual" are always already in question in a language that foregrounds the rules of the linguistic and formal codes; a subject is historically formulated in language precisely by subjection to a preexisting system that at once socializes and individuates it. Language produces the subject, not the other way around. The lyric "I" is a metaleptic figure, an Apollonian illusion of an "individual" projected upon, to use Nietzsche's words, "a piece of fate" (1979, 54).

The current forms of disciplinary censoring of poetry themselves trace back to the nineteenth century. T. S. Eliot writes that at the end of the eighteenth century "the attitude towards poetry" and "the expectations and demands made upon it" changed significantly, as the "decay of religion, and the attrition of political institutions left dubious frontiers upon which the poet encroached." Wordsworth and Coleridge are not just "demolishing a debased tradition, but revolting against a whole social order; they begin to make claims for poetry which reach their highest point of exaggeration in Shelley's famous phrase, 'poets are the unacknowledged legislators of mankind.'" While in Shelley we get a first in "this tradition" of poets as "Nature's M.P.'s," the other reading of the poet as "priest" results in Matthew Arnold's notion of poetry as substitute religion—"coffee without caffeine, tea without tannin"—which is "extended" and "travestied" by the "art for art's sake" position (1986, 16).

The exaggerated expectations placed on poetry in the nineteenth century leads to a kind of criticism that views poetry as a pretext for discourses compelled by other agendas. "For Johnson," Eliot writes, "poetry was still poetry, and not another thing"; in the nineteenth century, however, we have "critics who do not so much practice criticism as make use of it for other purposes" (1986, 57). If lyric poetry is dismissed today as an anachronistic, nineteenth-century phenomenon, the criteria used for this judgment are nineteenth-century, moralistic, normative criteria following from expectations that poetry do something other than poetry—the expectations of a last-ditch humanism.

And when it turns out that poetry doesn't do anything other than poetry—that it does not do what it "should" or "could" do—it disappoints and becomes irrelevant to the huge social and political problems that are understood to be the moral burden of literary study to address, and thus redress, so to speak, the failure of poetry to do so.[16]

Literary study is a rational enterprise, of course, and if, as Eliot put it, the question "What is poetry?" posits the critical function (1986, 10), it also necessarily posits a discursive erasure of poetry. Poetry generates discourses of "truth," given its constitutive split between sound and sense, "appearances" and "reality." Yet it becomes dispensable to the discourses it generates, reducing to a means to the end of truth—whether the "real" meaning of the text or its refusal of stable meanings, or its historical, social, political, or ideological determinants or agendas. Truth keeps receding behind representational "appearances" of various sorts. In all cases, though, the physical materials of the text, the ground of all sorts of discursive "appearances," remain superfluous, outside the game of meaning and the disciplinary borders of literary study.

Wlad Godzich, discussing Paul de Man, points out that criticism is "a form of language trained upon reason" and it aims to "permit" meaning to speak directly, "in its own voice," rather than through representation and mediating figures (1983, xxvi). Criticism aims at transparency, at stripping the text of its figural "appearances"; it works with "the premise that meaning, or the truth, is not 'at home' in the language of representation of the primary text" (xxiii). This is no doubt true. Yet if "appearances" is only a figure for figurative language, the specialness of poetry again disappears from view, for we are again within the framework of a discourse of representation and truth or the lack thereof. This is, in effect, "transparency" at another level, for the material reality of poetic language is now relegated to the category of "appearances" at a different level—and this done so "naturally" that it doesn't seem to need mentioning. For the "premise" *here* is that the discourse of truth and representation is not "at home" in the materiality of the primary text. But figural and "rational" languages alike depend on a prior material language and a prior operation that gets us from the material letters and sounds to words. And that operation cannot be subsumed under the rubric of figuration because it has a history. We did not come with language; we have all had to learn it. To dismiss the materiality of language is to dismiss the emotionally charged history that made us who we are—subjects in language, which is the subject of the lyric.

As important as de Man's work is for reading the rhetoric of poetry, it draws the line at the rhetoric of the linguistic code itself and the history of our emotional relationship to the code. Here his insight into the blindness of theory is disarming, and I want to consider in some detail his resistance to what resists theory. Writing on Walter Benjamin's "The Task of the Translator," de Man explains the demystification translation performs as it foregrounds the slippage between what one means and the way one means:

> To mean "bread," when I need to name bread, I have the word *Brot*, so that the way in which I mean is by using the word *Brot*. The translation will reveal a fundamental discrepancy between the intent to name *Brot* and the word *Brot* itself in its materiality, as a device of meaning. If you hear *Brot* in this context of Hölderlin, . . . I hear *Brot und Wein* necessarily, which is the great Hölderlin text that is very much present in this [text]— which in French becomes *Pain et vin*. "*Pain et vin*" is what you get for free in a restaurant, in a cheap restaurant where it is still included, so *pain et vin* has very different connotations from *Brot und Wein*. It brings to mind the *pain français, baguette, ficelle, bâtard,* all those things—I now hear in *Brot* "bastard." This upsets the stability of the quotidian. I was very happy with the word *Brot*, which I hear as a native because my native language is Flemish and you say *brood*, just like in German, but if I have to think that *Brot [brood]* and *pain* are the same thing, I get very upset. It is all right in English because "bread" is close enough to *Brot [brood]*, despite the idiom "bread" for money, which has its problems. But the stability of my quotidian, of my daily bread, the reassuring quotidian aspects of the word "bread," daily bread, is upset by the French word *pain*. What I mean is upset by the way in which I mean—the way in which it is *pain*, the phoneme, the term *pain*, which has its set of connotations which take you in a completely different direction. (1989, 87)

This lively account of what "upsets" a "native speaker" goes to the heart of poetic language, the "disarticulation"—the suffering, the pain—of language that Benjamin talks about and that Nietzsche addressed before him. But de Man reduces the issue to one of quotidian comforts, and his tone already makes light of it. Later, he wants to take back this passage; it was just aiming for a "cheap laugh."[17] He admits and backs off from feelings for words in the mother tongue—surely not irrelevant to a writer, reader, or theorist of poetry. For poetic experience is at once an experience of the inhumanity of the linguistic code, its obliviousness to meaning, and of the personal feelings that are nevertheless attached to its material elements.

The paragraph immediately following the passage above begins, "This disjunction is best understood (to take it to a more familiar theoretical problem) in terms of the difficult relationship between the hermeneutics and the poetics of literature" (1989, 87–88). Recasting the disjunction between meaning and the way of meaning in the terms of hermeneutics and poetics—the mutually exclusive pursuits of attending to the extralinguistic meaning or to the form of poetic language—theoretically neutralizes precisely that which, in language, constitutes the "resistance to theory." As de Man admits, when one tries to achieve a "complementarity" of hermeneutics and poetics, "the poetics always drops out, and what one always does is hermeneutics. One is so attracted by problems of meaning that it is impossible to do hermeneutics and poetics at the same time. . . . The two are not complementary, the two may be mutually exclusive . . ." (88). The "one" who "always" prefers to do hermeneutics is the one who draws his disciplinary limit on this side of the "I" who is "upset" by *pain*. Another "one" may "always" prefer to do poetics but would draw the same line, excising emotion.

The "familiar theoretical problem" recuperates "quotidian" comforts, dismissing the historical and emotional charge of words in the native tongue. And to erase linguistic affect or emotion, whether one is doing hermeneutics or poetics, is to erase linguistic intention or motivation—precisely what enables meaningful language, the conditions for which poetry spells out. Only a theoretical accounting of the rhetoric of the language itself—and thus, at another level, of poetic forms—would get us out of the hermeneutics/poetics binary by instituting the history formative of the subject at that divide, as what generates that divide.

The passage I have quoted presents a phenomenon that does not come under hermeneutics or poetics, because it raises the question of personal and cultural histories in the native tongue. A cultural and personal connotational intension (*intensio*) historically intentionalizes the word in the mother tongue. This kind of history falls in the crack of the disciplinary binary; it is voiced as an "I" who *prefers* to say "*Brot*" to intend bread because, for example, he "hears" it in the "context of Hölderlin." But this "I" also prefers to say "*Brot*" because he has had to say "*Brot*": he has had to *intend* the phonemic sequence that constitutes the word "*Brot*." Here a personal history of intention embedded in the prescriptive word, rather than in Hölderlin, is at issue.

Insofar as "we obey the law" to "function within language," de Man writes, "there can be no intent; there may be an intent of meaning, but there is no intent in the purely formal way in which we will use language independently of the sense or the meaning" (1989, 87). That is, I can intend the object bread but not the word "bread," for it is already a "given." Yet I have *already* intended to say "bread"; I have a history of desiring and learning to produce the sounds of that word out of random noise and muscular activity. "I" am *constituted* as one who has inaugurally intended the word "bread"—and thus did "my" part to make sure that it stays a "given." The word "in its materiality" is not just "a device of meaning," and the way we use language is not "purely formal," because we are historically bonded to the physical materials of words. Thus it is not only the cultural connotations that make words in different languages mean differently but the sound shape of words and the auditory and muscular memories that cluster around word sounds and make for one's emotional relationships to them: *pain* just doesn't feel anything like *Brot* in one's mouth.

The divide between meaning and the way of meaning, which can only be duplicated on a theoretical register, is historically created, and it is the foundation of a history that is not just a constant deferral but a constant choice and motivation of meaning, which de Man's wording represses: "the phoneme, the term *pain*, which has its connotations" conflates a "phoneme" with a "term," a meaningful set of phonemes. Perhaps it is the English "pain" that underwrites this passage and tells the real story: the pain of the phoneme that must be subsumed by the "term *pain*" in order to carry on discourse and make sure that "pleasure and pain" will not be the "rulers in our state." De Man evades the question whether, for a native speaker, the phonemes themselves might not be connotationally intensified; he evades the historical event of the phoneme and the history whereby sounds come to be phonemes and phonemes come to make up "terms." In the beginning was not a phoneme, let alone a word.

As for Benjamin, the apocalyptic thrust of his essay is that translation gestures toward a pure language, stripped of emotional connotations, history, and therefore the possibility of intention. Such "meaning-less" language obviates a subject and becomes a sort of god, and translation points the way to that "Word": it "provisionally" comes to terms "with the foreignness of languages" (1969, 75)—above all one's own—by cleansing language of personal and cultural connotational histories and revealing its "inhumanity"—its independence, in de Man's words, "of any intent or any drive or any wish or any desire we might have" (96). Language "does things so radically out of control," he adds, that "they cannot be assimilated into the human at all" (101).

Is a "human" a rational creature, a given prior to or outside of language, who *ought* to be in control of language? Is a "human" one who "forgets" the inhumanity of the code in which he or she became a "human"? The revealed "foreignness" of the inhuman code "upsets" the personal and historical at-home-ness in the mother tongue. It is an alienation from the "human." Yet this is what poetry does in the first place: it remembers what the "human" forgot—that he is not God.[18] With poetry, we must think of language as a foreign mechanism *and* an intimate, constitutive history *at the same time*. We are never at home in poetry, for we experience at once the foreignness of the familiar language and the intimacy of the alien code. Translation "rationalizes" the alienation and loses the sense of the *unheimlich* that is at the heart of poetry, the experience of the intimate otherness of the mechanical operations of the linguistic code and of our histories, both personal and communal. This is an experience of the nothingness of the "human." A subject produced in language can only mean by means of an inhuman code, which it has had to master in order to be "human"—that is, a medium to pass on the linguistic code, along with the genetic code. The subject of poetry, the "I," is "human" only insofar as she is able to maintain and communicate an intimacy with the inhuman linguistic code by which she became "human."[19] This is why the subject in language is not "human" in any ordinary sense of the term, and we need to think poetry outside humanism.[20]

The critical opposition of poetics and hermeneutics duplicates the oppositions forced by the irreducible formality of poetic language: form/content,
sound/sense, materiality/reference, signifier/signified, semiotic/semantic, lan-
guage/discourse, appearances/reality, body/mind, and so on. Poetic language
generates these hierarchical theoretical oppositions yet resists their terms because, clearly, the hierarchies do not hold in poetry. Two different kinds of
language are at work simultaneously in a poetic text. What are merely distinct
linguistic practices are cast as theoretical oppositions only from a discursive
perspective that necessarily privileges meaning over the way of meaning. In the
largest terms, my argument is that poetic language generates such theoretical
oppositions yet resists their terms because it remembers the history that creates
the gaps internal to language. These distinctions come to be posited through
a lived history of language acquisition, the passage from body language into
symbolic language.

This very process by which a generic subject, one who can say "I," comes to
be formulated in language also formulates an individuated "I," one with a specific history of acquiring a specific language. The lyric "remembers" both an
individuating history and the generic history that draws the boundary of the
mind as it draws the boundary of the body. But "remembers" is in quotation
marks, because that traumatic history is consigned to oblivion by infantile amnesia; poetry "remembers" by dismembering abstract language into its materials and by "re-membering" the materials of words into coherent abstract meanings. Thus, perhaps, remembers also should not be in quotation marks, because
the possibility of such an operation requires access, at some level, to what
infantile amnesia "forgets."

The lyric "I" stands at the divide between the semiotic[21] and the semantic
systems and underwrites symbolic language—or endorses it with its signature.[22] The lyric confirms the *necessity* for an "I" to intentionalize the linguistic
code. It is the site of a choice, an ethical "meta-phoring" of the material language into meaning. The historical crossing that creates the conceptual gap is
recrossed by the individuated/socialized "I" created in that process. The fateful
crossing is intentionalized in its repetition by an "I," an emotion, an ethos, a
character, a rhythmic pulse between sound and sense. The "I" sounds the status
of the "human" itself—an animal with a past. But, because the "I" crosses into
language in a mother tongue, its character or ethos also sounds the historical
truth of a linguistic community—those who share a particular experience of
the trauma that produces "humans." Poetry invokes the emotional texture of
the materials of the mother tongue so as to remember and transmit this
personal-communal history.

The first part of my study develops my theory of lyric language, and central to
my theory is the phenomenon of a mother tongue. The universality of lyric
poetry suggests that it has a general social function apart from the varieties of

local functions different poetic practices may serve in different times, places, and cultures. Any such general function, however, can only be understood in terms of a specific mother tongue. The phenomenon of a mother tongue has not received much notice in poetic theory, which is surprising, because it is a fact that poetry lives only in its native tongue; it does not translate without a loss of its emotional charge.[23] Certainly, the sound shape of a poem, formally spelling the necessities of a specific language, cannot be translated. But why should that entail an emotional loss? How do the necessities of linguistic and formal codes make for an untranslatable "excess" emotion distinct from the translatable emotions that may comprise the content of a poem? Since poetry communicates emotional experiences, these questions are crucial, and they lead me to consider the process of language acquisition in order to account for the affective charge of the mother tongue and the emotional function of the formality of poetic language.

The mother tongue is charged with individuating emotional histories, both personal and communal, and poetic forms focus this charge by stylizing the distinguishing sonic and rhythmic qualities of a language. The emotions that make for the subject matter of poetry tend to be associated with such universal experiences as love, loss, and death. Such real-life emotions are not of poetic concern, and they are relatively translatable to other languages, as are thoughts and images. Yet they are experienced differently in translation, because the sound shape, the measures, and the rhythm of a poem, the way the material properties of a language are patterned to make for, in Wallace Stevens's words, "the particular tingle in a proclamation / That makes it say the little thing it says," will not translate (1951, 84). The emotional charge of a poem dissipates in translation because specifically poetic emotion—properly, literary emotion—is produced by a formal deployment of the emotional values of linguistic materials. And the formality of the language, its "beautiful necessities,"[24] grants the lyric an authority to speak of such universal givens as love, loss, time, and death, which constitute generic lyric topics. Because poetic language invokes the intrinsic authority of the linguistic code and affirms its necessities, it elicits in the reader an experience of recognizing "truth."[25] Native readers recognize both the necessities of the code as facts and their constitutive emotional history in that code. Thus they are predisposed to an acute personal recognition of the real-life givens that they might otherwise feel as only vaguely concerning themselves.

Again, poetry forces us to think of language as formal mechanism and as history at the same time. The formal disciplining of language that stresses the prescriptive shape and rules of the linguistic code also licenses variable, untheorizable responses to sounds. Meter, for example, is a regimentation of ordinary language, but it serves precisely to relax the discipline of referential use and set us free among the materials of language. Yet the network of associations proliferating around linguistic materials cannot be regulated by the linguistic code or by its formal representation. These associations draw on a historically accrued surplus emotion, in excess of the code per se. The emotions that the lyric may express are entirely different from this surplus emotion, which is an experienced event, not the hallucinated emotion of identification with a speaker and his or her emotions on the mimetic model. Feelings for words, feelings "inhering for the writer in particular words or phrases," are distinct, as Eliot argues, from emotions that are not of the order of art, emotions that art may express (1932, 8). Such feelings for words are specific to the authors and readers in the native tongue,[26] and the lyric subject articulates personal relationships to the material code with the communal emotional texture of the language. The speaking "I," whose position any reader occupies, is a radically social construct within a linguistic community.[27]

The lyric "I" makes the communal personality of a people audible. It both resounds individuating histories and formally transmits public traditions of how a linguistic community has patterned and remembered the material in excess of referential functions. It does not exist apart from these constitutive histories; it articulates them as what articulate it. Communities cohere around linguistic experience, and poetry is the ritualized confirmation of that coherence—explicitly so in preliterate languages. The communal being is audible in the materials of language, not in what a poem says. For with the material losses of translation, the historical textures of a language—its connotational resources, allusive networks, emotional associations, rhythmic memories, and so on—are all lost. Poetry transmits a cultural history that coheres around the systematic mechanisms of language. Translation loses that historical texture; it reduces language to merely an arbitrary system, silences both the "I" and the communal being, and nullifies the generic, language-specific authority and social power of poetry.

Because I focus on the formality of poetic language in order to engage its nonformal work, I venture into a number of disciplinary territories to provide a series of different perspectives on poetic language. My excursionary method aims to present a "virtual" subjectivity, a mother tongue, poetic form, and individuating personal and communal emotional histories as a gestalt that may be engaged via any one of its constituents, each of which hinges on the others and positions them in different configurations. There is no established disciplinary procedure or terminology for engaging poetic language as both linguistic and formal structures and personal and communal emotional histories. Thus I approach poetry not only through poetics but by way of linguistics, psychology, psychoanalytic theory, and studies of language acquisition.

The process of language acquisition is central to my theory of the lyric. Insofar as we are not born with language, we are not born "human." We become human through the historical experience of acquiring a language. Without this universal historicizing passage that each human must undergo, there would be no history of any kind.[28] But the specifics of this history are infinitely variable, depending on specific languages; time and place; social systems, classes, and cultures; and sets of caretakers and domestic arrangements—all imaginable variables of historically and culturally specific circumstances. Poetic language remembers the history that constitutes a speaking subject in a given language, and this history must be factored into a theoretical accounting of poetry and poetic form. Poetry commemorates a universal historical experience and rests on the historical specificity of the experience of becoming human by mastering a specific code and entering a linguistic and social system. There is no a priori human in poetry.

Language is emotionally charged *because* it has to be acquired. Infants are socialized into language by learning to hear and communicate emotion and thus intentionalize acoustic and muscular phenomena. And clearly, emotion would be differently contoured and communicated in different linguistic communities. But learning language is both an emotional training and a physiological disciplining of the organic body, to make it produce recognizable phonemes, the elements of a linguistic code. This is a primal history, so to speak, of the training of the oral zone—a sexually charged zone because of its link to alimentary functions and survival—to produce linguistic sounds. Infants are seduced into discipline, and the individuated/socialized subject is formulated at a crux of pain and pleasure. Poetry formally returns to that crux, to the emotionally charged history of the disciplining and seduction into language; it affirms the seductions of laws and the pleasures of discipline, always keeping in view the alien code and the pain of language.

Learning language involves training oral muscular activity to zone the noises produced in the larynx—in response not just to auditory but to multimedia reception—into segments of a linguistic code and of that code into sense or symbolic value. The code is a learned mechanism that historically sutures the organic body to symbolic language. And the lyric is grounded not on the body but on its history, which is what we hear in the materiality of lyric language.[29] Poetic language reveals that machinery and the constitutive alienation of the "human," as bodily produced events are "meta-phored" or translated into signifying units and come to circulate as social currency.[30]

The only ground, the only "outside" of poetic language is this lived history of somatically mastering the mechanisms of the linguistic code (mental mastery cannot be in question for creatures who cannot add one and one and get two) and the socializing emotional training that motivates and enables such mastery. Thus the "outside" of poetry constitutes its core, a history that shows the "other"—of both mind and body—to be "me." Poetry is the discourse of the constitutive alienation of the subject in language—the alienation that constitutes the genesis of the "human." And it speaks a kind of "second language," which must also be acquired, to graph the vernacular of communication into the grid of a cultural discourse called "poetry"—a set of conventions, forms, devices, and schemes that foreground the linguistic code, which must then be re-turned into sense.

This is not to say that ordinary language genetically or generically precedes poetic language; the sequencing above is for the purposes of argument. It cannot be said that ordinary language exists prior to poetic language, which articulates the rules of the semiotic code that must be passed on to ensure the cultural survival of the linguistic community and to enable ordinary language to carry on its business. It could be argued that ordinary language is a refinement of the poetic exercise of the rhetorical power of the material medium itself. Thus poetic devices that focus this power cannot be construed as decorative additions to some prior discursive language; rather, these devices foreground the emergence of discourse out of the mechanisms of the code—and even *their* emergence out of noise. Poetic forms remember that the code precedes the symbolic, not the other way around. Eliot writes: "Poetry begins, I dare say, with a savage beating a drum in a jungle, and it retains that essential percussion and rhythm; hyperbolically, one might say that the poet is *older* than other human beings" (1986, 148).

The incommensurability of the semiotic/formal and the semantic/symbolic systems is perceivable as an immediate experience in poetic language, for they work at each other's expense. A poem, far from being a text where sound and sense, form and meaning, are indissolubly one, is a text where we witness the *distinct* operations of the two systems. We can always yield to the seductive call to "stop making sense" and attend to the patterning of non-sense. Or we can choose to switch to the symbolic and make sense. We cannot do both at once, and poetic language will not allow us to ignore either system. Because poetic language is always on the verge of disintegrating into the elements of the code, it forces constant choice. The moat between the two systems—the historically produced gap that produces history—can only be bridged by a groundless choice to mean. The choice of language—willing sounds to make sense and willing sense to be sounded—entails an alienation from the body *and* the mind, from nature *and* reason, and this is the site of the historical and ethical subject, one who subjects herself to language, who freely chooses her fate, because, the second time around, she is in a position to choose and thus validate the socializing/individuating history that constitutes her—that makes her who or what she is.

A subject has this choice because she has a history of intentionalizing sounds; if we came with language, there could be no such choice. And this is an ethical moment—a choice to articulate and affirm an *ethos*, at once a personal and a communal character. Thus the "I" sounds the "communal being" in the act of voicing itself; it confirms and validates both personal and communal histories in language, and its intention to mean is *heard as* a speaking "voice," a rhythm, an *emotion*. Only in these terms can we speak of an "I"—as precisely what sounds the hollowness of the idol "sovereign subject." In poetry we hear, as Stevens puts it, "the inhuman making choice of a human self" (1951, 89). Thus the lyric "I" must be engaged not at the level of representation but both below and above the level of figuration, in terms both of formal schemes and literal processes—meter, rhyme, alliteration, assonance, and all kinds of wordplays that destabilize reference and foreground the mechanism of the code—and the phenomena of rhythm, voice, and emotion motivating the mechanical code.

The process of learning language, the "inscription" of signifying phonemes and words on bodily produced sounds, is intimately implicated in the concurrent process of the erotogenic inscription of a symbolic body over the organic body.[31] This is another individuating/socializing process and another crux of pleasure and pain, of seduction and discipline. Thus language is as sexually charged as sexuality is linguistically charged, and the concurrency of the two processes renders the borders between elements of language and the "textual," erotogenic body permeable, as is clearly seen in psychopathological confusions of the body and language. While psychoanalytic literature engages the operations of the elements of the signifier—letters and phonemes—in the "unconscious" and amply documents the imbrication of language and sexuality, the notion of an "unconscious" is of little help in understanding the poetic "I" because it rests on the repression of the crucial, formative history of language acquisition. It is astonishing that Freud's "science," which covers all facets of sexual development and relies on the operations of the literal and phonemic elements of the signifier in psychic life, never addresses the history of language acquisition and its inseparability from the concurrent history of sexualization.

Instead, Freud isolates the sexualization process and narrativizes it in order not to contaminate language for his rationalist project. A meaningful language must be kept out of the game—it must be something that is always already there. That is the rule of disciplinarity. Subjects coming apart in language, whole sexual scenarios unfolding in linguistic particles, which prove both the foreignness of the code and its emotional, psychosexual hold, would seem to demand attention to the passage into language, an inaugural breach that posits, on the discursive plane, the gap between the material body and the psychic or symbolic body. The "unconscious" is the text of the residual memories of being corralled into language, the most important (in discursive terms) aspect of the general project of disciplining bodily productions. The history of learning language is the repressed element of the "discipline" of psychoanalytic theory; it is the "unconscious" of Freudian theory itself, and it pops up on every page, in the very insistence on the particles of words as they are theoretically re-enlisted in a different signifying system, the "language" of the "unconscious."[32]

The histories of language acquisition and eroticization are as specific to each person as childhood experiences and memories are—or, for that matter, adult histories. Just as each reader has different associations with and responses to an image or a figure based on specific experiences and memories, each reader similarly has different emotional responses to particular verbal sounds and rhythms and is more responsive to some than to others. A poet will move one reader but leave another cold; a given poem will affect different readers differently; an "author's tone of voice" may "repel" or "compel" us (Moore 1987, 32). The history that such personal responses to sounds and rhythms rest on has been "forgotten" by infantile amnesia; as Giorgio Agamben puts it, though, we can consign to oblivion only that which we can never forget—that which makes us who we are (1995, 45). Lyric poetry is a culturally sanctioned discourse that allows us to remember—without remembering—the history that we are. In poetry, we recognize ourselves in an uncanny return of something long forgotten, our origins in the passage into symbolic language.

In view of the remarkable phenomenon of infantile amnesia, I consider the histories that produce human subjects as, properly, traumatic histories. As such, the history of the psychosexual and social subject in language is in principle not recoverable, and the subject thus produced can only be an "other" to itself. This belatedness is properly the structure of a traumatic history, a history we cannot possess the "meaning" of, for *it* possesses *us*. It has already happened before we could know it was happening; we can only "know" *after* language. Poetry recalls the emotional histories attached to the elements of the code "before" they were "forgotten" in language. These emotions are necessarily individuated, since each person lives this trauma differently. But each person's individual emotional relationship to the code is not functional in the operations of instrumental language. While socialization into language individuates a speaker emotionally, the institution of the symbolic has no place for the emotional history left in the wake of the coming of the Word. Poetry does. It provides a room—a *stanza*, in Italian—to recognize our personal relationship to the code, to what produced us and made us who we are. This, however, always entails a recognition of our otherness, of our constitutive split in the entry into language.

The historical breach that produces the subject as an other, the otherness of the bodily produced language to the "body" that can only be articulated in that language, leads me to the topic of hysteria. My purpose in engaging hysteria is to approach the formulation of the subject in language from the perspective offered by its disintegration into the materials and mechanisms of language. I am interested in the linguistic disturbances in hysteria and hysterical symptom formation along paths of figural and phonemic linkages. While the poet insists on the materiality and the somatic production of symbolic language, the hysteric somatizes symbolic language and "speaks" or communicates through the body. Hysterical symptom formation attests to the concurrence of the formulation of the linguistic subject and the erotogenic body; the imbrication of language and sexuality, which informs the linguistic disturbances of hysteria and generates the historically specific notion of an "unconscious" in the work of Freud, is the open secret of lyric language.

The second part of my study explores the kinds of reading practices my theoretical framework would enable. In terms of the genesis of this project, certain reading procedures that poetic texts themselves seemed to call for instigated an account of the centrality of linguistic and formal processes—an account that did not implicitly reduce the surfaces of poetry, the materials of language, and the forms and devices that organize them, to rhetorical reinforcements of the text's import.

My readings of four twentieth-century American poets focus on textual operations and the priority of the linguistic and poetic codes to what each poet may be "saying." The operations of these codes will not allow a reduction of poetry to an expression of an "individual" and his or her theology, ideology, or psychology, and I resist assimilating form to the content of the poems.[33] The order of the chapters in the second part roughly corresponds to the order of the chapters in part 1, and the chapters in the two parts could be interleaved. But I present the two parts separately, for my readings are not meant exactly to illustrate the theoretical arguments. My whole point is that poems do not illustrate any "theories," not even those of the poets. Rather, my readings are meant to show how starting with the perspective of poetic language as such, and thus engaging the texts at the level of the poetic code, opens them up in ways that challenge the canonical criticism of these poets' work.

My choice of poets is neither inevitable nor entirely arbitrary. I have chapters on T. S. Eliot, Wallace Stevens, Ezra Pound, and Anne Sexton. I chose to discuss *Four Quartets* and the *Cantos* because they are works with ideological content, and there exists a body of canonical criticism on them by which to measure the difference of readings that focus on the poems' language, without privileging content. *Four Quartets*, for example, is generally read, through the lens of Eliot's conversion, as a Christian text, presumably positing, and depending on, a prior God/Word to redeem the code. In a microrhetorical reading, however, the poem resolves itself into a set of strategies by which discourse generates itself out of the play of the linguistic code, the discursive productivity of the material elements of the code. Such a reading also historicizes the text I will focus on, "Burnt Norton" (1935), more accurately and less anachronistically by situating it not in the context of Eliot's personal beliefs and politics but in the 1930s at the moment of an economic crisis of representation, which, I would argue, marks the postmodern turn. A microrhetorical reading shows that the only history that is specific enough to be relevant to the poem is audible or detectible in the texture of its language. In "Burnt Norton," the governing rules of the code produce the "value" of a metaphysical surplus—not the other way around.

The canonical defense of Ezra Pound's *Cantos* is that its epic "openness," inclusiveness, and polyvocality cancel out the ideological closure of the poem, with the corollary that such openness makes Pound a source for postmodern poetries that spell the death of the lyric, as perennially announced by Marjorie

Perloff and others.[34] I propose, instead, that it is the lyric instability of Pound's language that argues against argument and saves the poem, making light of its ideological burden. It also actually brings Pound into the twentieth century by making light of the "EZthority" (1971, 291) of the legislator or "Nature's M.P." and his nostalgia for an Adamic language, the "right naming" that is the mantra of the *Cantos*.

The critical polarization of the Pound-Stevens camps that Perloff first proposed in 1982 still holds.[35] What is remarkable about that polarization is that both camps agree on how to read Stevens. Thus Perloff is in perfect agreement with Harold Bloom: Stevens is a Romantic humanist. She may be critical of this figure of the poet, while Bloom may defend it, but neither questions the figure itself. This is odd, since Stevens devoted his career to a relentless interrogation of just that figure. It is the humanist subject that Stevens calls into question, insisting that the subject *is* its "inhuman" language. I chose to write on Stevens because his work explicitly engages the status of the subject in language and because the sounds of words are crucial for him—both in theory and in practice. Thus, his work offers a site where we can engage the interrelationship of subjectivity in language and the emotional values of the materials of words. Stevens is also important because, like Eliot, he asks the modern question: "What is the social function of poetry *as* poetry?"—a question Pound represses or subjects to other agendas. Since Stevens's work is a kind of philosophical speculation on this question—what James Merrill aptly termed "involuntary philosophy" (1986, 117), an inflection of poetic language—I also engage his thought on emotions, irrationality, and the function of the sounds of words in poetry.

The second part of my book concludes with a discussion of Anne Sexton. This chapter is somewhat different, for her work is not on the scale of that of the three modern poets—partly because she belongs to a different generation of poets. Her more "naked poetry," however, offers a chance to engage the intricate relationship between the elements of the linguistic code, the subject in language, and the psychosexual subject. Because she deals with autobiographical material, and because she started writing in therapy, the border between her existential and textual selves is quite porous and this registers more directly in her verse, in ways that Eliot's "rest" in Lausanne or Pound's stint at St. Elizabeths do not. Classified as confessional poetry, Sexton's work is read as the public expression of the private thoughts, emotions, and experiences of a prior individual. Yet Sexton herself radically questions the figure of a coherent "I" in poetry, and while she works with autobiographical materials, the operations of her language clearly disarticulate the concept of an "individual" in charge of her words. Sexton was diagnosed with hysteria, and she wrote only on a typewriter, and this additional mechanization of language in her work also allows me to engage the relationship between the subject and the mechanical nature of the poetic code, as "Anne Sexton" keeps disintegrating into the mechanisms of the code and the machinery of their reproduction.

Notes

1. Plato 1974, 77. Responding to Plato's gendering, Barbara Johnson proposes that "expelling poets is expelling femininity; expelling femininity is expelling women" (2003, 5). I suggest that something more fundamental is at stake. In discursive terms, banishing poets is "excommunicating" the nonrational, emotional power of language in order to clear the ground for rational discourse and position language as its instrument and servant. At issue is the status of philosophical discourse itself; the gendering is a predictable rhetorical strategy. For the status of women is a "given," but the link between poetry and women is not, and the feminine is not the threat that needs to be reduced to the poetic. Poetry is the threat that Plato's gendering would neutralize.

2. For "affections"—"desire and pain and pleasure"—are "held to be inseparable from every action" (Plato, 1974, 76), and emotions can move people to irrational action. "Emotion" has a number of obsolete meanings that register the threat it poses. The earliest use of the word cited by the OED is a 1579 sense of "political or social agitation; a tumult, popular disturbance." Other early uses include "a moving, stirring, agitation, perturbation," and any "disturbance of mind, feeling, passion." The psychological sense of "a mental 'feeling' or 'affection,' . . . as distinguished from cognitive or volitional states of consciousness," comes in the nineteenth century. The threat of loss of control threads through these usages, and it is a social threat.

3. Plato is trying to establish philosophy against a popular form more "influential than what [he] calls 'philosophy' "; he is "setting himself against popular culture as he knew it," writes Charles Griswold (2004, 3, 2). Philosophy as a discipline begins by positioning itself as the discourse of Truth, the other of poetry, a "useless" and "irrational" practice. But Griswold notes how "sweeping" and "trans-historical" Plato's critique is and states that "for Plato what is at stake is a clash between what we might call comprehensive world-views; it seems that matters of grave importance in ethics, politics, metaphysics, theology, and epistemology are at stake" (2).

4. The mimetic theory safeguards reference: it posits the footholds of a stable reality (whether ideal or phenomenal) and thus a stable subject, whereas there are no such footholds in poetic language.

5. Sidney 1948, 407. The defense is a genre of nostalgia that would resist the "decline" of poetry. But poetry will continue to "decline"; as it keeps telling us, all is subject to change. Defensive projects in effect confirm the precedence—and reinscribe the authority—of a "normal," "rational," instrumental language that judges poetry to be in need of defending. Plus, it turns out that defenses of poetry often defend something else—something that poetry might be useful for. And the pathos of attempts to mobilize poetry for political purposes is that they play by Plato's rules and on his home field. This is one of the problems, for example, with Julia Kristeva's impossible project: "Poetic mimesis"—"mimesis and the poetic language inseparable from it" (1984, 58)—will "set in motion what dogma represses" and lead the way to "social revolution" (61). Plato was right: mimesis will do that.

6. *Its* definition of "irrational," in Greek and Latin prosody, is a syllable whose length does not fit the metrical pattern.

7. It is not self-evident that rational language is not a deviation from the norm of poetic language, which transmits the shape of the linguistic code that must be passed

on. If the priority of rational language were a given, why would philosophy quarrel with poetry, which, in that case, would be beneath comment?

Nietzsche writes: "If one needs to make a tyrant of reason, as Socrates did, then there must exist no little danger of something else playing the tyrant. . . . The fanaticism with which the whole Greek thought throws itself at rationality betrays a state of emergency: one was in peril, one only had one choice: either to perish or—be absurdly rational," absolutely ruling out the "instincts" and the "unconscious" (1979, 33). Clearly, I'm not positing "instincts" or an "unconscious"; what philosophy rules out is poetry, which is, before all else, the discourse of the linguistic code itself and the emotional power that it commands *as such*.

8. It is difficult to give a sense of this essential nonrationality after Romanticism and modernism. Varieties of defensive irrationalities—which implicitly confirm rational language as the norm—and organicist forms that would naturalize poetic language all cede poetic ground. The "freer" and more "naturalized" the verse gets, the more it consents to the authority of reason; the modern breaking of forms is a sign of surrender of the public power of poetry. The public power—and the real threat—of poetry lies not in local disturbances of grammar and form but precisely in its formality, in the systemic orders of the medium, the "message" of which is that, in Eliot's words, "there is no freedom in art" (in Gioia, Mason, and Schoerke 2004, 108). Sadly, "poetry" has become a screen on which to project our real-life fantasies of freedom. This particular "decline" goes back to the nineteenth century.

9. It cannot afford to think what it means for language, and therefore reason, to be materially produced by a body that is itself produced by the training that enables it to produce a language and a mind.

10. In Solomon 1979, 4; my emphasis.

11. Jonathan Culler writes: "Poetry lies at the centre of the literary experience because it is the form that most clearly asserts the specificity of literature"; its formality differentiates it from ordinary discourse, "altering the circuit of communication within which it is inscribed" (1975, 162).

12. The lyric is a universal genre and it is the foundational genre in diverse languages. It is as old as recorded literature. Given its original connection to song, the most public and socially coded way of formulating emotion in language, the lyric has an even longer communal prehistory. Its connection to ritual and the sacred—as in magic formulas, funerary verses, and prayers—takes it even further back. J. W. Johnson writes: "It is logical to suppose that the first 'lyrical' poems came into being when men discovered the pleasure that arises from combining words in a coherent, meaningful sequence with the almost physical process of uttering rhythmical and tonal sounds to convey feelings. The instinctive human tendency to croon or hum or intone as an expression of emotional mood is evidenced in the child's babbling; and the socialization of this tendency in primitive cultures by the chanting or singing of nonsense syllables to emphasize tribal rites is a well documented phenomenon" (1965, 460–62). Earl Miner points out that mimesis-drama is the privileged genre only in the Western tradition. By defining poetry as the art of "imitation" and including everything from lyre playing to treatises in verse to drama under that rubric, Aristotle could not distinguish the lyric as a genre. In all other world literatures, the lyric, which, operates under an expressive-affective rather than mimetic conception of language, is the "foundational genre" (1990, 82; 85).

Kristin Hanson and Paul Kiparsky place the lyric as the foundational genre from a linguistic perspective. Because verse is characterized by the recurrence of linguistic equivalencies that "inhere" in the structure of a language, they argue, it is the "unmarked form of literary language while prose is the marked form; and . . . the unmarked function of verse is lyric, while the unmarked function of prose is narrative" (1997, 17–18). The marked element of an opposition depends on the existence of the unmarked (Ducrot and Todorov 1987, 112). Narrative verse and prose, then, could not appear before lyric verse.

13. Theodor Adorno, for example, considers the lyric a product of "an individualistic and ultimately atomistic society" (1991, 38); "the traditional lyric, as the most rigorous aesthetic negation of bourgeois convention, has by that very token been tied to bourgeois society" (46).

14. Poetic language is a thoroughly historical and social medium. Words; grammar; poetic forms and the modes of their dissemination and circulation; speech sounds and their representations; and the shape and social status of emotions are all subject to constant change, and the function of poetry also changes in tandem with social change. Moreover, poetic language is itself a medium of history. Not only is each word a palimpsest but words and poetic forms carry communal histories of constantly changing usages and functions.

15. The idea of the lyric as the discourse of the bourgeois subject is a questionable model for even the nineteenth-century lyric; it would be more historically credible to argue that the "individual" represented in the poem, the private inner self and its trials and tribulations, emerges at a certain time in response to the emergence of a market for such a commodity.

16. To say this is not to subscribe to an art for Art's sake position, which remains within the framework of the nineteenth century. It is to raise the question that Eliot himself raises: what is the social function of poetry *as* poetry, not as an "adjunct" to some other discourse or agenda, including, I would add, that of "Art." For "aesthetics" is another discursive spoil of the "quarrel" between poetry and philosophy.

17. 1989, 96. Barbara Johnson links de Man's retreat to Freud's moment in the Irma dream, where he backs off from his analysis: "Frankly, I had no desire to penetrate more deeply at this point." Both de Man and Freud back off from "individual psychology," she says, to safeguard the general validity of their theories (2003, 59). Freud's Irma dream, which I discuss in my conclusion, explicitly acknowledges professional anxieties about psychoanalysis—whether or not he may be overlooking physiological problems—and is not unlike de Man's professional anxiety about the affective charge of language—about what can be admitted for serious consideration. Freud writes about the limits of interpretation: "There's at least one spot in every dream that is unplumbable—a navel as it were, that is its contact with the unknown" (1989, 134). The "unknown" is what is not knowable within the limits and the structure of one's own discipline—what must remain out of bounds to validate one's disciplinary procedures and the "knowledge" they yield.

18. I am not suggesting that de Man is unaware of "the nothingness of human matters" (Rousseau, qtd. in de Man 1983, 18). Here I am interested only in the disciplinary line he draws at the rhetoric of the mother tongue, which is *something*. It carries the history of the passage from bodily language into symbolic language—a history of becoming "nothing."

19. The communication of that intimacy also secures cultural conservation and transmission in language—of, say, "*Brot und Wein.*"

20. The common understanding of lyric poetry in terms of the "human"—an a priori, nonlinguistic entity, with a given "nature"—represses that foundational "nothingness" of the "human." For example, Susan Stewart's wide-ranging study of artistic creation proposes that poetic forms rise "out of sense experience" and produce "intersubjective meaning" as they "make sense experience intelligible to others" (2002, ix). She posits a human drive to "wrest" "form from nature": "The self (. . . lost in absolute darkness) is compelled to make forms" (12, 15). And by making forms and thus "making sense impressions intelligible to others . . . we are able to situate ourselves and our experiences within what is universal" (3). For her transhistorical, transcultural, and translinguistic approach, terms like "individual," "human," or "universal" are not problematic. But when we think poetry outside humanism, without assuming a "human" outside its history in language, these concepts that have dominated discussions of poetry are put radically in question. And since poetry is not an invention of humanism, it needs to be thought outside that framework.

21. I use "semiotic" to refer to the material aspects of language—the linguistic system and the somatic production of its materials; it marks the interface of the institutional and the somatic in language. It should be clear that mine is not Kristeva's "semiotic" of drives and the *chora*, a retrospectively posited "nourishing and maternal," rhythmic, prelinguistic "receptacle" (1984, 27, 29). I also use "semiotic" to designate the formal aspect of poetry as distinct from its semantic/symbolic aspect. Thus the sounds of words and the devices that organize them in poetry would constitute the semiotic axis.

22. This figure communicates and guarantees personal experiences of language to motivate the transmission of the semiotic code, which is, of course, necessary for the very survival of the linguistic community and its culture. Yet, because poetry remembers our bodily intimacy with symbolic language, it not only transmits the code but reinforces the symbolic. This deeply conservative function may partly account for the universality of the genre.

23. Translating the emotion that is the subject matter of the poem, however, can create different but equally powerful emotional experiences specific to the different material and historical textures of the new language.

24. "Beautiful necessity" is Emerson's term (1904, 6:49); Jakobson uses it to compare the geometric principles that make for the "beautiful necessity" of a painting to the linguistic and grammatical necessities that structure a poem (1987, 133).

25. Hanson and Kiparsky argue that because the recurrences that make for verse "are drawn from a set of possibilities given by language, and hence from a world beyond the control of the speaker," verse claims a textual authority not attributable to the speaker but "to a truth beyond him" (1997, 21, 41). A native reader of a language would apprehend formal structures (such as meter and rhyme) as resting on incontrovertible facts, and this recognition would seem to lend authority to the "content" of the poem as well, inducing an experience of recognizing truth (42). This is also what compels a reader to respond to what the poem is saying, acknowledging the authority of the code to speak about whatever it is speaking about. For this reason, a translated emotion—of a love poem, say—is not as convincing as it is in the original. Eliot writes: "A thought expressed in a different language may be practically the same thought, but a feeling or

emotion expressed in a different language is not the same feeling or emotion" (1979, 18). This impoverishing proves the emotional power of the code as such.

26. Eliot points out that "in a homogeneous people the feelings of the most refined and complex have something in common with those of the most crude and simple, which they have not in common with those of people of their own level speaking another language" (1979, 9). Linguistic communities feel differently; they come by general feelings by different routes and nuances.

27. When I speak of the social function of poetry, I have in mind a linguistic community, not an abstraction "social"—nor "the vast empire of human society" (Wordsworth 1981, 1:881). Marx writes, "Language itself is just as much the product of a community, as in another respect it is the existence of the community; it is, as it were, the communal being speaking for itself" (in Solomon 1979, 74). Eliot concurs: in poetry, "emotion and feeling" are "best expressed in the language common to all classes: the structure, the rhythm, the sound, the idiom of a language, express the personality of the people which speaks it" (1979, 8–9). Hence poetry is "stubbornly national"; it "differs from every other art in having a value for the people of the poet's race and language, which it can have for no other" (7).

28. As Agamben argues, this passage opens the possibility of history. There is no nature or culture or history before this foundational lived history, which is prior to the possibility of any exchange, substitution, and production of value—all third terms. This inaugural history is a transformation of bodily produced events into signs; the general equivalent here is socially shaped emotional motivation.

29. I want to stress that I speak of a linguistic body formulated in the historical process of learning to produce language. Poetic theory has to content itself with the linguistic body rather than invoking biological "drives" or a mystical, sublime "body as 'God'" beyond the reach of language (Kristeva 1984; Aviram 1994, 22). And the body that is trained to produce language cannot be opposed to the mind: because the body that comes to produce language is historically produced, it is not easily distinguished from the memory/mind that is formed and continues to function through its apparatus. In poetry, we cannot assume a body that is separable from the "forgotten" memory of its linguistic formulation. The linguistic body is the text of a history. While this is the case with the bodies of other discourses as well, poetry is, again, different, for it is the language of the history of a body that entails the very *possibility* of discourse. A mind that "remembers" the body's entry into language, by which it came to be a mind, and a body that bears witness to a mind produced by the linguistic—and, therefore, emotional and social—training of that body can only converse in poetry. Poetry is the site of recognizing the foundationally historical nature of the subject in language—as "body" and as "mind."

30. This "translation" happens before the logic of substitution and metaphor can kick in. The "human" is constituted in and as that originary mediation; it is an originary metaphor.

31. The history of the "linguistic body" overlaps with the inscription of the psychosexual body, and my point in engaging that process is to provide the context of a different, concurrent history of symbolization that is inextricable from language acquisition; it affects the language-producing body, even as language effects the formulation of the sexual body.

32. To address what is entailed in learning a language would risk the theory, for the "unconscious" may be the repository of a linguistic rather than a psychosexual history—the archeological remains, to use Freud's figure, of the history of language acquisition. A "scientist" as interested as Freud in language and literature would be aware of the need to supress the history of language in order to draw his disciplinary borders. Indeed, we could see Freudian theory as a kind of hysterical displacement of the trauma of language onto the sexual inscription of the body—a theoretical somatizing, so to speak.

33. The standard critical procedure affirms a hierarchy and accounts for particular forms on the grounds of their suitability for what the poem is saying. One accounts for the choice of a sonnet, for example, by showing how this form fits a particular content, assuming that the author knew what he wanted to say and chose the best means to that end. But a poem is a metaleptic figure and one needs to work without prioritizing content; one has to be able to also argue, for example, why a certain kind of thought is most suitable for a sonnet.

34. See, for example, "The Supreme Fiction and the Impasse of the Modernist Lyric" (1985b) and "Postmodernism and the Impasse of the Lyric" (1985a, 172–200).

35. See "Pound/Stevens: Whose Era?" (1985a, 1–23).

PART ONE

Lyric Theory

Chapter 1

✿

THE LYRIC SUBJECT

SOUNDS, SENSE, AND THE "I"

*I or me are the words associated with voice. They are like
the meaning of voice itself.*
—*Paul Valéry*

IMPLICITLY OR explicitly, the speaker in a lyric poem is an "I." This figure is a generic "I," not to be confused with an extralinguistic entity. The "I" in discourse is a universal, an indexical function. In Hegel's terms, "when I say 'I,' 'this individual I,' I say quite generally 'all I's,' every one is what I say, every one is 'I,' this individual I" (1967, 154). Yet the poetic "I" is also heard as an individuated voice, for we can "hear" the distinct voices of different poets working in the same language and at the same historical moment, with the same linguistic and cultural necessities and resources. The audibility of a distinctive written voice is a remarkable phenomenon: how does an individuated "I" become audible through the universal "I" of language in poetry, a discourse that foregrounds conventions and rules? Clearly, the generic "I" and the individuated "I" cannot to be understood as oppositional: the "I" in poetry is both the generic "I" of language and an individuated "I" sounded by the materials of language. My argument is that the experienced effect of an individuated speaker lies in an experience of linguistic materials that are in excess of what can be categorically processed—an experience guaranteed by the formality of poetry.

The lyric works with the material experience of the somatic production and reproduction of words as sounds and sounds as words, whether spoken, written, or read.[1] Formal schemes that abstract and stylize the distinctive sonic and grammatical shape of a language serve to foreground its material reality and put up an organized resistance to meaning, both as sense and as intention. Sounds are not without semantic resonances—whether associations specific to a particular poet and/or a given language, or "universal"[2]—but their formal system operates independently of signification and keeps in constant view the intractably nonsensical, sensory basis and medium of meaning, of sense and intention. We are not allowed to forget or "overhear" the nonmeaning body of words, the somatically produced and processed material events. Lyric language presents—to the ear[3]—that which resists communication and the will of an individual "speaker." Thus, oddly, an individuated speaker is heard in a language that foregrounds the materiality of the linguistic code and resists an individual will.[4]

Bodily produced acoustic phenomena and signifying sounds converge and diverge in their separate, overlapping patternings. The phonemes are organized in two different systems: the formal patterns of recurring sounds in such schemes as rhyme, alliteration, assonance, and consonance, and the linear phoneme sequences that organize sounds for sense. We process the sounds both acoustically and cognitively. As we hear both sounds and signifying units, we process both relations of similarity and relations of difference on the combinatorial axis. On another level, metrical order and syntactic order, with their different patterns of accent and stress, exist alongside, and interfere with, each other.[5] While metrical variations, as well as the choice of meters, can do semantic work, the organizational principle aims not to communicate meaning but to represent the sound shape of a language.[6]

The formal systems have a certain autonomy, even an automatism, and appear partly independent of the will of the poet.[7] Sounds recall and call forth other sounds, repeating and reproducing themselves with a kind of impulsion that questions the agency of the speaker—the voice in the poem—if not the poet herself. At the same time, the sound movements are conventionally coded or theoretically codable; we can formulate a grammar for their behavior. The self-propulsion of the material sign, then, is reemphasized and socially sanctioned by formal devices, whose responsibilities are to the phonic properties of a given language and the sound system of a given poem. Thus formal devices and conventions, which carry a history, regulate and render audible the material "body" in an internal, systematic resistance to "meaning" in both senses of the word. Conventions that stylize the rules of a language represent the body, and in the lyric there is an excess of "body," but all affected—at once prescripted (by the givens of the language and convention or social consensus) and histrionic. The lyric performs the material grounds of language.

In lyric poetry, reference is also challenged by an excess of potential meanings. The very resistance of the material medium to reference instigates a proliferation of possible meanings at the same time that it renders them all speculative. Faced with rhyming words, for example, the reader speculates sense connections.[8] Thus a resistant materiality and the surplus semantic production of paradigmatic linkages that it speculates both challenge the ends of communication. The signifier is indeterminate or unstable, and this indeterminacy is a matter not just of a figural complexity of layered meanings but of new senses being generated out of sound affinities. Alternate subliminal meanings and arguments can run along a sequence of rhymes or sound-related words, whether systematized or not; such syntactic liberties as inversions or sentence fragments—which may themselves be partly serving the formal imperatives of meter, rhyme, and sound patterns—facilitate this production of surplus sense.

Signification or reference, then, is destabilized from both ends: the word as sound has its own obligations foremost, and the word as signifier will not be fixed, for it, too, is thus granted *its* autonomy, producing "senses" seemingly without need of agency. There is an excess of "sense" in the lyric, but all on the brink of nonsense—all "precarious" or "dependent on prayer," as in the root sense of the word.

If sounds dominate, sense is compromised; if sense is too fixed, sounds are not free to do their kind of affective signifying work. In lyric poetry, the distinct operations of both the formal system organizing the material properties of the signifier for the voice and the ear and the symbolic system of referential language must be perceivable in their *difference*, their noncoincidence. Neither system can be transparent. The excessiveness of each system to the other necessitates a constant negotiation, a constant choosing and intentionalizing not only of sounds as words but also—and herein lies the difference of poetry—of words as sounds. Each system is made to intentionalize the other's automatisms.

The figure of the lyric "I" governs this intentionalizing operation: it tropes— "meta-phors," moves, and motivates—acoustic phenomena as signifying phenomena, and vice versa. The gap "between" the systemic operations of sound and sense—or of sound as oral-aural sensation and sound as sense—is the site of the "subject," a speaking agent, an audible voice. On another level, the "I" inhabits the gap between the formal—phonemic, metrical, and grammatical— orders and the semantic and propositional content. The gap that the "I" occupies is the internal gap of language, and it is also the site that the reader must occupy. The reader who repeats the speaker's words experiences herself as a requirement of meaningful language, which depends on an "I." Grammatically, "I" is a shifter; empty of lexical value, it indicates that discourse is taking place.[9] Thus, although the shifter, the sign *I*, is a conventional symbol—that is, it varies from language to language (I, *je, ich*, etc.)—it cannot represent its object "without 'being in existential relation' with this object: the word *I* designating the utterer is existentially related to his utterance, and hence functions as an index."[10]

The indexical "I," whose position is occupied by anyone reading or speaking a poem, marks an intention to mean, prior to any specific meanings. Applying Agamben's terms of the voice-Voice-meaning progression (1991, 35) to poetic language, we could say that this "I" speaks in the Voice, which is no longer mere bodily sound and not yet meaning but the pure intention to mean. The "I" as the site of the Voice indicates that discourse is taking place. It converts *langue* into *parole* at the same time that it effects the movement from voice as animal sound to sense. In either case, the "I," situated between the code and the message, enables the code to communicate and the message to be comprehensible. It not only converts *langue* into *parole* but the *parole* into sense. In Gilles Deleuze's terms, "In the order of speech, it is the I which begins, and begins absolutely"—even if this is silent speech (1990, 15). A linguistic act that begins with, or is initiated by, an "I" is positioned as "speech," and "sense is always presupposed as soon as *I* begin to speak; I would not be able to begin without this presupposition" (28). For sense, as distinct from propositional content, is what is meant by what is said.[11] Thus "I" and sense are coeval, voiced events of intention.

In the figure of a lyric speaker, sounds come to mean or assume the "air" of having a meaning, in *this* instance, by being meant or intended. Marianne Moore writes, "what is said should at least have the air of having meant something to the person who wrote it" (1987, 508). The intentionalizing, delimiting figure of an "I" is a requirement of the meaning function,[12] and it does rhetorical work. Always courting nonsense, lyric language would persuade us that sounds that make sense, formal and grammatical structures that mean, and a "meaning" or intending language-user choosing and voicing those sounds are coeval and reciprocal.

Thus one answer to the question "Why is there lyric poetry?" lies in this event of an "I" as the agent of language—the figure of a subject that makes language mean by intending it. Sounds that *can* mean—a condition prior to any specific meanings—are sounds we can ascribe to an "I," and the subject thus produced is at once an irreducibly linguistic construct—a verbal object—and an "I" "choosing the words he lives by," as James Merrill puts it (1986, 21). This is not to "reduce" the "I" to a poetic effect but to point to the concurrence of poetics and ethics in the event of lyric subjectivity.

And it is the sound of intention, the rhetoric of the voice that we hear as an individuating inflection of language. We hear the "I" that is the voice of intention, a motivating emotion. Intention individuates: it determines the way "I" sound the words—"my" inflection, tone of voice, and rhythm—and distinguishes the way "I" sound from the way "you" sound and the way "we" sound from the way the computer sounds.

By making audible the necessity for an "I" to motivate the linguistic code, poetry marks the inauguration of the subject in language as it inaugurates meaningful language at the crux of intention. We do not expect the language of first-person prose to need motivating because the material mechanisms of language are not *officially* sanctioned to interfere with sense. In lyric poetry, form—publicly sanctioned conventions of organizing the materiality of language—puts meaningful language and the subject radically in question and shows that the event of meaning in language requires an intending "I"—properly an ethical subject. Thus the given necessities of the linguistic and formal codes force a foundational choice to mean. Thus the formality of poetry forces the issue of intention and a subject. It forces an ethical function—to *choose* necessity in order to be an "I" who means.

If the "subject" is a verbal object that is, above all, sounds, it is an acoustic event. The lyric poem, where the poet is presumably speaking to himself or to no one in particular,[13] depends, in fact, on being heard by a "you" *as* an "I" speaking. The reason the lyric poet turns her back to the audience, without which she cannot exist, is that she *must* be heard. And she must first be heard by herself. If she is the figure of pure intention to mean, a "you" and an "I" are coeval in the act of speech. Thus the lyric "I" must also always be a "you," if it is to mean—if it is to spell out the condition for meaning. For the lyric "I" is not prior to its words, and its words have nothing to do with "self-expression."[14] The referent of the lyric poem is not a preexisting individual entity we can see or imagine but an "I" that must be heard *as choosing words*, intending sounds to make sense and troping the gap between sensation and cognition. The poem does not express some prior intention or meaning; it is an act of intending to mean. The "I" metaleptically tropes the gap words open by choosing words. Because the lyric involves such will and persuasion, because the lyric subject is the rhetorical construct of a voice and depends on an auditor, the "I" is a socially and historically specific formation. If a set of sounds, an acoustic event, must be heard as an intention to mean for there to be an "I"—for sounds to make sense and for sense to be sensible or audible to another—the "I" is utterly dependent on an audience, an other or others with the ear to hear this "turn," which is the event of language itself.

The interface of genre and history rhetorically positions the lyric speaker and allows the inscription of the "I" in the poem to be read as a *self*-inscription. Put differently, in the lyric an "I" that can only speak within the textual system of the linguistic and formal codes and an "I" that can be heard and realized only outside that system—an existential and historical subject-agent—must *seem* to coincide. That rhetorical coincidence is, properly, a moral ground, a figural coincidence that would convince us that the speaking "I" stands by his words. Thus the intending "I" as accountable for his words marks the ethical turn of the formal system, as well as linking the author and reader in a community sharing that intentionalizing turn of the "I." We need not share the personal history, experiences, or beliefs of a particular poet; instead, we share the process of re-cognizing the words that re-produce(d) the poet as an "I" that produces his words and history. We recognize the "I's" production of the language that has produced him. Metalepsis is the figure that governs poetic logic.

METALEPSIS

> There is no more dangerous error than that of mistaking
> the consequence for the cause.
> —*Nietzsche*

Metalepsis or transumption figures a "consequent" as an "antecedent," or the other way around. John Hollander, who proposes metalepsis as the trope of "allusive echo," distinguishes it from other figures that operate in a kind of conceptual space. In most descriptions of rhetorical figures, he writes, an "implicitly spatial language connects the representation with what it replaces—part for whole or vice versa, proximate or otherwise associated object or quality . . . and so forth" (1981, 113, 134). But transumption is a diachronic figure that involves a temporal sequence. In the case of allusive echo, the "process of taking hold of something poetically in order to revise it upward, as it were, canceling and transforming . . . is a metaleptic act in the broadest sense. It is taking after—in the sense of 'pursuing'—what one has been fated to take after as a resembling descendent" (147).

There is confusion among the rhetoricians about the function of the trope: it may substitute "the effect for the cause, the subsequent for the antecedent, the late for the early, for example, but there is a general sense that it is a kind of meta-trope, or figure of linkage between figures, and that there will be one or more unstated middle terms which are leapt over, or alluded to, by the figure" (Hollander 1981, 114). Hollander also points out that in a number of the examples of the trope cited by the rhetoricians, the substitution seems to involve a path of "like sound[s]," phonemic similarities, and "near-puns" (141, 135).

The figure seems to have two functions: it may reverse temporal sequence and it may allude to an unstated middle term between two tropes. If we think of these two functions together, figuring temporal sequence as reversible would appear as the "metaphysical" middle term. As such, metalepsis is an intentionalizing trope that "motivates" time and, in the broadest sense, history itself. A "meaningful" history is a typological history, where historical lateness is motivated as an earliness, as the fulfillment of a precursor, the antitype of a type. Indeed, historical and narrative meaning in general—all meaning that rests on the order of precursors and fulfillments, causes and effects, where each gains significance in a reciprocal motivation across time—rests on metalepsis. What holds for the Christian model of history and for certain models of literary history also holds for the psychoanalytic model of the history of the subject. Psychoanalysis is a metaleptic search for antecedents to motivate consequents in a way that grants meaning to the present and to the past, as an "I" created by the narrativizing comes to figure itself as the agent of the narrative.

If the intentionalizing trope of metalepsis also moves along the lines of like sounds and phonemic connections—that is, not only "above" but "below" tropological substitutions—it would seem to be involved in the specifically poetic motivation of sound as sense *and* of sense as sound. The metaleptic figure of the lyric "I" tropes the discursive and the formal systems, sense and sounds, by willing sounds to mean *and* willing meanings to be sounds—to be sounded. This intentionalizing inaugurates time within the word and motivates its temporal or "historical" lateness as a logical priority. It takes the word-concept as prior to the word-sound and a consequent "I," created in sounds of words, as an antecedent "I," the source of words. But the radical difference of poetry is that it also works the other way around, always exposing such priority to be a retroactive effect of the event of a voice and oral-acoustic sensations, the material production, patterning, and processing of sounds. Such a reversal is possible in poetic language only because the shape of the linguistic givens is always audible and we are not allowed to mistake a consequence for a cause.

THE POET'S SIGNATURE

You were created of your name, the word
Is that of which you were the personage.
—*Wallace Stevens*

What am I after all but a child, pleas'd with the sound of my
own name? repeating it over and over;
I stand apart to hear—it never tires me.
—*Walt Whitman*

The author's self . . . the soul is a cypher, in the sense
of a cryptograph.
—*Edgar Allan Poe*

The difficult question of the relation of the poet to her textual "I" confronts us with another gap, duplicating the divide between the symbolic and semiotic aspects of language on a different scale, in terms of a divide between the existential and the textual worlds. Even in documentably autobiographical poetry, a moat separates the person of the poet from the textual subject. The poet is responsible for the credibility of her "I"—as at once an experiencing "I" and this particular set of words, at once a psychological, social, and historical self and a verbal entity. Apart from what content it may have and whatever thoughts, feelings, or experiences it may express, the *generic* credibility of a lyric poem hinges on the speaker's rhetorical credibility—on both registers.

The poet makes certain "choices" to shape her text. These choices are not necessarily all conscious choices; they operate on the subjective and linguistic experiences and materials governed by the primary process of free associations and substitutions of senses and sounds.[15] Yet they also operate under public constraints. The poet negotiates personal materials and public languages—the given phonological, syntactic, and semantic logic of the language, the history and conventions of the genre in that language, and the network of other discourses and "idioms" of the time and place. In the words of the textual "I," these other languages also become audible. Most important, the systemic operations of the code are audible, for this "I" who "chooses the words he lives by" is also chosen by the language he lives in. At this level, the figure of the lyric "I" with its two-way intentionalization negotiates two kinds of rhetoric: a discursive "macrorhetoric" deployed by the poet and a "microrhetoric" of the linguistic code,[16] operating not with signifiers but with the constituent elements of the signifiers. The "I" in the poem is the interface of the rhetoric of the poet and that of the code. Neither rhetoric is dispensable if a poem is to be other than a social document or some curious artifact.

At the macrorhetorical level, persuasive rhetoric depends, Aristotle points out, on the "character" of the person presenting it: the orator must "make his own character look right," so that he can induce his hearers "to believe a thing apart from any proof of it" (1984, 90–91). In an oral situation, where the speaker and the audience are face to face, persuasion depends on the physical act of speech. The sounds of the words, their pronunciation and mode of delivery, the tone of voice, facial expressions, and bodily gestures all work to affect the audience. Rhetoric is an art of seduction; it aims to affect, to move, to transport an audience.[17] The only "truth" rhetoric can claim lies in the social *power* of the material, physical act of speech.[18] "Truth" inheres in the *event* of discourse and the relation between a speaker and a hearer; it is neither "inside" discourse—in what is said—nor outside the discourse, in some natural or metaphysical given. Thus it is a social truth, with psychological, ethical, and political dimensions.[19] And it incurs responsibilities, for words are like a "powerful narcotic": it is "impossible to resist their strong fascination" (Barilli 1989, viii–ix, 5).

Insofar as its truth is neither outside nor inside discourse but lies in the act of a discourse that exploits the emotional power of words, poetry aligns with rhetoric.[20] And the lyric is the most rhetorical of poetic genres, entirely dependent on the cultural audibility and credibility of the speaker. The referent of the lyric is hypothetical—the perceptions, emotions, thoughts, and memories of an "I" that refers only to the given instance of discourse. Since the lyric poet's subject matter is his hypothetical subjectivity, "himself" and his emotions, it is imperative that he "sound right." Poetic texts, emphasizing the physical media of sounds and letters, their tones and rhythmic arrangements, are designed to deploy the full resources of the medium for persuasion: the "I" has to persuade "you," the reader-auditor, to hear him as an "I,"[21] to believe him, and it does that by invoking the rhetorical and emotional authority of the material code.

The discursive and material persuasions of a poem coincide in the speaking "I," which we could call the signature of the poet, the crux of an existential and a graphic person. The signature is an "ethical" institution,[22] and a poet's signature, his "I," endorses the symbolic language with his personal, identifying inflection of the linguistic and formal codes. The poet persuades by inscribing his signature into the code. In the broadest sense, a poetic "signature" includes an individuating prosodic and syntactic rhythm, a distinct voice, and distinguishing audible or visible textual marks—all that makes for a personal inflection of the code—and it underwrites the macrorhetoric of discursive persuasions.[23] More specifically, the signature as the proper name is always encoded in the texts. The name of the poet both designates a specific historical person and operates within the discourse, as a textual entity. It both yields to the code and lays claims on the code, making it yield his "name," the letters of his "character." The proper name is the most fertile ground for letter play, as a range of practices—from Walt Whitman's naming himself within the poems to all poets' playing on their names in homophones, puns, and anagrams—testifies.[24] The signature links the author to his "I" and establishes historical authenticity and ethical accountability in a textual mark; it places a text inside existential, historical experience, even as it places that experience inside a text.

The textual signature, then, links and separates the macrorhetoric of the "existential" person and the microrhetoric of the textual code that is equally in play in lyric language. A speaker who must seem to be convincing as both an existential person and a textual construct must both use language to move an audience and be used and moved by language—if the text is to be poetry and not oratory. To the extent that the grammatical, literal, and sonic shape of the given language is audible in the articulation of the speaking "I," the "I" convinces. A convincing lyric subject is spoken by the words she speaks. She must draw on the authority of the code, and language must be audible through her as much as she is audible through language. For what individuates her is not what she says but the particular ways in which she makes audible the shape, the "beautiful necessities," of the language.

While a kind of macrorhetoric, stressing the sensory dimension of language and the I-you configuration, aligns poetry with rhetoric, the formal rules of poetry distinguish the two practices. Forms emphasize the sensory dimension of language and thus have a macrorhetorical function, but they also guarantee a space for the workings of microrhetorical processes that make light of the coherency of the word unit. Rhymes, assonance, consonance, and wordplays like anagrams and puns all work to destabilize reference. What distinguishes poetry from other discourses that may equally rely on figures and tropes is its official sanctioning of intraverbal condensations, substitutions and displacements of the elements of the signifier. Poetic language, which deploys all varieties of tropes, itself works both below and above the threshold of figuration. It breaks down the signifier into its material elements to disclose a kind of microrhetoric and thus the necessity for an intending subject choosing what it could not choose.[25] It institutes the ethical figure of an intending speaker and marks a will to mean even as it secures a full view of the abyss. Poetry is a rhythmic beat between sense and nonsense, an intending speaker and "hollow sounds" perpetually emerging from and resolving themselves into one another.

Such microrhetorical processes compromise authorial intention. Saussure's work with anagrams raises just this issue. He "discovers" a complex web of phonemic echoes and linkages that are as independent of the formal order per se as they are of lexical divisions. It can not be determined whether these are intentional—whether the microrhetoric is motivated by the poet or the code, or even the reader—in this case, Saussure. He identifies a kind of obsessive, ritual phonemic patterning, where words seem to be generated by the phonemic shape of anteceding words rather than "directly chosen *by the formative consciousness*" (Starobinski 1979, 26, 121). Saussure is reading ancient Latin verse. But any poem will yield a phonemic organization independent of the lexical and formal units. A phonemic and syllabic systemicity must be audible or perceivable precisely in order to raise the question of intention. Authorial intention must be questionable—but not determinable—if the text is to be a poem, a crux of intention. Sequences of words might be systemically generated—or appear to be so generated—by the linguistic code *or* by patterns of usage, current or remembered. If we can retroactively intentionalize what might appear as a proactive, "mechanical" psycholinguistic process, we are on the ground of lyric language. For example, Bishop's "The Map" opens:

> Land lies in water; it is shadowed green.
> Shadows, or are they shallows, at its edges
> showing the line of long sea-weeded ledges
> where weeds hang to the simple blue from green.
> Or does the land lean down to lift the sea from under,
> drawing it unperturbed around itself?
> Along the fine tan sandy shelf
> is the land tugging at the sea from under? (1979, 3)

The stanza proceeds by reverberating the phonemic shape of the opening lines. It produces itself as variations on a set of letters and phonemes that are in play and generates its content—the "metaphysical" speculation about ground and figure relationships—as a figure set on *its* ground.

If authorial intention does not at least appear to be somewhat compromised, the credibility, the persuasiveness of lyric language itself will be compromised. For the microrhetoric that destabilizes reference in the lyric also renders perceptible the necessity for an "I" and its foundational intention to mean. The foregrounded systemicity of the linguistic and formal codes renders all sense hypothetical and ensures that the text will not reduce to its macrorhetoric. The system is positioned as the ground, with rules that govern its operations independently of the ideas and ideologies that it might host in any given instance. The system must in a sense cancel ideologies to ensure its self-perpetuation; it must outlast ideas and ideologies. This is no less true of poetic language than of language itself.

Microrhetorical processes make light of macrorhetoric, most certainly of polemical rhetoric and its motivation. For example, here is a well-known passage from "Hugh Selwyn Mauberly":

Died some, pro patria
        non "dulce" non "et decor". . .
walked eye-deep in hell
be**lie**ving in old men's **lies**, then unbe**lie**ving
came home, home to a **lie**,
home to many deceits
home to old **lies** and new infamy;
usury age-old and age-thick
and **liars** in public places

. . . .

frankness as never before,
disillusions as never told in the old days,
hysterias, trench confessions,
laughter out of dead bel**lies**. (1990, 188; emphases mine)

This is a highly rhetorical, public language, depending on conscious repetitions of words and syntactic phrases. While the message motivates the word choice, a microrhetoric is also at work, as a web of **lies** weaves through the passage, quite literally dismantling, "belying," be**lie**fs. But it *also* dismantles the opposite of "beliefs in lies," the truth—the frankness, disillusions, confessions, the slaughter, the "dead bellies"—in the final syllable of the poem: **lies**. Some linguistic compulsion might have yielded the final **lies**—after the **bel** of "be-lief"—but Pound, who works at the level of letters, phonemes, and syllables, would not be unaware of the final **lies**. "Laughter" and "slaughter" (line 8) have a similar letteral link that again works to tell a different story. This kind of rhetoric makes the performance convincing by undermining the message; the microrhetoric dissociates the poet from his own Horatian rhetoric, and positions Horace's rhetoric among "old men's lies." By belying his own rhetoric, by allowing his language to argue against the truth claims of the orator's macrorhetoric, the speaker convinces that he in fact tells of "disillusions as never told in the old days."

"Hugh Selwyn Mauberly" has many such passages, with a tension between two kinds of rhetoric, where a microrhetoric of puns and letter play makes the speaker credible even as it may compromise his message:

The **age** demanded an im**age**
Of its accele**rated grimace**,
Something for the modern st**age**,
Not, at any **rate**, an A**ttic grace** (1990, 186; emphases mine)

Pound grants a linguistic and poetic motivation for what "the age demanded," which compromises the irony and the argument. The "tic" in "Attic," for example, registers a dangerous ambivalence, and we are justified in noting the "tic" not only because of the preceding "grimace" and the "grimace"-"grace" rhyme but because the palindromic symmetry of "**at an**y . . . **an At**tic" forces us to read at the syllabic level. The series of alternations between "at" and "an"—"**at any rate an At**tic"—works to the same effect. Indeed, the whole stanza—if not the whole poem—asks to be read at the letteral and syllabic level. And at this level, tone is no guide, for a different kind of argumentation subverts the macrorhetoric. For a final example, is it possible not to hear "Flaubert," the "true Penelope" of "E.P.," in "Mauberly"?[26] There is an inequity and promiscuity—as Pound's eroticizing the aesthetic in the first poem of the sequence acknowledges—a usurious excess of interest without regard to use or production of meaning in the workings of language itself, which threatens not only stable meanings and reference but all kinds of stability and order in individual and social life and values. Pound's *Cantos*, as I will argue at greater length, sing of this war between two kinds of rhetoric, two kinds of power. The microrhetorical excess makes for a speaker who is more or other than the *user* of language. This surplus is outside the economy of use and wobbles the system of referential and economic equity. Pound, being a lyric poet before he is an epic poet, always acknowledges this remainder. A line like "Azure hath a canker by usura," for example, rescues that "useless" residue that is in danger of disappearing in tendentious verse and its referential norm. The "Ezra" scripted into "Azure hath a canker by usura" is the lyric poet—in excess of his biblical namesake the scribe and of the epic poet-hero Ezra with his plans. Wordplays and literal links, always pointing to the linguistic code, exercise power over those who would exercise power over words and thus ensure that the medium outlasts messages.[27]

Whether this kind of rhetoric sounds the nature of the unconscious or of language, whether it betrays the hidden wish of the speaker or "the hidden wish of words," as Merrill puts it (1986, 111), it operates at the semiotic level to shape the aspect of poetic language that is untranslatable. And such code-specific microrhetorical processes also individuate subjects within the symbolic and formal systems. This language-specific and individuating rhetoric leads me to a consideration of language acquisition, for in that process, the signifier is experienced as a space-time event that varies from person to person. The individual subject *is* that history of the intimate and unstable relationship between words and physical experiences, long before it can come to verbalize the narrative of his history. Lacan proposes that the figures of style and the tropes used by the analysand are not mere figures of speech but are themselves "the active principle of the rhetoric" of the analysand's discourse (1977, 169). That is, the discourse and, therefore, the subject are produced by these figures that mark the "precise point at which sense emerges from non-sense" (158). But the point at which non-sense reemerges from figural sense is what marks the individuated subject. When the analyst stops listening to sense, to meaning, Serge Leclaire writes, he can hear the letters that compose the secret name of each individual psychosexual subject. Somewhat similarly, when we stop listening to sense, we can hear each poet's signature, the microrhetoric that distinguishes his voice/text in resounding the code.[28]

NOTES

1. The relationship between spoken and written language is obviously very complicated, but it is a separate issue. The best way to limit it to the question that interests me might be to grant Agamben's point that the spoken word—the signifying word—is already a *gramma*, a trace of a sound, the sign of the loss of the animal sound (1991, 35, 39). That loss is the condition of speech itself, the mark of the human difference, a "writing" that marks the human. What interest me, however, are the implications of the occurrence of the poetic word in the "mother tongue," where the animal sound does not just disappear. There is an echoic, rhythmic return—in the mind's ear—that resounds, re-voices the "animal phone." In this "echoic" return, we hear the passage from phone to the word.

2. Jakobson's work shows that emotional tones of different sounds are encoded semantically in a variety of languages.

3. Even a written text addresses the ear, what Stevens calls "the delicatest ear of the mind" (1954, 240). The ear certainly hears more than the eye can see in a text because we have to sound out the words internally, silently imitating the muscular activity of producing sounds in order to *recognize* the visual data that the eye has registered *as words*. Perception of words in poetry depends on the mouth-ear circuit; even when words are not sounded, their "acoustic and motor images" are invoked (as in "interior speech") to make for words (Jakobson 1978, 37). Groups of jumbled letters may be visually registered, but they don't become words or sentences unless the ear can hear them said; they must be processed through the mouth-ear circuit. Some of e. e. cummings's poems offer this liminal experience.

4. In one sense, the linguistic code speaks the "I," since it is prior to it. But insofar as the "I" is individuated, it cannot be an after-effect of the code. The individuated "I" proves the dependency of the code on an "I" to give it voice. Before the code can assume discursive meanings, its formations have to be sounded/voiced by a speaker and re-sounded by an auditor/reader.

5. This noncoincidence is the basis of Agamben's definition of poetry as an "opposition between metrical segmentation and semantic segmentation." Thus the possibility of enjambment—a "disconnection between the metrical and syntactic elements" (1995, 40)—is what distinguishes poetry from prose (1999, 109).

6. Similarly, syntax, which represents the no-less-binding grammatical givens of a language, can do formal work, as in syntactic parallelisms and repetitions. But it is perceived as intending to make sense, while sound forms work against sense. Marianne

Moore's poems are interesting in this context. While she places poetry and prose on a continuum, the texts considered poems present for "inspection" the noncoincidence of several ways of organizing linguistic material: metrical stress patterns, syllabic orders, syntactic orders, stanzaic patterns, rhyme schemes, and visual patterns all coexist without coinciding, as each order follows the imperatives of its distinct system.

7. This is especially true for rhyme, where the choices are limited to a finite number. Jakobson, in "Subliminal Verbal Patterning in Poetry," argues that complex verbal designs may occur without a poet's "apprehension and volition" and cites many poets' testimony to this effect, including William Blake's "without Premeditation and even against my Will" (1985, 60).

8. "This propensity to infer a connection in meaning from similarity in sounds illustrates the poetic function of language," writes Jakobson (1985, 157). This "propensity" also points to the deep knowledge that informs poetic language: in the mother tongue, the signifier-signified relationship, as Benveniste has argued against Saussure, is not arbitrary but, on the contrary, necessary (Jakobson 1985, 28). That felt necessity motivates the reader to speculate sense connections between like sounds. A perceived sound similarity, a *material* likeness, thus instigates a desire for a "metaphysical" shared meaning, which confirms the priority of the linguistic code to whatever we do with it—the priority of sounds to sense. We do not, after all, expect two words with similar meanings to have similar sounds.

9. A shifter is a form that references the given speech act in which it appears. The first-person pronoun is a shifter, in Jakobson's terms, "because the basic meaning of the first person involves a reference to the author of the given act of speech" (1985, 23). Benveniste writes that pronouns are "indicators of the utterance": "What is the 'reality' to which *I* or *you* refers? Only a 'reality of discourse' . . . *I* signifies 'the person who utters the present instance of discourse containing *I*'" (qtd. in Agamben 1991, 23). In linguistic terms, speech moves from *langue* to *parole* via shifters: pronouns are "'empty signs,' which become 'full' as soon as the speaker assumes them in an instance of discourse. Their scope is to enact 'the conversion of language into discourse' and to permit the passage from *langue* to *parole*" (24).

10. Jakobson, qtd. in Agamben 1991, 24.

11. This also "confirms," Deleuze adds, the "possibility of a profound link between the logic of sense and ethics, morals or morality" (1990, 31).

12. An "I" is one who intends by speaking, who means to make sense and thus motivate a "you" to listen. Ashbery's poetics rests on the recognition that the intention to make sense, the desire to communicate, and the reciprocal desire to understand matter more than what is communicated. He insists on the primacy of the rhetorical situation, "the fact of addressing someone" (in Packard 1974, 123). Elsewhere, he says, "The pathos and liveliness of ordinary human communication is poetry to me" (1983, 56). Poetry turns on this desire for communication per se:

> The extreme austerity of an almost empty mind
> Colliding with the lush, Rousseau-like foliage of its desire to communicate
> Something between breaths, if only for the sake
> Of others and their desire to understand you and desert you
> For other centers of communication, so that understanding
> May begin, and in doing so be undone. (1977, 45–46)

Or, as Eliot has it, "while poetry attempts to convey something beyond what can be conveyed in prose rhythm, it remains, all the same, one person talking to another; this is just as true if you sing it, for singing is another way of talking" (1979, 23).

13. This is Eliot's definition of the lyric voice, which he prefers to call the "meditative" voice: "the voice of the poet talking to himself—or to nobody" (1979, 96).

14. The question this subject raises is the question Lacan formulates about the psychoanalytic I: "It is not a question of knowing whether I speak of myself in a way that conforms to what I am, but rather of knowing whether I am the same as that of which I speak" (1977, 165). When the two coincide, the words will have formulated who I am. As Merrill puts it, words discover who "I" am. That of which I speak comes into being in my speech, not the other way around. Or, in Anne Sexton's version, the words in the poem say "something I might have said . . . / but did not" (1981, 12). The poet's "I," of course, is produced not by narrating but by reproducing the material language; this intentionalization of the medium is prior to the possibility of any narrative operation.

15. Northrop Frye describes lyric creation as "an associative rhetorical process, most of it below the threshold of consciousness, a chaos of paronomasia, sound-links, ambiguous sense-links, and memory-links very like that of the dream. Out of this the distinctly lyrical union of sound and sense emerges" (1957, 271–72). On another scale, Eliot speaks of "a simultaneous development of form and material" in lyric poetry: "the 'psychic material' tends to create its own form" and "the form affects the material at every stage" (1979, 110). The poet "cannot know what words he wants until he has found the words": "When you have the words for it, the 'thing' for which the words had to be found has disappeared, replaced by a poem" (106). The poet does not start by choosing what to say; he is partly chosen to speak certain words in a certain order that sounds right and "relieves" him of his "burden" (107).

16. This is Renato Barilli's apt term for intraverbal figures that work "below the verbal threshold" (1989, 110).

17. See Barilli 1989, vii, x.

18. By contrast, the Platonic notion of truth has "contempt for the materiality of language" and privileges things over words, demanding transparent, instrumental language (Barilli 1989, 7). The early modern dissociation of the senses and the intellect and of the different senses reinforces this notion. The eye and the ear offer different modes of knowledge: "on one side is the belief in the presence of truth, something everybody can reach 'through their eyes' and through intuition. The other side is marked by the absence of an absolute truth, which is replaced by arguments with varying degrees of probability, about which one must talk and to which one must listen: the stress is on the mouth-ears circuit. The spread of printing . . . provides crucial help . . . to the success of the first model" (66).

19. Foucault traces a crucial moment in the history of "truth" in just these terms: with the sixth-century Greek poets, "the highest truth . . . resided in what discourse *was*, . . . what it *did*"; a century later "truth" lay in "what was *said*. The day dawned when truth moved over from the ritualised act—potent and just—of enunciation to settle on what was enunciated itself: its meaning, its form, its object and its relation to what it referred to. . . . [H]enceforth, true discourse . . . ceased to be discourse linked to the exercise of power" (1972, 218). Thus, "effective, ritual discourse, charged with

power and peril, gradually arranged itself into a disjunction between true and false discourse" (232). This repression of the rhetorical power of pure discourse is exercised by one of the "great systems of exclusion governing discourse"—"the will to truth" (219).

20. The history of rhetoric and poetics attests to the early recognition of the lyric's rhetorical status. In the classical division, poetics concerns meter and the technical art of constructing poetry, especially the long forms of epic and drama, while brief forms and emotional languages come under the rubric of rhetoric. Rhetoric treats forms such as epigrams, elegies, and hymns; focuses on style and diction; and addresses emotions and how they are produced. Thus, Barilli argues that the "gap between the practice of rhetorical discourse and that of certain poetic genres or brief texts exhibiting a lyric flavor is rather small" (1993, 5–6, 68).

21. W. R. Johnson's study of the classical lyric stresses the rhetorical I-You configuration. Essential to the classical lyric is rhetoric, and essential to "lyrical rhetoric," he argues, is the "pronomial form and lyric identity": the lyricist, like the orator, means to persuade and educate his hearer about human passions, which to embrace and which to shun, "what configurations of identity . . . are possible or preferable." The lyric offers "paradigms of identity, patterns of schooled volition" (1982, 23, 30, 31).

The rhetoricity of lyric language and its relation to the audience is obscured with the emergence of "aesthetics," which registers a "modern" anxiety about how a public audience might be defined or conceived. According to Tzvetan Todorov, "Aesthetics begins precisely where rhetoric ends." In "the passage from classical to romantic ideology," aesthetics comes to substitute for rhetoric, and the devaluation of rhetoric sets in (1984, 111). In the romantic opposition of lyric and rhetoric, the lyric comes to be privileged but also purged, as it were, not just of baroque ornament and diction but of its public offices.

22. Sean Burke writes that it "installs the ethical within the graphic" (1997, 242–43). And, we could add, the other way around.

23. Eliot proposes that in writing nondramatic verse, "one is writing, so to speak, in terms of one's own voice: the way it sounds when you read it to yourself is the test. For it is yourself speaking. The question of communication, of what the reader will get from it, is not paramount" (1979, 100). "One's own voice" is what "sounds right" to one's own ear. Eliot does not say "for you are speaking it," but that "it is yourself speaking"; it is speaking yourself *as* yourself, and the test is, does it speak in your "own voice"? Eliot admits to "some confusion of pronouns in this passage," but he lets the confusion to stand. "Yourself" in poetry is a set of words that have their own rhetoric, their way of sounding right, but "When you read it to yourself," it must sound like "it is yourself speaking."

24. Whitman's "Souvenirs of Democracy" (1973, 615), incorporating his signature into the text he is bequeathing the future, is a clear case of how the signature that would link the text to the poet is itself a textual entity. It can exist only in a text; we put signatures only in writing. The moat of reference keeps duplicating itself, for the signature does not "refer" to Walt Whitman, the historical person. It only testifies that the printed text is the will of the signatory, represented in handwriting, who declares his accountability and responsibility to the future:

. . . I, my life surveying,
With nothing to show, to devise, from its idle years,
Nor houses, nor lands—nor tokens of gems or gold for my friends,
Only these Souvenirs of Democracy—in them—in
    all my songs—behind me leaving,
To You, whoever you are, (bathing, leavening this leaf especially with my
    breath—pressing on it a moment with my own hands;
—Here! feel how the pulse beats in my wrists!—
    how my heart's-blood is swelling, contracting!)
I will You, in all, Myself, with promise to never desert you,
To which I sign my name,

Walt Whitman [signed]

The "I" is both a textual entity—as is the signature—and lays a claim to a real future: after Walt Whitman is dead, "I" will live. "I was the man," but "I" am a text. My life was always already in the past tense: "I" live only in the future, only after *my* death.

25. Jonathan Culler writes: "What the functioning of puns reveals about language is, first, the importance of the urge to motivate, which comes to seem a powerful mechanism of language rather than a corruption that might be excluded"; "Precisely because the linguistic sign is arbitrary," he continues, "discourse works incessantly, deviously to motivate" (1988a, 11). It would seem that at this point we need a speaker for whom the linguistic sign is not arbitrary—a native discourser—to motivate the compulsive mechanisms of the code.

26. This poem would lend evidence to Saussure's argument that phonemes of sacred names are encrypted in funerary poems. The phonemes of a name, analyzed, recombined in various ways, and distributed throughout the text, make for an order independent of the formal orders of rhyme and other sound schemes such as assonance or consonance, which do not imply that a word or a name is being imitated. Pound's title gives us both the name and the significant consonantal cluster of Pound's initials, ELP—**E.P. Ode Pou**r L'Electio**n** de son **Sep**ulchre—that are also distributed through **Pe**nelo**pe** and the unnamed **Elp**enor, the one "with a name to come."

27. But such devices become problematic when used to establish power over words. In H.D. and Robert Duncan, for example, microrhetorical processes that would dissolve "truths" become instrumental devices for recuperating *the* occulted Truth. Such microrhetoric functions as a macrorhetoric, and the poet, under the guise of a mystical self-surrender, is instituted as pure will over language. The credibility of microrhetoric depends on a certain relaxation of attention, an *appearance* of unintentionality, of randomness, of an excess. Elizabeth Bishop is a master at this: a poem is very often over-organized with sonic and letteral patterns, but this surface organization runs alongside the referential import and the formal shape of the poem—its rhyme scheme or metrical frame—of which it seems happily oblivious. This is a "useless" excess that we cannot assimilate into a reading. Here neither aspect of language is made to serve the other, and both are audible in their separate systems; they will neither add up nor reduce to one another.

28. Unlike the analysand's "non-sense," the poet's may be a conscious appeal to the power of microrhetorical persuasions. Ashbery says, "Something I never understood

is why the rhyming word is the more convincing substitute for the word that means the same" (Bellamy 1984, 16). If one has, say, "pray" in a line, "fray" will be more convincing than, say, "unravel." Different sounds "argue" differently. But Ashbery also speaks of revising by "substituting a word that sounded like one that was there but had a different meaning" (16). If one had "pray," one might change it to "fray" or "play." This kind of "intraverbal" or "collapsed" rhyme substitutes along the axis of the code and might be subliminally audible for native speakers of a language, or for certain speakers of a language, when the context, meaning, and the reader's expectations factor in. For readings also individuate, partly on the basis of what different readers see/hear in the same text.

Chapter 2

⚜

THE HISTORICAL "I"

THE MOTHER TONGUE'S "I"

What kinds of noise assuage him, what kinds of music pleasure or repel him, what messages the receiving stations of his
senses are happy to pick up from the world around him and
what ones they automatically block out—all this unconscious
activity, at the pre-verbal level, is entirely relevant to the
intonations and appeasements offered by a poet's music.
　　　　　　　　　　　—*Seamus Heaney*

Even when two persons of taste like the same poetry, this
poetry will be arranged in their minds in slightly different
patterns; our individual taste in poetry bears the indelible
traces of our individual lives with all their experience
pleasurable and painful.
　　　　　　　　　　　—*T. S. Eliot*

QUESTIONED ABOUT WRITING in German after the war, Paul Celan responded:
"Only in the mother tongue can one speak one's own truth. In a foreign tongue
the poet lies" (Felstiner 1975, 46). "One's own truth" would seem to be distinct
from the propositional or factual truth content of what one says, which one
can say in any language. The truth spoken in the language in which one undergoes the transition into words is "one's own truth"; it is who one *is*. The lyric
"I," which has no reality other than its audibility as an "I," re-sounds the originary mediation of the mother tongue that makes for the socializing/individu-
ating history of a subject. The cultural institution of the lyric safeguards the
site for the re-cognition of that lived history. The poet's personal memories
and associations in the mother tongue are formalized and thus socialized as a
generic discourse of a virtual "I," so that other speakers with other, different,
memories and associations can recognize their "own truths" as socialized/indi-
viduated subjects in language.

　　The entry into symbolic language, which constitutes one's lived history *as*
an "I," is a "passage" from the semiotic to the semantic system of language. It
is a historical process, a "crossing" of what in theoretical retrospect becomes a
"gap." In Emile Benveniste's terms, the semiotic and semantic are two "discrete
and contrasting signifying modes" within language: "The semiotic (the sign)

must be RECOGNIZED; the semantic (discourse) must be UNDERSTOOD. The difference between recognition and understanding entails two separate faculties of the mind: the ability to perceive a correspondence between what is there and what has been there before, and the ability to perceive the meaning of a new enunciation."[1]

Drawing on this distinction, Agamben proposes that, in order to be "constituted as a subject within language," the infant must remove itself from infancy, break the "closed world of the sign," and transform "pure language into human discourse, the semiotic into the semantic" (1993, 55). The human in its historicity is located in this transformation: "Animals do not enter language, they are already inside it. Man, instead, by having an infancy, by preceding speech, splits this single language and, in order to speak, has to constitute himself as the subject of language—he has to say *I*." Thus "man's nature is split at its source," and "the historicity of the human being has its basis in this difference and discontinuity." Because the infant has to enter symbolic language to become a human subject, the origin of the human is a "historicizing" that founds "the possibility of there being any 'history' ": only because of this discontinuity between the semiotic and the symbolic is there "history"; "only because of this is man a historical being" (49, 52).

If the historicizing entry into language makes for a subject who can say "I," a kind of language use that foregrounds the very difference between the semiotic and the semantic systems would be the proper language of a generic historical "I," which is the "I" of the lyric. Lyric language rehabits the transition we make from the sign system to the discursive system in order to become "human" subjects. "The world of the sign is closed," Benveniste writes: "Between the sign and the sentence there is no transition. . . . A moat separates them."[2] The "moat" between the semiotic and discursive systems is historically created in the very constitution of the subject in language. And poetic language occupies that "moat": we both recognize the sign system *as such* and understand meanings.

The philosophical account of the historicizing entry into language tells a universal story; in order to engage lyric language, however, we need to consider the special status of the mother tongue and the lived history of the transformation of random muscular and sonic phenomena into recognizable elements of a sign system. This first stage of language acquisition makes for an individuating emotional history in language. All humans undergo this socializing process but under infinitely variable conditions, and these differences shape each person's emotionally charged relationship to the elements of the signifier. The separate history of the individuated "I" is that of the passage from the body to the linguistic system and on to the symbolic. If the history of the "human" is the passage from the code to the symbolic and makes for the generic "I" of language, the individuated "I" is historically encrypted in the materials of the linguistic code. This lived history accounts for the emotional charge of the elements of the signifier, and poetry returns to that history of seduction and discipline into language. Its pleasure is in the return to the site of pain. And that site, the historicizing origin of the human, is the mother tongue, the site of "one's own truth."

Poetic language remembers the history of the process of language acquisition. The poetic production of meaning out of material, acoustic phenomena reverberates an earlier transition from the production of sounds to the production of words. From the perspective of cognitive and psychological development, the acquisition of verbal language, sometime in the second year of the infant's history, is part of a general development of the symbolic function and entails profound changes both in mental operations and in the way sounds and voices signify. In Jean Piaget's terms, language becomes possible with a transition from sensory-motor intelligence and relation to the environment and others to symbolic, conceptual, or representational intelligence and relations. The activity of sound production via mutual imitation between the child and its caretaker is eventually replaced by the production of sounds as linguistic signs with referential content. In between is a stage where a sound may function as a sign that is not arbitrary but immediately associated with its referent. The production of such individual "symbol" or "image" representations is a continuation of the sensory-motor intelligence preceding the acquisition of language. At this stage, the sounds are not words but re-cognized sensory-motor productions that intend to signify. Such representations, unlike the arbitrary, conventional, social signs of language, remain "individual"; they are "translations" of "personal experiences" and they play a "unique role alongside the system of collective signs" (1962, 75, 68, 71).

Even after the earlier, sensory-motor language is "forgotten," the mother tongue carries somatic and emotional memory traces of this transitional activity of the socially undifferentiated "speaker," who uses sound images for individual representations. This "other" language cannot be forgotten because that transition makes us who we are—individuated speakers with particular associations and feelings for particular phonemes, words, and phrases. And such "forgetting" cannot be understood in Freudian terms, as repression, for the experience of infancy does not reach representation, which is a necessary condition for repression. Rather, infancy is "forgotten" in language, with the emergence of the very possibility of representation; the institution of the symbolic function rests on infantile amnesia.

But the mother tongue also holds the possibility for recall, and lyric poetry reverberates that history of "forgetfulness." It resounds the transition from somatic to representational language and recalls individual relationships to sound images. If an "I" comes into being in "forgetting" the archaic bodily language, the lyric looks back, as in a dream, to that passage into conceptual language. An I is not just one who can say "I" in a linguistic system but one who has a personal relationship to the sound images that mark its transition to symbolic language. The remainder in the wake of that transition, the experiences and associations not communicable in words, is the inheritance of the "individual." And the remainder that cannot be represented in verbal language is more, rather than less, in the mother tongue where one becomes an "I." In poetry, there is an uncanny return of the "forgotten," personally charged material body of language as something at once more strange and more familiar than sense.

Also possible in the mother tongue is a retrieval of undifferentiated perception, which characterizes a stage in language acquisition. Learning the verbal code by an intersubjective process of "mutually negotiated meanings" between the child and the mother physically and emotionally socializes the child.[3] What is lost in this process is "the conglomerate of feeling, sensation, perception, and cognition that constitutes global nonverbal experience." Such "global" personal experience, Daniel N. Stern writes, does not quite disappear; gradually driven "underground" with the development of language, it continues to have an un-represented, "unverbalized," "unnamed," but "nevertheless very real existence" (1994, 204, 207, 208).

Global experience is characterized by undifferentiated, amodal perception. The infant's perception of a "patch of yellow sunlight," for example, would be a mix of modal properties, such as the "intensity, warmth, shape, brightness," and so on, of the patch. This "omnidimensional perspective" is lost as language specifies sensory channels for the experience: "Someone will enter the room and say, 'Oh, *look* at the *yellow* sun*light*.'" Words separate and distinguish dif-ferent properties and assign them to separate sensory modalities;[4] they draw borders and institute unimodal perceptual qualities as "figures" on the multi-sensory "ground" of early childhood experience. The amodal and personal ex-periences that are driven underground can resurface under conditions that sup-press the linguistic version of the experience, and Stern cites certain "contemplative," "emotional" states and works of art, such as symbolist poetry, that aim to evoke "experiences defying verbal categorization" (1994, 208, 209).

The characteristic symbolist device of synesthesia certainly invokes the flux of amodal perception. But the device that the Romantics and Symbolists popu-larized is found throughout Western literature, going back to Homer and Aeschylus.[5] Some form of synesthesia seems to be at work in the mechanism of poetic thinking generally as well as in the construction of linguistic meaning in early childhood. As a psychological phenomenon, synesthesia is "an *involun-tary* joining in which the real information of one sense is accompanied by a perception in another sense."[6] Rare among adults but common in children before age seven, synesthesia, Kevin Dann argues, most often links colors with linguistic symbols, "letters, numbers, and words," which are "particularly sa-lient emotionally with children" (1998, 7–8). Synesthesia is both an emotional and a conceptual experience, for the phenomenon of undifferentiated or amo-dal perception appears to be "an essential mechanism in the construction of meaning" (95, 82).[7] Research in synesthesia suggests that it marks a necessary transitional stage in the development of language, serving as the "primary mediator between the described perceptual complexes of objects and the descriptive sound complexes of language."[8]

Terrence Deacon also proposes that the mediation of cross-modal, indexical associations is necessary for learning language. In the development of symbolic language, cross-modal associations of images and experiences with particular word sounds make for the indexical associations of words (1997, 302–3). But at a certain stage of language learning, "a referential shortcut" becomes possible and one can bypass the indexical mediation and use the "relationships implicit in combinations of signs (e.g., phrases and sentences)" to refer directly to the relationships between objects and events (301). Thus, cross-modal associations make for the crux of reference, mediate sign-object relations, and "ground" language. But such personal experiences that constitute an early and foundational form of thinking—of perception and conception (Dann 1998, 82)—are dispensable for the system they help institute.

The coherence of physiological sensations, psychological affect, and mental cognition in the production and reception of sounds constitutes a lived "global" experience that is lost in words. But even after sounds are channeled into linguistic use, these experiences of sounds and voices seem to continue a subliminal existence and can be recalled in certain kinds of language use. Poetry exploits the affective qualities of sounds, remembering the history of the production of speech sounds. Thus, the *necessary* historical "ground" of symbolic language may be "retrieved"—remembered or imagined—out of the "amnesia" of referential language, whose stability depends on infantile amnesia. Poems begin, many poets testify, with a rhythm—an experience that is not verbal and not consciously invoked—and the hold of the referential function relaxes with the entry into a rhythmic state, allowing for a greater sensitivity to the perceptual qualities of sounds. The rhythmic threshold is also a sensory mode threshold, rendering permeable the linguistically drawn borders between auditory and specular experience and perception. The rhythmic alternation between patterned repetitions of sounds and sense, music and image, the desire to annul and the desire to reinscribe the subject, is an essentially synesthetic lingering of the lyric "I" between auditory and visual sensations and senses.[9] This synesthetic site for the *event* of sense out of sensations on the verge of categorization functions, much as the indexical "I" functions, as a site of meaning.

Another kind of poetic retrieval recovers the emotional values of sounds, and it too recovers an experience that transgresses the boundaries drawn by linguistic experience. Acoustic and phonological phenomena are processed in different hemispheres of the brain, which become fully specialized around age twelve; while sounds are processed in the right hemisphere, speech is processed in the left. Poetic language must be processed both acoustically and phonologically, in both hemispheres, because it carries acoustic information in excess of the linguistic information. In processing the acoustic signal as speech, we attend away from the acoustic to "the combination of muscular acts that seem to have produced it," Reuven Tsur writes; and we attend away from these movements "*to* their joint purpose, the phoneme sequence" (1992, 11). Thus, in processing the acoustic signal, the listener "intentionalizes" it by moving "back to the articulatory gesture that produced it and thence, as it were, to the speaker's intent."[10] While speech processing intentionalizes the sound as a phoneme, acoustic processing responds to the emotional colors and tones, the perceptual qualities of speech sounds that are irrelevant to speech and escape categorical processing.

In processing acoustic information, a "universal" or shared history intersects with a personal and language-specific history, for the emotional associations of the sounds of words seem to be partly determined by the cognitive processes of speech recognition and hold across languages. The tonal qualities of different vowel sounds, for example, are not language-specific and seem to follow from the amount of cognitive effort required to process them. Thus /i/, the simplest vowel to process, is generally perceived as "light," while the back vowels, which take more effort, are perceived as "dark" (Tsur 1992, 23). The phonemes that take more effort to process are also those that are acquired later, and these sounds are more emotive than the phonemes that are acquired earlier and are simpler to process. More cognitive effort makes for a "delayed categorization" of the sound as a phoneme, and we could say that this delay in processing the signal as speech repeats or reproduces the historical "delay" in the acquisition of the phoneme. The distinct processing of sounds and phonemes that poetry calls for thus reinscribes a lived history.

In the process of language acquisition, the denotative and the expressive uses of sounds are distinct: while the child is mastering the sign system, Jakobson writes, "he constantly resorts to the other sounds, still unmastered, for sound gestures (interjections and onomatopoeia)."[11] The later a phoneme is acquired (such as nasal vowels), the longer it has been in the play of sounds as in onomatopoeia, and the more emotional value it has.[12] While the emotional tones of different phonemes seem to hold across languages, the particular correlation of phonetic and semantic values would be language-specific and make for personal emotional associations of the sounds of particular words. Thus, the emotional value of particular words, particular phonemic clusters, would be determined by the language-specific history of the speaker.

The denotative-rational and the expressive-emotional languages of the child cooperate in poetry. While sounds are differentiated into phonemes and linked to form words, they also enter independent patterns of repetition and similarity. Poetic devices organize, in patterns of repeats, the acoustic information not processed for speech—the remainder, as it were. In poetic sound patterns, each recurrence reinforces the lingering precategorical auditory information, aug-

menting the emotional quality of such sounds. Hypnotic poetry especially relies on periodic sounds (vowels, liquids, and nasals), and regularity of rhythm
reinforces the emotional resonance of such late-acquired phonemes that relax
attention and linger in memory (Tsur 1992, 43, 46).

Poetic effects thus entail a delay or a disruption of smooth cognitive functioning, and memory serves to reinforce the delay in recoding acoustic into
phonetic information, as each recurrence increases the resistence. Poetic forms
of repetition ensure the *experience* of such delay, which recalls the lived, "historical" delay in the acquisition of different phonemes. Attention to sounds that
linger in memory, the pleasure of lingering between acoustic and phonemic
processing, and the emotional value of this delay in cognition constitute a conscious, subjective experience of time that is a living history. Such delay in categorization also ensures that acoustic information is processed not only tempo-
rally but spatially, in the right hemisphere, thus facilitating a synesthetic
crossing between sound and figure.

Symbolic language, Deacon writes, enables us to share "a virtual common
mind," because it functions independently of any "indexical attachment to any
particular experiences." But when a listener "reconstructs" an idea or a narrative
of someone else's experience, he "regrounds" it "by interpreting it in terms of
the iconic and indexical representations that constitute the listener's memory"
(1997, 427). Listeners intentionalize what they hear by supplying their own
indexical mnemonics. Thus, "[L]anguage functions as a sort of shared code
for translating certain essential attributes of memories and images between
individuals who otherwise have entirely idiosyncratic experiences" (451).

Something similar might be said about the lyric: it enables us to share a
"virtual common subjectivity," which exists only at the symbolic, thoroughly
social, level. A shared virtual subjectivity is actualized by each reader articulating herself, her experiences, memories, and emotions, with the words of the
model "I." In the case of poetry, the listener's indexical mnemonics include not
only representations but muscular, auditory, rhythmic, and emotional memories. By patterning and emphasizing the linguistic "remainder," the lyric preserves a space for the experience of individuating relationships to those non-
symbolic aspects of the code that are functional in learning and processing
symbolic language: the somatic memories of sensory-motor and oral-aural experiences, the amodal and specific personal perceptions that cannot be represented in verbal language, and an "individual" system of image representations
of auditory and phonic sensations. The special emotional and historical texture
of the mother tongue that makes for the history of an "individual" can return
only in the specific language that produces itself on that "foundation."

The formality of lyric language not only allows for the reinscription of subjective experience into the symbolic medium but also carries a cultural memory.
An intersubjective history of subjectivity constructed around the "I" bonds

communities of speakers—not only of contemporaneous subjects but subjects across different times and places. Pound proposes this "measure" for poetry: "No man can read Hardy's poems collected but that his own life, and forgotten moments of it, will come back to him, a flash here and an hour there. Have you a better test of true poetry?" (1970, 286). Such conscious subjective experience originates not with or within the subject but with a social process and a social medium that carries a communal history—the language-specific history of poetry; its conventions; its historical store of usages of specific words, forms, devices; its accumulated rhythmic practices; and so on. Linguistic communities transmit their experience of language into discourse in ways as variable as the individuals' transmissions of their experience of words into discourse. Lyric language "remembers" the initial acquisition of language that individuates/socializes subjects in the medium of a discourse that requires the acquisition of a second language and a second set of "poet-parents," more hero-sized than the first, merely mortal set. The lyric poet is both an individuated/socialized speaker in the mother tongue *and* a discursive "I," individuated and socialized over again in a tradition to ensure the linguistic community's historical truth and its reproduction.

Poetry is the tradition of the mother tongue's "I," the record of how the linguistic "remainder" that makes for one "I" among others has been coded to translate subjects across time. The lyric puts on record an "I" who exists nowhere else but in the language she sounds and the discourse of the "I" that she resounds. It is a social medium safeguarding a personal experience of language. On both counts, the poet must submit to the rules of how things may be said in words and how they may be said "poetically," "now," in order to enter the discourse and the record. This necessity to resuscitate a tradition ensures the audibility of the "I" and safeguards its history against "blackout." For without that history, it does not exist.

RHYTHM

You don't devise a rhythm, rhythm is the person.
—*Marianne Moore*

The phenomenon of rhythm offers an approach to both the social formation of an individuated "I" in the process of language acquisition and the poetic recovery of that history in the formulation of a lyric "I." The individuated, historical subject who says "I" is a diachronic figure audible in a distinctive rhythm. Rhythm is not to be understood as a representation of an "I." And it belongs to neither the semiotic nor the semantic order, neither to the formal systems of meter and rhyme nor to the discursive organization of figure and meaning, but it *intentionalizes* both systems. The indexical function of rhythm renders both language and speech meaningful and sounds a metaphysically groundless, and historically grounding, intention to mean. It makes sounds/words interpretable as intended; it makes them intelligible to a "you" in time. Rhythm, a pattern of recurrence that is experienced in and as time, both renders language sensible and reveals the experienced temporality of an intending "I" to be a necessary condition for meaningful language. My argument here is that we need to think of the "I," intention, character, and rhythm as terms that may substitute for one another—as different ways of formulating the condition for the event of meaningful language.

Rhythm is the crux of language acquisition. Learning language depends on a rhythmic training that precedes and enables meaningful speech. The stage of babbling, where the infant can produce the phonemes of all possible languages, entails recognizing aural sensations and reproducing them orally. Physical training in recognizing and reproducing sounds as such, without regard to signification, involves pure imitation and rhythmic repetition and serves to establish a rhythmic mouth-ear connection. Thus it is more accurate to say that babbling is not simply a stage in language acquisition but a *different* language, a different kind of rhythmic communication system. The training in *vocal* rhythmization, in the prosody of human speech, entails hearing and communicating emotion, which establishes the mouth-ear circuit and motivates phonemic production; it precedes speech, which could not happen without it.

The expressive features of speech—its nonverbal, intonational and rhythmic qualities, its stress patterns, the pace and timing of its flow—all convey emotional information, and Ellen Dissanayake argues that the human brain is "programmed to respond to emotional/intonational aspects of the human voice"; even newborns respond to variations in "frequency, intensity, duration, and temporal or spatial patterning of sounds."[13] Infants seem to come with "innate intersubjectivity"—a capacity for "eliciting and responding to emotional communication with another."[14] This initial language involves responding not only to voice rhythms but to facial expressions and body movements;[15] it is a "multimedia" interaction between the infant and the people around him (1999, 373). Rhythmic sounds and movements give enjoyment through means that involve right-hemisphere capabilities—processing facial and intonational expression and prosodic contours, whole pattern recognition, "regulation of emotional information," and *crossmodal perception or analogy*" (381). Thus vocal rhythmization seems to involve negotiating a variety of sensory stimuli; it emerges in—and is located within—a "global" experience. The particulars of this language, within a given culture and linguistic community, will vary with each mother-infant unit,[16] but its procedures of attunement seem to be universal. Voluntary and involuntary imitations, repetitions, and modulations of each other's gestures and tempo offer mutual pleasure, and such harmonizing has significant benefits, not only for the infant's emotional development but for his "intellectual, linguistic, psychosocial, and cultural development" (374, 375). In this dialog, children learn to perceive nonverbal gestures, sounds, tones, and rhythms of intention and emotion as an "intrinsic part of their society's communication system."[17] Infants are not particularly encouraged to produce words, for this preverbal, rhythmic communication system has to be in place before speech can take place. The child first has to hear vocal rhythm, the rhetoric of the voice as such, as communicating intention and emotion.

The capacity to respond to speech sounds as communicative and to recognize intentionality and emotion may or may not be innate; what is important is its development through the rhythmic interaction—first somatic, then social and linguistic—of the infant and the mother. It seems that rhythm *cues* the infant to speech sounds—to intentionalize acoustic phenomena. Colwyn Trevarthen writes: "the strong response of a newborn to the periodic motion of an object in an otherwise inactive field must contribute to his perception of persons and their communication signals. All voluntary movement is periodic. . . . It has rhythmic coherence" (1994, 223). Jakobson also suggests a link between rhythmic repetition and intentionality; repetition of syllables, he writes, signals that "their phonation is not babbling, but a verbal message" (qtd. in Tsur 1992, 54). Rhythm seems to communicate and teach intentionality, as the child's sounds are intentionalized in a rhythmic, repetitive dialog with the caretaker.[18] Intending is learned and involves interpretation: an auditor, interpreting the infant's sounds, intentionalizes the sounds as communicative, and this, in turn, guides and limits how the infant will next use that particular sound. The acquired word, John Dore writes, "is not merely the symbolic consequence of intentional development. It is, specifically, the consequence of *interpreted* intentions" (1994, 243), and it is developed through social interaction.

Rhythm is learned. It structures the intersubjective process of the transition between somatic and verbal languages and articulates a coherent ego across that passage. Biological and environmental rhythms may be givens, but social rhythms are learned. And verbal rhythm is social. The ground of the somatic language of infancy, it becomes functional in the proper understanding of lexical meaning in the semantic mode of signification. A constant between the two languages, rhythm transcodes one into the other and constitutes an essential part of meaning in language, if not the very *possibility* of meaning. Certainly, literary meaning depends on hearing the rhythm that intentionalizes the lexical components of a sentence, interpreting what is meant by the sentence. Unlike meter, rhythm has an indexical function and enables hearing—ensures the audibility of—what is meant by what is said.[19] Nietzsche emphasizes that literary meaning depends on hearing rhythm. A *"third* ear"—Stevens's "delicatest ear of the mind"—hears rhythm *as* meaning, for the rhythm of a sentence must be apprehended if the sentence is to be *understood*:[20] "If there is a misunderstanding about its *tempo*, for instance, the sentence itself is misunderstood!" Reading "for the ear" involves listening to the "*art and intention* in language."[21] Rhythm is a meaning function, and it is operative in prose as well as in poetry. In poetry, however, it becomes sensible as such against the backdrop of grammar and meter and thus establishes itself as a meaning function.

Reading demands not only attention to sounds and verbal signs but the recognition of motivation to hear the speaker that is produced in and as rhythm. And a lyric "I" that must be heard—that is a rhetorical excess of the formal and discursive codes—exists only in its social reception or its receivability. An auditor is necessary for any rhetorical event, which is precisely what the lyric "I" is—an intersubjective, persuasive rhythmic movement. Rhythm is a rhetorical relation between a speaking "I" and a hearing "you," and it affects both the sounds (including meters) and the sense of the words. The double event of language and the subject in lyric poetry turns on rhythm, which makes for the audibility of the "I" by making its sounds/words intelligible to a "you."

Because the "I" that is produced as a rhythm is prescribed by the mother tongue and the specific history of each mother-infant pair, rhythm is an "individual" and individuating trait. "A man's rhythm," as Pound has it, is "in the end, his own, uncounterfeiting, uncounterfeitable" (1968a, 9). It is a signature that stamps and authenticates the currency of language. A subject that is not discursively formulated, "narrated," or formed-formalized—an "I" that is prior to the possibility of such operations—exists in an audible rhythm and voice. Poetic rhythm can be "heard" in a text; it is a mentally audible movement of sounds that will not reduce to discursive meanings or formal effects. Pound calls it melopoeia, a "perfection of movement," apart from anything "salient in the thought or the rhyme scheme" (1960, 55). Rhythm has no symbolic value, and it is distinct from meter, insofar as meter is an abstract representation of the sound shape of a language and can be represented as an abstract scheme. Rhythm is experienced in and as time, as a persuasive movement of the voice. It does not represent and is not representable; it does not measure and is not measurable. And the rhythm that motivates an acoustic event to be receivable as a signifying event is not an acoustic phenomenon, even though it may be "heard" in an acoustic event. Rhythm persuades, even compels, our hearing in a certain way, our hearing sounds as meaning; it makes audible an intending "I."

The individuating rhythm of a poet is at once his "voiceprint," his "character" or "signature," and makes audible the prosodic "music" of the mother tongue. The phenomenon of the voice, Philippe Lacoue-Labarthe writes, comprises "intonation, elocution, tone, inflections, melisma, rhythm, even timber (or what Barthes calls 'grain'). Or color."[22] Classical rhetoric addresses these phenomena that do not fall

> under the jurisdiction of linguistic distinctions in the proper sense (of the type semiotic/semantic, for example) because, more fundamentally, they escape the metaphysical (theoretical) distinctions that always underlie

them (sensible/intelligible, matter/form, body/spirit, thing/idea, and so on). A phenomenon of this sort is, finally, untheorizable. (1988, 159–60)

Rhythm is a phenomenon that is not of the order of language, but it "affects a language" (159) and affirms an *ethos*—both the communal character of a language and a personal character, or "signature." The rhythmic signature imprints the phonemic flow.

Distinct from meter, which belongs to the formal system, rhythm makes for the perceptibility of time.[23] For rhythm is not simply the fact of temporal repetition or periodicity; it requires a perception of periodicity *as* rhythmic.[24] As such, it involves the auditor's participation in structuring time and movement. Nicolas Abraham writes that rhythm trains and compels us to experience an event as rhythmic. Poetic rhythm thus requires a rhetoric on the part of both the speaker and the auditor. The rhythmic event happens only if we will it: "We have only to reject a rhythm and it will not occur" (1995, 73). Thus the criterion of rhythm is not a quality of the rhythmic object but lies in the beholder, in our "rhythmizing consciousness," which emerges as an "expectation of a return," motivating a future and, retrospectively, a past (79). Rhythmizing consciousness creates itself as a temporal, intending subject in creating a future with "its own decisive act of will" (72).

Thus metrical time and the experienced time of rhythm are distinct. Meter organizes objective time and institutes patterns of periodicity, whereas rhythm organizes subjective time and makes for the *experience* of periodicity. But formal meter may facilitate rhythmic perception. John Crowe Ransom writes that "formal metre impresses us as a way of regulating very drastically the material, and we do not stop to remark (that is, as readers) that it has no particular aim except some nominal form of regimentation" (1949, 70). I would say that such "regimentation" calls for and enables a subjective perception of rhythm—a subjective rhythmizing of repetition, the way that one rhythmically structures physically identical events like clock ticks. It is not quite the case, then, that the metrical foot and "lived time" connect "only occasionally and by chance," as Abraham claims (1995, 80). At the level of rhythm as well, we have to think of poetic language as a two-way intentionalizing: the metrical code is intentionalized by our rhythmizing response, which emerges in response to the orders of the code. The sonic system of a given language, as it is encoded in the formal system, and subjective responses to that system are both operative in poetic rhythm.

In organizing subjective time along a past-present-future continuum, we alternate between recognizing a difference, a new event, as a repetition and anticipating a repetition as a new event. Perceiving formal repetitions as rhythmic realizes a present in relation to a past and a future; it makes for a system of sonic echoes that is experienced outside of or "beyond" consecutive time and involves a subjective, auditory memory and desire. Yet any expectation of return can arise only if the initial perception of rhythm is already a re-cognition. The temporal delay and functional difference involved in processing acoustic phenomena as phonemic information would entail some process of representation of the acoustic as both itself and something different. The phoneme is something like an "interpretation" or an echo effect of the acoustic: a sound returns "now," and elsewhere, and is re-cognized as intending to make sense. This return positions the original experience as that of a "pure" sound, as distinct from a signifying sound. If the word is an echo of acoustic sensations, a temporal delay and spatial displacement are constitutive of signifying sounds themselves. Rhythm enables the perception of time and space in a *re-cognition* of a temporal and spatial difference between acoustic and verbal phenomena. Representation depends on this temporal-spatial difference but cannot generate the categories of space and time. The temporal-spatial difference of meaning posits a past that can never be known but only re-cognized, and the expectation of a future repetition emerges because the present itself is a recognition—a repetition. Another way of putting this point is that rhythm becomes audible when the present is perceived *as* repetition, which renders the past recognizable as such. Thus the present is perceived as a repetition of a past that can only be known as a repetition-in-reverse of what is re-cognized at present. In other words, sound is *not* "sound" before it is "sense." Or, voice is not "voice" before it is "meaning." This rhythmically articulated two-way intentionalization constitutes a subjective experience of time.

I focus on rhythm rather than meter because I am interested in the subject function. The individuating and intentionalizing function of rhythm enables meaning in language and renders audible an intending subject. Meter does not serve the same purpose. It is not a crux of an intending "I," for it does not cross systems; it is not a "transcoder."[25] Meter belongs to the linguistic/formal system and represents the generic phonic shape or even phonic grammar, so to speak, of a language.[26] Sounds come in a continuous flow, and meter is a periodizing segmentation of the sonic flow. It would seem to organize the flow and perhaps stress what needs to be stressed for the meaning function. In an accented language like English, the given syllabic stress patterns do not necessarily coincide with metrical feet; thus meter may also counteract the lexical fragmentation of the flow. To help make sense of the phonemic flow, we have two, noncoinciding systems of segmentation—the metrical and the lexical, and they are in dialog. But neither system can generate meaning. Rhythm transcodes these systems and secures the production of sense, of meaningful language. It makes for a speaker.

As a subject function that involves emotion, intention, motivation, and the choice of meaning, poetic rhythm must be distinguished from meter. John Hollander, following I. A. Richards, proposes that meter produces a "'frame' effect" to isolate poetic experience;[27] along with other sonic patternings, it helps establish what Jonathan Culler calls the "monumentality and impersonality" of poetry (1975, 187). In Valéry's wording, "The exigencies of a strict prosody constitute the artifice which bestows upon natural speech the qualities of an unyielding material, foreign to our spirit, and almost deaf to our desires."[28] Meter sounds the "inhumanity" of language and necessitates an "I," a motivating function that, on this register, is performed by rhythm. The formality of poetry necessitates intentionalizing for its language to "mean," and rhythm sounds the "humanizing" inflection of intention. The socialized/individuated "I" is heard as a rhythmic inflection of the generic "I" of language and against a metrical norm—or against any patterning that functions as a norm and makes for the isolating "monumentality" of poetry. Rhythm entails interpretation, both in its production and its reception. It is a subjective, mental echo or interpretation of the metrical measure, and it intervenes in the fatality of meter.

Meter and rhythm, then, cannot be conflated without annulling the poetic subject and its intentionalizing function. Amittai Aviram, for example, does not distinguish the two and proposes rhythm to be a "sublime" force that brings about "a physical response," engaging "the reader's or listener's body" and disrupting "the orderly process of meaning" (1994, 5, 223). "The metrical rhythms of poetry," he writes, appeal not "to our limited intellects" but to "the body in its fundamental existence, prior to or outside the ideologies that construct the body within any social code" (23, 35).[29] But meter *is* a social code and, as T.V.F. Brogan puts it, "strictly speaking, meter has no rhythm. Meters provide structure; rhythms provide movement" (1993, 1068). Moreover, while meter may not "participate in the process of signification," there is no "signification" without rhythm, which is the condition for meaning and cannot be understood as a "disruption" of meaning.

My argument in this discussion of rhythm has been that the rhythmic body *is* the "socially constructed body";[30] rhythmization *is* socialization, and it secures meaning. And it is difficult to tell apart bodily responses to poetic rhythm from our total memory of verbal rhythms. Our sensory experience of the materials of words is already emotionally and historically charged, and we cannot physically experience verbal rhythm in a way that is distinguishable from a mental experience. "The sounds of a poem," Susan Stewart observes, "are not heard in the room of the poem, but they are heard within the memory of hearing that is the total auditory experience of the listener" (2002, 75); certainly, a total rhythmic memory shapes our experience of poetic rhythm. The mind holds an individuated memory of verbal rhythms; it is already inside a linguistic body, and, in poetry, the rhythmic body is already inside a verbal mind.

Meter keeps in view both linguistic constraints and conventional imperatives, and the poet must be heard within that given framework. Here, too, the speaking "I" has to be figured as an alternation or a rhythmic pulse between metrical rules and the prosody of speech—of what one means or *wants* to "say" within a metrical system that is indifferent to—"deaf to"—one's desires. Robert Frost's comments on "the sound of sense" point to this difference on another scale:

> The best place to get the abstract sound of sense is from voices behind a door that cuts off the words. Ask yourself how these sentences would sound without the words in which they are embodied:
>
> > You mean to tell me you can't read?
> > I said no such thing.
> > Well read then.
> > You're not my teacher.
> > .   .   .   .
>
> Those sounds are summoned by the audile imagination and they must be positive, strong, and definitely and unmistakably indicated by the context. The reader must be at no loss to give his voice the posture proper to the sentence.

The "sound of sense," the "abstract vitality of our speech," is "pure sound." And "if one is to be a poet he must learn to get cadences by skillfully breaking the sounds of sense with all their irregularity of accent across the regular beat of the metre." This "mingling of sound sense and word accent" is allowed by the "possibility of emotional expression" (in Gioia, Mason, and Schoerke 2004, 10). It is a matter of a negotiation or a rhythmic transcoding of the two orders of speech prosody and metrical pattern so as to make a particular emotional inflection audible.

The Trauma of the Word

> Ethos, the habitual dwelling place of man is that
> which lacerates and divides.
> —*Heraclitus*

Lyric language, I have argued, transmits the history of the subject in language. Yet this constitutive history of language acquisition is utterly "forgotten." The remarkable phenomenon of infantile amnesia leads me to approach this history with the model of trauma and suggest that such "amnesia" is a different kind of memory that poetry transmits. In most general terms, a traumatic experience is an immediate event that leaves an enduring memory trace but cannot, in principle, be recovered as itself. If, in Freud's terms, "*Consciousness arises instead of a memory trace,*" it follows that memory traces are "most powerful and most enduring when the process which left them behind was one which never entered consciousness." Consciousness functions as a protective shield against external stimuli, and any "excitation" that is "powerful enough to break through the protective shield" may be described as "traumatic" (1989, 606–7). Such a shock event leaves behind an enduring memory trace of an experience that has never entered consciousness and, therefore, can never be known in and as itself. It can only be repeated or reproduced.

Cathy Caruth's work develops the implications of Freud's model. "The traumatized," she writes, "carry an impossible history within them"; they are themselves the "symptom of history," of an occurrence that, in its repetition, remains "absolutely *true*" to the original event, precisely because the event was not "known" in the first place (1995, 5). A history of trauma "can only be grasped in the very inaccessibility of its occurrence," and the traumatized is possessed by a historical truth, the *knowledge* of which he does not, and cannot, possess:

> The experience of trauma, the fact of latency, would thus seem to consist, not in the forgetting of a reality that can hence never be fully known, but in an inherent latency within the experience itself. The historical power of trauma is not just that the experience is repeated after its forgetting, but that it is only in and through its inherent forgetting that it is first experienced at all. And it is this inherent latency of the event that paradoxically explains the peculiar, temporal structure, the belatedness, of historical experience. (7–8)

Thus "the historical and personal truth" (8) trauma transmits is "the difficult truth of a history that is constituted by the very incomprehensibility of its occurrence" (153)—the properly historical truth of a formative yet unassimilable history.

I would like to focus on a particular moment in the process of language acquisition, the passage from babbling to a word, with this model of a traumatic history in mind. The historical event of the passage into language "crosses" the gap between sounds and words, the semiotic and the symbolic. More accurately, this originary historical event opens the theoretical gap in producing a subject—the one who will come to say "I"—at that site. The historical and personal truth of this subject is transmitted in the very word itself.

For Freud, "[v]erbal residues are derived primarily from auditory perceptions": "In essence a word is after all the mnemic residue of a word that has been heard."[31] But an auditory perception would leave an acoustic memory trace, not a "verbal" trace. An auditory sensation would have to be somehow *heard as* a word—it would have to be perceived *as* a word—in order to form the mnemic trace of a *word* heard, rather than of sounds. The "moat" that separates sound and sense, material/acoustic and conceptual/linguistic phenomena, and now acoustic memory traces and consciousness of words opens with a "word heard"—an *echo* of sounds in a conceptual register,[32] a return or reverberation of sounds elsewhere.

This involves crossing two kinds of hearing. The child does not hear with the same ear as the adult, Robert Pujol writes. The relations of phonemes escape the adult, because he is "attuned to the sense which comes from sonority and no longer to the sonority itself. We suggest that the subject *infans* does not hear this with the same ear; he is sensitive only to the phonemic opposition of the signifying chain."[33] And Deleuze adds, "If the child comes to a preexisting language which she cannot yet understand, perhaps, conversely, she grasps that which we no longer grasp in our own language, namely, the phonemic relations, the differential relations of phonemes" (1990, 230). On another scale, as Deacon argues, the child hears relations of syntax—parts of speech to parts of speech and symbol to symbol—before she hears discrete units on the referential plane of meanings. She is learning a code, oblivious to semantics, and she hears "globally"—sees the forest before the trees (1997, 135). These relations constitute the given constraints of the semiotic code the child is born into and no doubt the child would have to hear at this level in order to master the code.[34]

To go from hearing the necessities of the semiotic code, the phonemic relations, to hearing semantemes and words, one has to cross systems. The experience of "a word heard," then, can only be an "incomprehensible" experience of pure difference. Hearing-sounds-*as*-a-word would be an immediate experience of the difference between acoustic and linguistic phenomena. The birth of the subject, the possibility of history and a psychic life, lies in an *experience* of an otherness internal to the auditory perception of words. At this threshold between sensation and representation, an immediate, felt sensation is also recognized as not itself, as a representation. The possibility of such an experience rests on a time-space interval opening within the experience itself. If something must be re-cognized to be perceived, difference is the condition for this *initial* experience; it opens up *inside* the event of experience. Such an originary experience, one that originates memory itself,[35] is properly a traumatic event where an immediate experience is also not itself. Nothing can bridge this originary gap, the traumatic event of language that inaugurates the subject. The word is the memory trace of a wound, the scar of a cut delineating the boundary that draws apart and distinguishes a mind and a body. This separation that delivers one into language at the same time inaugurates one's psychic life; it is an experience of loss, of an otherness that constitutes one's most intimate self.[36] And this is an emotionally charged event, insofar as the child hearing the code is also hearing the voice that motivates him to listen to the code; he is hearing emotion. The original pain of hearing a word is a trauma suffered passively, by the ear, in the pleasures of the voice.

The intimate otherness of the symbolic system accounts for the insistence of the phoneme and the letter in the Freudian and Lacanian unconscious. The "unconscious" is the repository of the elements of the signifier—not mere sounds but signifying sounds, sounds with personal associations, below the threshold of the word. What is suppressed—and what Freudian theory re-presses—is the history of the transformation of animal sounds to symbolic language. But the phonemic threshold of that transition is not just forgotten. Indeed the resonances of these linguistic elements constitute who we are as individuated beings in a given language. An individuating preverbal hoard is the inheritance of the person. The mere bodily sounds before linguistic sounds and the semantic/symbolic system after linguistic sounds are all overdeter-mined; only this history, which I "forget," marks me.

Referential language forgets the trauma, just as the narrative "I" forgets the truth of its history. The truth of the subject's history is "mastered" or "cured" in fictions of history, in narrativization, a sublimation that is, of course, neces-sary for there to be History.[37] But what this covers up is the other history of the otherness of the "I," the alien intimacy of the symbolic language. This knowledge, which registers in neurotic and psychotic disorders, is public—an open secret—in poetic language. Insofar as the lyric "I" resists narrativization, it resists rationalizing or "understanding" the trauma, for to do so would lose the truth of *its* history, which is the history of the "human." Poetry wills to reopen the wound, to repeat the violence that opens the history of the human subject, so that we can re-cognize our selves in the experience, as Stevens puts it, of "the inhuman making choice of a human self" (1951, 89). Poetry keeps the record of that history in the words of a hypothetical "I" inhabiting the gap of language. The lyric rests on the voiced recall of words, where symbolic language dissolves into sounds *and* where physiology resolves into signifiers.[38]

   Poetic conventions socially sanction a kind of language use that undoes, even as it reinstitutes, the illusion of meaning in language; they carry a history of communal acknowledgment of a shared trauma of individuation/socializa-tion.[39] Like post-traumatic repetitions, they keep the unassimilable trauma—the truth of the subject—still audible: they make for the audibility of the truth of history. Thus the re-turn of lyric poetry to an earlier relationship to words is not a regression but a *willed* return to a site of pain. For it is the affirmation of a history and of the possibility of a history. The direction of the will is reversed, retrojected: it means to bring about again, to repeat, a future it *already* occupies, since it speaks in words. It is more of a Nietzschean return: "now" "I" will it to happen one more time, since it will have to happen anyway, since "I" will have to say "I" again to be "human." It is the repeat that intentionalizes. The return of poetry is not to dwell on loss or to retrieve what is lost—these are thematic dodges—but an affirmation of loss. The "universal" lyric themes are variations on this generic move: the will to lose again, to choose language again. Regression to an earlier relationship to words may be pleasurable in a psychological sense, but the *power* of choosing, once again, one's fate, and the *pain* that that entails—as all power does—makes for pleasure in a poetic sense. This is the birth of tragedy, over and over, in lyric language *and* its inevitable dissolution, over and over, into lyric language. Its groundless ground is at once an individuating history and a human history.

Paul Celan, who lived the trauma of the mother tongue through a traumatic and incomprehensible history on an incomparable scale, understands that the *intimacy* of the symbolic, the alienation that is the history of the subject, is the mother tongue's traumatic "truth":

> And can you bear, Mother, as oh, at home, once on a time,
> The gentle, the German, the pain-laden rhyme? (qtd. in Felstiner 1975, 24).

John Felstiner says he took out "that schmaltzy 'oh, at home'" in translating the poem (24). But that cry and its location are crucial. The phrase registers the trauma of the mother tongue itself, "as oh, at home." The poet lies in a foreign language because it is merely a foreign language; the pain of the mother tongue is its intimate foreignness, its *constitutive* otherness. "The gentle, the German, the pain-laden rhyme" conflates historical trauma with the truth of the mother tongue. The lyric "I" does not forget that in the beginning was a violence, a cut into undifferentiated space-time, which instituted space, time, language, and the psyche. In poetry, the uncanny, the *unheimlich* that is "oh, at home," always resounds through the symbolic. The truth that the "I" tells in the mother tongue is the truth of its history, the incomprehensibility of its occurrence, which makes for its constitutive but unassimilable otherness.

ASIDE: THE TRADITION OF TRAUMA

> The light sinks today with an enthusiasm
> I have known elsewhere, and known why
> It seemed meaningful, that others felt this way
> Years ago.
> —*John Ashbery*

> . . . the roses
> Had the look of flowers that are looked at.
> —*T. S. Eliot*

> I am with you, you men and women of a generation, or ever
> so many generations hence,
> Just as you feel when you look on the river and sky, so I felt.
> —*Walt Whitman*

Poetry remembers the traumatic history that constitutes the individuated/so-cialized subject in language. It is a kind of language use that allows each reader to experience the intimacy and foreignness of the language that articulates him or her. Enabling such experiences also ensures the cultural transmission not only of the linguistic code but of a tradition of the "subject" by activating and maintaining both personal and cultural memory of what constitutes a subject in language. The "specialness" of poetry is that it is an art of the linguistic code per se yet also remembers a personal and communal history in language. I would like to engage this memory through Walter Benjamin's idea of "aura" to give a sense of the difference of the poetic word from other kinds of art objects.

Benjamin draws on Freud's theory that "*consciousness arises instead of a memory-trace*"[40] to distinguish conscious experiences of the moment—"of a certain hour of one's life"—that do not leave behind enduring memory traces from experience "in the strict sense of the word," which is "a matter of tradition," in both collective and private life (1969, 157). If experience in the strict sense of the word has to do with enduring memory traces, tradition in both individual and collective experience would have to consist of repetitions of traumatic events, events that can never be known in themselves but only in and as repetition. For Benjamin, experiences where "certain contents of the individual past" converge with the "material of the collective past" are marked by an "aura" of their uniqueness and permanence (159). The aura is "the unique phenomenon of a distance," however close the object may be, and it "disintegrates" in experiences of the moment that lack such texture and distance—that have "no breath of prehistory" surrounding them (222, 185).

In the case of a work of art, mechanical reproduction detaches the object from "the domain of tradition" and dissipates its aura, for the "uniqueness of a work of art is inseparable from its being embedded in the fabric of tradition," which is precisely what makes for its distance from us (Benjamin 1969, 221, 223). Benjamin is primarily concerned with visual media and the nature of "modern" experience, but in an endnote to his essay on Baudelaire, he adds that words, too, can have an aura and cites Karl Kraus's remarks on the common experience of the impenetrability of the word, often induced by repetition or reproduction itself: "The closer the look one takes at a word, the greater the distance from which it looks back" (200). This is true in more than one sense. The word certainly has a collective historical texture—a linguistic, cultural, and literary "etymology"—which is part of its distance from us. But in poetry, this history converges with our personal prehistory and a different experience of distance, an experience of the intimate otherness of the material code that constitutes us and our unrecoverable personal histories. This is why reproduction does not wither the aura of the poetic word.[41] Poetry is exempt from decay of aura because its experienced aura depends not on originality but on reproducibility. Without reproduction, it dies. Poetry is, in principle, a mass art and it forces us to relive the trauma of the word as a communal as well as a personal historical experience.

The poetic word retains an aura because it will not reduce to its referential function; it is outside a representational economy. The reduction of the word to its referential function, for discursive "consumption," would be comparable to mechanical reproduction of art objects, which in effect produces a referential object, reproducing the material object *as* referential. Poetic forms and schemes maintain a tradition devoted precisely to blocking such referential reduction. The word in poetry, however it is produced or reproduced, maintains the aura of "uniqueness and permanence" (Benjamin 1969, 223), for we have to physically reproduce it *as* a muscular, somatic experience to read poetry at all. In poetry, the word itself is the site of experience "in the strict sense of the word." And the materiality and distance of the word, its sounds and look, the texture of the voice it calls to re-sound it all evoke a personal and communal prehistory.

"To perceive the aura of an object we look at means to invest it with the ability to look at us in return," Benjamin writes, and notes that "This endowment is a well-spring of poetry" (1969, 188, 200).[42] Prosopopoeia, which objectifies the speaker by granting a face to objects, would be the operative device. But when the object is the word itself, we are already radically and intimately objectified. In the word, we are already looking back at ourselves. Mechanical reproduction does not touch the poetic word because the "distance" or the aura that makes for the unique experience of the word resides elsewhere, in *our* history. The distance is internal and measures who we are, both personally and collectively, as each reader can read herself and her history in a poetic text, an object that is also, literally, the "breath of prehistory."

Whitman's "Crossing Brooklyn Ferry" speaks to this intimate distance of words as they articulate a collective tradition of unique experiences of a shared history in language. Whitman begins with an apostrophe, granting the river scene a face and the power to look back at him:

> Flood-tide below me! I see you face to face!
> Clouds of the west—sun there half an hour high—I see you also
>   face to face.

The sense of sight dominates the poem, and the speaker's relation to his pre-text, the scene, is "face to face," seeing and being seen, reading and being read by objects. The speaker scripts the scene as that which prescripts him.

But Whitman's speaker also prescribes the future, for he addresses not only the contemporaneous cityscape but as-yet-unborn readers. He grants a face not only to the objects around him but to his text as *one more object* facing his readers. He insists on the textual object and our very act of reading his print-face, repeatedly addressing "you who peruse me now." Thus, Whitman's "I see you face to face" not only positions him at the river scene but also positions the reader at the scene of the text, for his "I" is a type- or page-face looking at the reader. And when I read the line and sound his "I," I both necessarily "prove" his text's claims and literally speak *my* truth: "I see you face to face."

Whitman's "I" speaks in the past tense, from beyond the grave. The "I" is not the Walt Whitman who was at work choosing his words; the speaker exists neither in 1856 nor in the text-object but in our reading/speaking his words. This is a signature effect: the textual object is the signature that severs and links the man and the "I" in the poem and requires a third party, a future reader, to countersign it—to recognize it. We have the power to endorse its authority, to look at him, to grant him a face. The epitaphic text positions itself as the prehistory of our history, in the poet's future, and insures a kind of literal, empirical "immortality." He lives on only if I pick up his book; my voice must be the fulfillment, the antitype, of his prescriptive text, his typeface. I prove "he" is not dead by the very act of reading him, lending him my body and my voice. But in thus reading and repeating his words, "I" too become a text, a typeface looking back at "me." In this uncanny recognition of ourselves in an object as one among other "objects than which none else is more lasting" (1973, 165), we experience the lyric objectification of subjectivity in the material medium of language: we as readers experience what a lyric "I" is.[43]

"Whoever You Are Holding Me Now in Hand" (Whitman 1973, 115–17) registers that the text poses a threat for the reader. Here, "signing" oneself "a candidate for [his] affections" involves an oral, sexualized exchange. The words are the "kiss," the contact between "your" lips and "mine." "To put your lips upon mine I permit you," he writes, but he proceeds to warn his reader:

> But these leaves conning you con at peril,
> For these leaves and me you will not understand,
>
> .   .   .   .
>
> For it is not for what I have put into it that I have written this book . . .

The difficult line "But these leaves conning you con at peril" suggests that if "you" "con"—study, master, memorize, know—"these leaves," "you" would be duped, for the material reality of the book's body will have "eluded" you: "Already you see I have escaped from you." But the subject of the clause could also be "these leaves," and the line also suggests that the leaves con "you" and "at peril." If I am not seduced and conned to sound his words, he does not exist: "In libraries I lie as one dumb, a gawk, or unborn, or dead" (116). A "gawk"—a slang word, part of living speech that is doomed to become obsolete—is what he would be in a library: extinct. Yet if he depends on my voice to reproduce him, don't I depend on him, on speaking the words that pronounced me as their countersigner, assigned my voice as the fulfillment of their typeface to transmit him through time? Am *I* not "at peril" in "these leaves conning"? At this juncture, we see that the transmission of a "tradition" of the subject is the fulfillment or the "antitype" of the "type," the transmission of language itself. For the entity that is at stake here, the "I," is the entity that is formulated in learning language, in repeating, mastering, and endorsing a prescriptive "text."

Gay Wilson Allen writes that Whitman "learned to write less with pen and ink than with the alphabet of the type cases" (1961, 17). His poetic self—his most intimate, "nighest name"—was also formulated as an object of typefaces, designed for transmission. And this printed or typed self exists only in commerce with readers. He is a "dumb" object until we "use" him, consent to see face to face a text that claims to see us. "Who knows, for all the distance, but I am as good as looking at you now, for all you cannot see me?" he writes; "Consider, you who peruse me, whether I may not in unknown ways be looking upon you." Such addresses, again, make for an uncanny experience of double or mutual objectification in typefaces to mutually enable subjectivity.

Whitman's "unfinished business" (Cowley 1959, 87) is concluded when the currency of the object of paper and type ferries the "I" to "you." The lyric exchange of "I" and "you" establishes the "similitudes of the past and those of the future" on the ground of physical experiences of material objects, above all the text object of words about other objects. Here, the physical, empirical reality of a bodily produced and reproduced text that "I" and "you" experience makes for "our" historical bond. What "I" and "you" establish in "our" textual exchange *is* the link between the past and the future.

Whitman asserts:

Others will enter the gates of the ferry and cross from shore to shore,
Others will watch the run of the flood-tide,
Others will see the shipping of Manhattan . . .
Fifty years hence, others will see . . . as they cross, the sun half an hour high.

The poem presents not only a transient moment in time—the sun "half an hour high"—but also a historical moment in a manmade scene, for Whitman stages his archetypal river crossing in a specific landscape of ferries and masted ships, factories and commerce. He foregrounds the inevitable historical difference between the speaker and the reader who will pick him up and "peruse" him "a hundred years from hence." While the poem will always present the same scene of the ferry crossing, we will see a different cityscape in our different historical moment. The only way that "others" can enter the "gates of the ferry" is in his words. He ensures his future by ensuring our present; he ensures "others who look back on me because I look'd forward to them." When everything will have changed, we will experience, in speaking his words, the uniqueness and permanence of his and *our* historical experience:

Closer yet I approach you,
What thought you have of me now, I had as much of you—I laid my stores
     in advance,
I consider'd you long and seriously before you were born.
  .   .   .   .

We understand then do we not
What I promised without mentioning it, have you not accepted?
What the study could not teach—what the preaching could not
    accomplish is accomplish'd, is it not?

What is "accomplish'd" is that, as we have "perused" and "used" his words
on the page and sounded his "dumb beautiful ministers," we have proved him
"lasting." His "ministers" represent us to ourselves, serving us to articulate our
personal and historical experience. The maddening closeness of Whitman's
words to us makes palpable their distance across space and history from us.
When we say his words in our voices and articulate his sounds, they are both
our words and alien words. The intimate otherness of poetic language—the
unique experience of distance—is the experience Whitman forces on us. This
experience makes for the inmost "I," and "we" connect across time and space
because of that distance, that intimate otherness of words. The other that we
speak and hear in his prescriptive words is the other who speaks us. And as we
sound the otherness of his text in our "now," in an existential relation to the
words of its "I," we experience the uniqueness of his and our history and in
that very act articulate their permanence. We prove that "It avails not, time
nor place—distance avails not / I am with you, you men and women of a
generation or ever so many generations hence."
    "I was chilled with the cold types and cylinder and wet paper between us /
I pass so poorly with paper and types. . . . I must pass with the contact of bodies
and souls," Whitman wrote in 1855 (Cowley 1959, 87). When he revised "A
Song for Occupations," he took out these lines. In "Brooklyn Ferry," he knows
that he passes with paper and types or not at all. His rhetorical job is to persuade us to reciprocate, to voice his typeface and invest his text with the power
to look back at us. Whitman's poem constructs this aura precisely out of the
urban experience of one "in a crowd" and by the very mechanical reproduction
that dissipates aura. Whitman's "print face"—the "cold types"—itself becomes
"auratic" when I voice his words.[44] "Uniqueness and permanence are as closely
linked" in authentic experience, Benjamin writes, as "transitoriness and reproducibility" are in mechanically reproduced experience (1969, 223). But a poem
like "Crossing Brooklyn Ferry" eludes this framework; it means to ensure the
reproducibility of its "transitory" crossing and thus make its reader bear witness
to its uniqueness and permanence. Mechanical reproduction does not erode its
authenticity; rather, it ensures access to others who will have to re-produce it
in their voices.[45]

The conscious and unconscious memories clustering around objects allow for
our construction of ourselves in terms of what we remember, both individually
and collectively. When our object is a poem, we articulate our personal experience of its words and establish a "tradition" of unique histories. But a memory

of a collective is also activated as we remember other poems by the same poet and poems by other poets and articulate our historical reality. The reader is a medium not only for the reproduction of the textual object but for the construction of a poet's oeuvre and of a collective tradition; the reader is articulated as both a historically specific, individuated social subject and as the medium of a collective history. Reading Whitman, we would remember, for example, Wordsworth's description of the poet's experience of the city and its "marvels":

> And now I looked upon the living scene;
> Familiarly *perused* it; oftentimes,
> In spite of strongest disappointment, pleased
> Through courteous self-submission, as a tax
> Paid to the object by prescriptive right.
>
> Rise up, thou monstrous ant-hill on the plain
> Of a too busy world! Before me flow,
> Thou endless stream of men and moving things!
> Thy every-day appearance, as it strikes—
> With wonder heightened, or sublimed by awe—
> On strangers, of all ages; the quick dance
> Of colours, lights, and forms; the deafening din,
> *The comers and the goers face to face*,
> *Face after face*; the string of dazzling wares,
> Shop after shop, with symbols, blazoned names,
> And all the tradesman's honours overhead:
> Here, *fronts of houses, like a title-page*,
> *With letters huge inscribed* from top to toe . . .
>   (1979, 233, 235; emphases mine)

The cityscape is presented as a text facing the speaker, its "peruser." The "fronts of houses," "huge inscribed" with letters, "like a title-page," explicitly links faces and typefaces or fronts and fonts. The speaker's imperative apostrophe— "Rise up, thou monstrous ant-hill"—signals both consent or submission to the city *and* a licensing, permitting it to be, a gesture Whitman repeats in the final section of "Crossing Brooklyn Ferry." Wordsworth's speaker submits to the prescriptive rights of the city-text to script his words, which are, in turn, prescriptive objects for Whitman.

But reading Whitman, we may also "remember" other texts he "predicted" or "prescripted" and script him into twentieth-century American poetry. By ferrying him to a future he addresses but could not have known, we countersign his "promise" and make for "our" history, as well as commemorating Whitman's historical reality. We remember the different futures of his past, confirming the historical uniqueness of our crossing as we grant his crossing its permanence. I remember, for example, Elizabeth Bishop's "Poem," which thematically engages the issue of tradition. My "memory" articulates a collective history that transmits itself through me, even as it marks my historical uniqueness. Bishop's poem, about the "use" value of a "useless" object, a painting, is her only work with a generic title, and it is about poetry as much as it is about a painting. Bishop first describes the painting as an object, specifying its approximate size and colors. "About the size of an old-style dollar bill" and with "the same whites, gray greens, and steel grays," it "has never earned any money in its life." "Useless and free," it has been "handed along collaterally" (1979, 176). Whether it earns any money or not, the painting exchanges hands, is inherited, and has an economic reality and value as a collateral. Both senses of "collaterally" will come into play: we will learn that she has received the painting of her great uncle through an aunt, and the painting is a property that will secure a transaction.

The description of the scene the painting represents pays close attention to the material medium. Bishop seems here to follow her own prescription: "What one seems to want in art, in experiencing it, is the same thing that is necessary for its creation, a self-forgetful, perfectly useless concentration."[46] The speaker moves in from the represented scene ("It must be Nova Scotia") "up closer" to the material details of paint on the board: cows that are "two brushstrokes," the "white and yellow, / fresh-squiggled from the tube," the "half inch of blue sky," the "titanium white, one dab," "that gray-blue wisp," the "filaments of brush-hairs," and so on. Obsessive attention to the "mantling" of the material object and the work involved in its construction, dissolves the representational illusion. Then comes the exclamation reinstituting the illusion, but elsewhere, in her memory: "Heavens, I recognize the place. I know it!" The "collateral" painting underwrites the "exchange" of recognitions, memories, knowledge, but only insofar as it is encountered and looked at as an object. The art object—painting or poem—is a site for the formation, articulation, and communication of subjects across time; it is a site where "our" "coinciding" looks form a community. These painted or verbal objects carry memory, and we articulate our personal memory around them. She lets the painting look back at her, position her within its scene—not the represented scene but the brushstrokes—and reconstructs the painting. The material object, not the representational illusion, allows for the coincidence of the "two looks" by two people and at two things—the object and the landscape—"years apart."

"Poem" presents the process of reading a text at the level of its material construction. When the representational/referential "illusion" dissolves into the material elements that construct it, an "I" emerges as one who reconstructs the represented "scene," or the referential content, by activating her individuating memories. The painting is "passed on" because she looks at it as an object produced by a subject and producing a subject in a specific medium. The coincidence of the two subjects in turn allows for the coincidence of different "I's" at different times in the speaker's life. The painter has objectified his experience of looking at a place that looks back at him. This object then serves as a mirror for the viewer to articulate her memory not only of the place but of the words of her aunt in "handing down" the painting to her; a six-line passage, set off in italics, places the speaker in a history involving her great-uncle, her aunt, her aunt's mother, and her earlier selves. Collateral communication across time and space is backed up by this collateral object:

I never knew him. We both knew this place,
apparently, this literal small backwater,
looked at it long enough to memorize it,
our years apart. How strange. And it's still loved,
or its memory is (it must have changed a lot).
Our visions coincided—"visions" is
too serious a word—our looks, two looks:
art "copying from life" and life itself. (Bishop 1979, 177)

The parenthetical phrase places the memory as a childhood memory; it refers to changes on the scale of a lifetime. The painting produces a memory and marks the speaker's present, distinct from the time of the painting, the time of her childhood memory—which "copied" from a "life" that would no longer be what it had been—and the time of her memory of receiving the painting. "Life itself" exists only in the "compression" of its various copyings by people— in paintings, looking at paintings, poems, readings of poems, memories of what "must have changed a lot." The past offers a now-alien surface on which we and our present—what we know, "remember," "love"—may be returned back to us as who we are.

This is

—the little that we get for free,
the little of our earthly trust. Not much.
About the size of our abidance
along with theirs: the munching cows,
the iris, crisp and shivering, the water
still standing from spring freshets,
the yet-to-be-dismantled elms, the geese.

Once again, "life and the memory of it" are so "compressed" that they turn into each other. For the final description is not of the painting or of her mem- ory; it is the compression of her life "now" and her memory of life; the "yet- to-be-dismantled" and the present tense place us in a precarious, "shivering" verbal illusion "now," a "now" that comes into focus as memory. We abide "now" in recognizing the look of things that have been looked at and thus "mantle" our history, even as the cows, the iris, the geese, the elms, and "we" along with them, are "dismantled." The text produces the history of which it is the product.

The formation or activation of a personal memory, a family history, a community of those who have looked at objects and felt things—all the facets of a subject—are reflected off of objects that are seen, represented, re-seen and re-presented again. The poem's internal movement of describing the same scene over and over repeats the repetitive descriptions of the same landscape in "Brooklyn Ferry." Both texts enact a continuous repetition and revision, in which not only individual subjects but a communal identity are formulated in and as a history. In such lyrics, the time-bound subject does not contemplate her difference from the timeless art object; rather, these lyric "objects" are commodities that "adequately" represent the temporality and the historicity of the subjects that make, peruse, and use them. Such an object has "authenticity," which, to cite Benjamin, is "the essence of all that is transmissable from its beginning, ranging from its substantive duration to its testimony to the history which it has experienced" (1969, 221). And that testimony requires a witness who accepts the object as a collateral for the "history" of the subject and its curiously permanent, continuous commerce and conversation with other histories that make for a tradition.

Notes

1. Qtd. in Agamben 1993, 54–55.
2. Qtd. in Agamben 1993, 55.
3. I use "mother" because of the term "the mother tongue," but I speak of the social and socializing relationship between the child and its primary caretaker; any caretaker would be in a "mother" position.
4. See R. H. Wheeler in Dann 1988, 82–83.
5. See Engstrom 1965, 839–40.
6. Cytowic, qtd. in Dann 1998, 5. I am basing this discussion on Dann's history of psychologists' work on synesthesia, which he uses to debunk the Romantics' and Symbolists' "misunderstanding" of synesthesia as a higher, transcendent mode of experience.
7. Dann cites the psychologist R. H. Wheeler's findings that "without their synaesthetic photisms, synaesthetes essentially could not hear, and the same was true for thought: if, during the thought process, the photisms were blocked, further thought was impossible" (1998, 83). In synesthesia, the distinction between thinking and feeling does not hold, for meaning and thought fail to develop without the imagery and sensations (84).
8. Erich Jaensch, qtd. in Dann 1998, 110.
9. This is a lingering between the Dionysian and the Apollonian, a desire to see oneself echoed in sounds and to hear oneself reflected in words. It is a desire for the impossible union of Narcissus and Echo. Heaney invokes this synesthetic crux in "Personal Helicon": "I rhyme / To see myself, to set the darkness echoing" (1990, 11).
10. Liberman, qtd. in Tsur 1992, 12. Deacon, also citing Liberman, writes that processing speech sounds entails "predicting" the "oral-vocal movements" that produced

them, ignoring other acoustic data. "Because the speech signal originates from a rather limited source, a human oral cavity, a full acoustic analysis is unnecessary; only the linguistically relevant information about what movement generated the sounds needs to be separated from the sound. What is important is the speaker's *intended* words, which are reflected in intended movements of oral and vocal muscles" (1997, 359). Speech sounds, then, are perceived in terms of intention and "articulatory (i.e., somato-motor) features, not just sound features" (360).

11. "All normal children in all cultures go through a stage in the language acquisition process in which they invent or repeat rhymes, play with sound, etc.—in other words, they play with the poetic function," writes Linda R. Waugh (1985, 146).

12. Jakobson, qtd. in Tsur 1992, 54. The phonemes acquired latest have a "double edge": "On the one hand, they appear to constitute the highest linguistic layer, the most rational accessories of referential language (and the first to dissolve in aphasia). On the other hand, of all the acquired phonological systems, the last acquisitions served for the longest time exclusively as gestures (onomatopoeia and interjections). In the last phases of speech-learning (and the first stages of aphasia) they may be seen as 'especially charged with emotion' when used as sound gestures and, at the same time, unavailable for 'arbitrary linguistic signs' " (Jakobson, qtd. in Tsur 1992, 65). These late-acquired sounds may also assume greater aesthetic value; among late acquisitions, continuous and periodic sounds, such as nasal vowels, are "beautiful," whereas aperiodic sounds, such as the affricates /pf/ and /ts/, are "ugly" (Tsur 1992, 66).

13. 1999, 370, 371. In infants, "the two hemispheres are not as specialized as they later become," she writes, and children depend on the right-hemisphere capabilities "for producing, processing, and responding to the affective prosodic components of speech" (371).

14. Colwyn Trevarthen, qtd. in Dissanayake 1999, 373.

15. Deacon, in his study of the coevolution of language and the brain, suggests an interesting phylogenic parallel. Early speech, like "motherese," he proposes, would have been "embedded in a richer nonspoken matrix of gestures and exaggerated intonation" (1997, 363). With the development of fully articulate speech, "gestural and prosodic" features have been "recruited," in modern languages, to contribute to greater effectiveness and efficiency of verbal communication. "The one class of paralinguistic functions which probably had the longest co-evolutionary relationship with language," he writes, "is speech prosody: the changes in rhythm, volume, and tonality of speech that are used both to direct attention to what the speaker deems to be more salient elements and to communicate correlated emotional tone" (364). The whole passage on the complimentarity of the anatomical, neurological pathways governing rhythm and vocalization is of interest.

16. This is, for the infant, an inaugural social and linguistic unit of a "you" and an "I." My interest is in a social and emotional history in language, and the "mother" is the one who teaches vocal rhythmization.

17. Not only are prosodic features processed in the right hemisphere, but they are "primarily produced by the larynx and lungs, and not articulated by the mouth and tongue," Deacon writes (1997, 418). He links the prosodic features of speech to the vocalizations of other primates (313). Like stereotypic vocalizations, they communicate "arousal level, emotional states, and attention"; unlike such vocalizations, of course, they are "continuous and highly correlated with the speech process" (418).

18. See the case studies John Dore (1994) provides.

19. Linguists maintain that "the meaning of a sentence cannot be calculated . . . from the meaning of its lexical components." Prosody "indicates how the information marked by such means is to be interpreted in a given context" (Auer, Couper-Kuhlen, and Muller 1999, 5, 27, 10).

20. Current knowledge "supports" Nietzsche. Deacon writes: "[S]ites of brain damage that produce aprosodic speech or difficulties in analyzing emotional information encoded in prosody often involve the right cerebral cortex, opposite the 'language-dominant' hemisphere" (1997, 365).

21. *Beyond Good and Evil*, no. 246; emphases mine. Reading for the ear requires "that one must not be doubtful about the rhythm-determining syllables, that one should feel the breaking of the too-rigid symmetry as intentional and as a charm, that one should lend a fine and patient ear to every *staccato* and every *rubato*, that one should divine the sense in the sequence of the vowels and diphthongs." But "the German does not read aloud, he does not read for the ear, but only with his eyes; he has put his ears away in the drawer for the time" (no. 247).

22. The qualities that make for the voice entail personal definition or self-possession, but they are acquired. Pound writes that one must "master all known forms and systems of metric" (1968a, 9) in order to be able to sound one's "uncounterfeitable" rhythm. Merrill writes that the greater the poet's mastery of syntactic and formal resources, the more "individual" his voice will be, even as it becomes more of a pastiche (1986, 80). Individuating rhythmic inflections become audible only within a given system and in proportion to how well one is "socialized" within that system.

23. Piaget writes that musical rhythm is, in fact, "the most intuitive of all time measurements and is most certainly not imposed on us from outside" (1971, 303).

24. Auer, Couper-Kuhlen, and Muller support the claim that perception plays an active role in the construction of rhythm: "for a given set of stimuli to be perceived as rhythmic, the factual durations making up this set are less relevant than the time structure we impose on it." Such "subjective rhythmization" accounts, for example, for "the well-documented finding that even physically identical stimuli (such as the dripping of a water tap or the tick tock . . . of a clock) are heard as rhythmically structured in groups of two or, more rarely, three elements" (1999, 13). The perception of rhythm, then, is not "automatically related to (or derivative of)" physical events: "the human receptor of the acoustic signal must perform a number of interpretive tasks to hear its rhythm" (23). The perception of rhythm is a constructive process of interpreting physical data, and it involves the imposition of a temporal order (27).

25. This is Deleuze and Guattari's term, and the concept is relevant, even though they are thinking on a cosmic scale. They propose that rhythm organizes "milieus" out of chaos; "milieus" are blocks of "space-time constituted by the periodic repetition of the component," which distinguishes them from chaos. But milieus are open to chaos: "not only does the living thing continually pass from one milieu to another, but the milieus pass into one another." Rhythm transcodes one milieu into another and enables their coordination. This intermilieu transcoding distinguishes it from meter, which operates in a "noncommunicating milieu": "Productive repetition has nothing to do with reproductive meter," for "whenever there is transcoding, we can be sure that there is not a simple addition, but the constitution of a new plane, as of a surplus value. A melodic

or rhythmic plane, surplus value of passage or bridging" (1987, 313, 314). Meter doesn't cross systems and cannot generate the surplus value—in my case, the subject.

26. For meter may represent the phonic "structure" of meaning in a language. Paul Boomsliter and Warren Creel propose that "language uses an elaborate system of prominence devices that make it possible to convey complex meanings," and poetic devices are "organized extensions" of these devices (1977, 296). Thus meter may stylize those phonic properties of a language that are essential to the meaning function; in the case of English, this would be the alternation of accented and unaccented syllables. Meter, then, may stress what needs to be heard—in English, the accented syllable of a word, which "serves as the meaning-flag for the whole word" (297).

27. Hollander writes: "The word of flow, 'rhythm,' characterizes the series of actual effects upon our consciousness of a line or a passage of verse: it is the road along which we read. The meter, then, would apply to whatever it was that might constitute the framing, the isolating; its presence we infer from our scanning." He suggests that this distinction comprehends "other sets of linguistic and literary dimensions": "design and particular; norm and instance; spatial, or at least schematic and temporal; singing or speaking and writing; and ultimately, in the matter of the angles of vision of linguistic theory itself, synchronic and diachronic, phenomenological and historical" (1975, 135–36).

28. Qtd. in Hollander 1975, 195 (his translation).

29. Aviram's view of rhythm is not unlike that of Kristeva, for whom the rhythmic pulsion of the *chora* is an eruption of an "asocial drive" that disrupts the sociosymbolic order (1984, 71, 81). Aviram, too—although his is not Kristeva's project of retooling Freud to the end of revolution—insists on a firm distinction between the "sublime," "rhythmic body" and the "socially constructed body" that poetry, predictably, "challenges" (1994, 223).

30. Monique David-Menard proposes that the ego image begins to be formed by rhythmic movements of body parts and that rhythm serves to integrate the body in communication with an other. The noncoherent motor activity of the newborn comes to organize itself through the self-limitation of rhythmic movement (1989, 145–47). For example, if the infant is distracted from the breast into noncoordinated motion, restoring the object of the oral reflex assures rhythmic movement, and the infant abandons "hallucinatory jouissance" for rhythmic sucking (Landauer, qtd. in David-Menard 1989, 157). Through such self-limitation, rhythm institutes a reality principle and creates a space where a body and an ego—a mental projection of the body—may be configured. Rhythm thus articulates a subject and protects it from disorganization: "Every rhythmic movement and every erotic scenario bears the mark of a charmed-away threat of loss of self" (David-Menard 1989, 4, 155). Arrhythmic muscular movements, convulsions, and contortions in disorders of linguistic-somatic symbolization, such as hysteria, attest to the function of rhythm in the social formulation of a coherent body and ego.

31. 1989, 633. Perceptions, according to Freud, become potentially available to consciousness when their mnemic traces enter the Preconscious system and are there brought into connection with word-presentations. Consciousness depends on word presentations, which depend on traces of auditory stimuli. The "special sensory source" of the *Pcs.* system is the auditory (633). But this model cannot explain the phenomenon of the word.

32. Sounds or clusters of phonemes may be associated with objects. For example, the phonemic sequence "table" might be a quality of a particular object, on the order of its size, color, shape, and so on. But the passage into referential language would entail an experience of the *difference* between the articulated, feedbacked phonemic cluster "table" and the particular object. And in certain psychopathological regressions from abstract language, words "held in memory" may be used as "properties of objects" on the order of color and size (see Abse 1966, 108–9).

33. Qtd. in Deleuze 1990, 357.

34. Implicit in Saussure's work with anagrams is the idea that poets in some sense also hear or listen to language at this level.

35. It originates time itself as a beat between hearing and hearing-as—that is, as a metaleptic crossing. Deacon proposes that infants, incapable of the most basic motor operations or of abstract thought—such as adding two and two—are capable of learning the most complicated human system, language, because they are amnesiac. Amnesia enables exclusive attention to the present, without the interference of memory. But the hearing of semantemes would entail memory; it would be a re-cognition, a hearing-as—and here we cross systems. And that crossing is a traumatic event experienced in an "inherent forgetting" (Caruth 1995, 7–8). This is the trauma infantile amnesia forgets in instituting memory.

36. The psychic dimension is generated in the drafting of the existential, experienced necessity of the semiotic system into symbolic language. If, as Freud and Lacan propose, the unconscious works as a poetic text, the reason is that the "unconscious" is a concept conjured at the site of the internal gap of language, a historical site in which poetic texts dwell.

37. For Lacan, the subject is formulated when the patient makes the traumatic event "pass into the *verbe*, or, more precisely, into the *epos*." Thus, "he brings back into present time the origins of his own person" in a language that "allows his discourse to be understood by his contemporaries." The formation of a persistent ego entails a narrativizing that links the present subject to "his" past, so that the subject may be constituted "as being the one who thus has been" (1977, 46–47).

38. Lyric poetry entertains all kinds of third terms—the metaphysical and its permutations, including the psychoanalytic—that trope this gap, *and* it exposes them as terms that would make sense of a history that has already happened before one could know it and made possible that one can "know" anything at all. A traumatic history that initiates the possibility of knowing anything withholds the possibility of *its* comprehension.

39. Emily Dickinson is one poet who "dwells" in the traumatic event of language. She tests the limits of sense, dismembering words and disarticulating meaningful language to syllables, sounds, and ABC's. Her language occupies the gap/threshold between syllable and sound, sense and nonsense, which generates all other dualisms of the material and the nonmaterial. The material medium of sounds and letters and the huge topics—God, love, death, and so on—keep collapsing into each other, living in each other's death, at the site of pain, the initial trauma of the wounding word. But she stops at this frontier of pain, the threshold of a traumatic surfacing or severance from the body into "metaphysical" surfaces. She disintegrates the word back into letters, syllables, and phonemes, but that's her limit: these cannot further disintegrate into the

body. They must remain the elements of an intimate, alien code. That is what it means not to be a schizophrenic: it means there is no body, no further material base. While she must not "condescend" to words, she has to "consent" to them (no. 1651).

40. See Benjamin 1969, 160ff. In Freud's terms, "becoming conscious and leaving behind a memory-trace are processes incompatible with each other within one and the same system" (1989, 607, 606).

41. Benjamin touches on printing, "the mechanical reproduction of writing" (1969, 218–19), and the immense changes it brought about in the evolution of forms of writing that appeal to the masses by reproducing the masses—so that they can see themselves "face to face." But poetry would not seem to be in the category of writing shaped by the fact of "technical reproducibility" (220), and the aura of the word seems largely immune to the effects of mechanical reproduction.

42. "Wherever a human being, an animal, or an inanimate object thus endowed by the poet lifts up its eyes, it draws him into the distance" (Benjamin 1969, 200).

43. Writer and reader, text and voice, constitute a cycle of displacements where neither "I" nor "you" are self-identical and therefore are exactly what an "I" and a "you" are.

44. Benjamin distinguishes "trace" and "aura": "The trace is the appearance of proximity, however remote the object that left it behind. Aura is the appearance of distance, however close the object that evokes it. In the trace we take possession of the object; in aura it takes possession of us" (qtd. in Rolleston 1989, 17). But in Whitman's text, we experience the aura of a trace—the distance of a proximity of words and of our present.

45. It is possible that only reproducing poetry in another discourse erodes its aura. An interesting question, for example, is what happens to poetry and the intimate distance of its words when criticism quotes it, when it enters into and is appropriated by another discourse? Criticism is a discourse generated by print media and market needs, and unlike marginal commentary that the text absorbs as part of its history, criticism absorbs the text. Benjamin distinguishes concentration and distraction: "A man who concentrates before a work of art is absorbed by it. . . . [T]he distracted mass absorbs the work of art" (1969, 239). Absorption of the poem would dissipate aura; the text would now be a counter in another discourse and would not offer that too close / too distant experience.

46. Qtd. in Schwartz and Estess 1983, 288.

Chapter 3

⚜

THE SCRIPTED "I"

THE ERATO-GENIC "I"

Erato is the lyric muse, and eros is a generic subject matter of the lyric. Thus, what relation the pains and pleasures of lyric language may bear to sexuality is an askable question, and it may be posed in terms of the relation of the lyric subject to the psychosexual subject that is concurrently formulated in the mother tongue. Language learning and erotogenic formulation of a coherent body are inextricable processes, and pleasure in language has an erotic resonance, just as erotic pleasure has a linguistic aspect.

Pleasure will not reduce to an organic function because it has a history. Serge Leclaire's account of this history is most germane to the linguistic history that I am focusing on. The erotogenic body, he proposes, is a symbolic or represented body comprising a set of zones selected through a series of "originary" representations (1998, 44–45). An area of the body experiences an "immediately accessible, felt difference—pleasure or unpleasure"—and registers the mark of that difference, and the erotogenic body is formulated as a text bearing the memory traces of these sensations (46).[1] The "textual" inscription of the erotogenic body on the undifferentiated physiological body of the infant entails a process of selection and zoning of the body into surfaces and is concurrent with the selection and zoning of acoustic into phonemic phenomena.

The inscription of erotogenic zones thus effects another passage from sensations to signifying marks. An erotogenic zone is a signifying zone, a repeatable "letter trace" of what cannot be repeated, an originary representation of a bliss that exists only as a memory trace marking its loss. The letter that "fixates and annuls *jouissance*" (Leclaire 1998, 53) is both a trope of a trace—a pleasurable or unpleasurable experience leaves a mnemic trace "in the form of a graphic, acoustic, visual, tactile, or olfactory trait" (93)—and rather literally a letter trace, as Leclaire shows in case analyses of the recurrent literal linkages that make for symptoms. Thus "To take the body literally is . . . to learn to spell out the orthography of the name composed by the erotogenic zones that constitute it" (59). Each letter fixes a singular zone of pain or pleasure, and one's body is as distinct as a "secret name" made up of one's singular letters.[2] Again, this is quite literally the case, for the letters of names come into play in the inscription of the body, and often there is a "resemblance between a patient's fundamental phantasm and his name" (83).

Linguistic and erotogenic symbolization, which together formulate the sub-ject, thus converge in a microrhetoric, a distinguishing *signature*, and the ana-lyst must listen to the literal code. For the individuating literal trait to be heard, the "meaningful echo [must] exhaust itself in the unfolding of its reverberation" (Leclaire 1998, 81). Draining away "the mirages of meaning" will render audi-ble the "stripped-down formality of a literal network." The "meaningless," the literal formula "deprived of meaning" (83), is the "meaning" of the individual—what motivates him and what makes sense of his motives. Leclaire's literally analytic reading of the subject's discourse is essentially a poetic procedure, one that Saussure uses to read Saturnian funerary verse. Just as for Leclaire mean-ing is a "mirage," for Saussure, the "poetic message" is "the superfluous luxury of the hypogram" (Starobinski 1979, 121), a theme word, usually a proper name, whose phonemes are dispersed over the extent of the whole text. Both procedures involve hearing at the literal and phonemic level and tending to the formality of the system that precedes and underwrites the "meaning" or "message." Thus, to hear the subject or to hear the poem, one must hear pre-cisely at the level that the infant hears language.

The individuated erotogenic body is an intersubjectively produced text. Sexual pleasure is "born from a play within the memory of satisfaction," Leclaire writes, but for a satisfaction to be so "inscribed," a "supplementary factor" is necessary: the satisfaction must be "regarded as *jouissance* in the eyes of an-other." For what invests the zone with sexual value is the other's pleasure in the experience. He gives an example:

> [T]he softness of a mother's finger playing 'innocently,' as during love-making, with the exquisite dimple next to the baby's neck and the baby's face lighting up in a smile. We can say that the finger, with its loving caress, imprints a mark in this hollow, opens a crater of *jouissance*. . . . In the hollow of the dimple, an erotogenic zone is opened, an interval is fixated that nothing will be able to erase. This is where the play of pleasure will be produced in an elective manner provided an object, any object, comes along to revive in this place the brilliance of the smile fixed by the letter. (Leclaire 1998, 49–50)

In this example, "what makes the erotogenic inscription possible is the fact that the caressing finger is itself, for the mother, an erotogenic zone" (50). Here, the mother writes the text of the erotogenic body; she marks the inscription or incision, which the organic body supports "just as the page in a book sustains, causes to appear, and in a sense constitutes the letter inscribed there" (52).

The mother seems to teach sexual pleasure, and the breast-mouth connec-tion would be especially charged, for in the mother's clear pleasure in breastfeeding, the infant learns to associate an additional, interpersonal rhyth-mic pleasure with the solitary pleasures of sucking and feeding the physical body. The mother both satisfies hunger and institutes a need for "love." In Freud's formulation, a child's "intercourse with anyone responsible for his care affords him an unending source of sexual excitation and satisfaction from his erotogenic zones. This is especially so since the person in charge of him, who, after all, is as a rule his mother, herself regards him with feelings that are derived from her own sexual life: she strokes him, kisses him, rocks him and quite clearly treats him as a substitute for a complete sexual object." Lest anyone is "horrified" by this, he reassures us that "She is only fulfilling her task in teaching the child to love" (1975, 89).

The teaching and learning of desire in the erotogenization of the body is not simply analogous to but is inseparable from the concurrent teaching and learning of intention in the acquisition of language. For Gilles Deleuze, "sexual organization is a prefiguration of the organization of language, just as the physical surface [is] a preparation for the metaphysical surface" (1990, 241–42). He proposes an analogical relationship between language and sexuality: in the infant, the formative elements of language—phonemes, morphemes, and semantemes—are not yet "organized into formed linguistic units which would be able to denote things, manifest persons, and signify concepts. This is why these elements have not yet a reference other than a sexual one, as if the child was learning to speak on his own body—with phonemes referring to the erogenous zones, morphemes to the phallus of coordination, and semantemes to the phallus of castration" (232). Throughout all that which language will come to do—designate, manifest, and signify—Deleuze writes, "there will be a sexual history that will never be designated, manifested, or signified in itself, but which will coexist with all the operations of language, recalling the sexual appurtenance of the formative linguistic elements."[3]

Deleuze, of course, prioritizes the organization of the sexual body as "prefiguring" the organization of language. But there are no grounds for such prioritizing; language and sexuality are concurrent and mutually negotiated organizations, which accounts not only for the sexual charge of language but also for the linguistic charge of sexuality. The oral zone is both an erotogenic zone and the site of the earliest and most intimate presymbolic connection between language and the body, and it remains the physical site of the mutual negotiation of the erotogenic and the linguistic functions. Both language learning and the erotogenization of the body are intersubjective processes that render physiological phenomena into signifying phenomena, and both are individuating/socializing processes. For what also gives the mother pleasure is to hear the infant make sounds, *and then* to hear it make *signifying* sounds. She teaches interpersonal pleasure and she socializes into language; she ensures socialization by making it pleasurable. Just as the other's pleasure sexually charges a zone, the rhythmic production of imitative sounds, then of phonemes and words, are eroticized by the communicated pleasure of the other in hearing and responding to sounds.[4] This imbrication allows for the eroticization of language at the same time that it produces/imprints the erotogenic body as a language. Linguistic and erotogenic symbolization are co-implicated in the rhythmic emergency of the individuated/socialized sexual subject in and as a language. And they overlap in the oral zone, a "core" or a "depth" that comes to function as a switchboard between different codes.

If the production of speech is pleasurable because it gives the other pleasure, there is a sexual investment in the production of signifying sounds, in the *loss* of the alimentary pleasures of the feeding mouth, of the intimacy with the mother's—and one's own—body. The mother teaches and convinces the infant to intend, to desire, the loss of the other's and his own body. She seduces the infant to be "himself," to speak. This socialization into an "I" is by way of an annulment of all that an "I" cannot be, and the mouth, the zone of primal pleasure, itself becomes instrumental in this loss.

From this perspective, sexuality—like the "I," rhythm, and intention—will not reduce to the physical or to the metaphysical. It is another mark of the *history* by which these termini come to be posited. The "in-between" phenomena place in the divide that they articulate in time and as history. "Sexuality is in between eating and speaking," Deleuze writes; "at the same time that the sexual drives are detached from the destructive alimentary drives, they inspire the first words made up of phonemes, morphemes, and semantemes." But we could also say that speaking is between sexuality and eating—that the socializing linguistic articulations channel sexual drives away from the alimentary and into symbolization. "Sexuality is neither denoted, nor manifested, nor signified" by these linguistic elements, Deleuze writes, and when words finally achieve the status of ordered linguistic units, phonemes, morphemes, and semantemes lose their "sexual resonance" and operate on a symbolic plane. With full mastery of language, the "sexual resonance is repressed or neutralized"; henceforth "sexuality exists only as an allusion, as vapor or dust, showing a path along which language has passed" (1990, 242). But, again, if we do not prioritize sexuality, we can also say that with full sexual development, the linguistic resonance of sexuality is neutralized and language exists only as an allusion, a vapor trail marking the path of the passage of sexuality.

Lyric language remembers both passages. If sexual pleasure produces words and sounds (from the infantile language of "lovers' talk" back to the pure cry), in poetry sounds and words produce pleasure. Sexuality and language are two paths of individuation, two ways of objectification to produce a subject. Both entail pain and pleasure at once, since the subject who doesn't exist otherwise desires both to appear and to be annulled. Lyric language remembers the language of the pleasure body and its pain. This memory is the difference of the mother tongue—"between" the symbolic language and the organic body. Only in the mother tongue can the pleasure body "speak" and be heard in the "sounds of words." The body of words, produced by and producing pleasure, is the trace of the passage between sensory motor and representational experience, between physiology and erotogeneity, between sounds and sense. It belongs to the mother tongue that has made and unmade it, for this passage is also a site of pain.

Poetry, then, is also a revenge on the mother who seduces and betrays, who delivers into verbal language and the symbolic; she turns out to be the father in disguise, "a bearded queen, wicked in her dead light," as Stevens represents her (1954, 507).[5] And she is avenged for her betrayal, castrated again and again, dissolved back into nonsense sounds. But that does not get rid of her, for in the mother tongue, on the mother's stage, the phallogocentric word is as hallucinatory as the imaginary penis. And one really has no desire to get rid of her, for she is the foothold of the poet's history, a "ground" on which the metaphysical and physical "footholds" are figures. Neither sounds nor words but their intimate and irreducible distance from each other marks the historical ground of the "I" in the sounds of words:

> It was nothing he could be told.
> It was a language he spoke, because he must, yet did not know.
> It was a page he had found in the handbook of heartbreak.
> (Stevens 1954, 507)

Postscript

From a different perspective and on a different scale, sexuality and speaking, as well as eating, are necessary for the survival of the discursive species, the linguistic community, and the individual speaker. The mother seduces into language, which necessarily imbricates speech with sexual pleasure and alimentary satisfaction, to ensure the transmission of the linguistic code. Linguistic communities are in competition and languages, like genes, need to reproduce themselves for the survival of the community. And, as Deacon argues, in this arena, children are "the only game in town": they reproduce language (1997, 109). For they hear language at the level of the code that *must* be reproduced. A viable community has to reproduce children to insure the reproduction of language and guarantee the further reproduction of both the linguistic and the genetic codes. Whatever makes the linguistic code more easily transmissible— more infant-friendly and less hospitable to semantic interference—is selected over alternatives. Languages are in constant change, for they have to keep adapting themselves to children. For the object is seduction. Languages, Deacon points out, "need children more than children need languages" (109). It is not the infants who are at the mercy of the symbolic system, into which they are inserted, but the other way around; the symbolic order needs to "abduct children." I would say "seduce" children, and here, too, I would stress the priority of language. Children must be able to pass on the language—and, therefore, the culture, which is inscribed in them with the acquisition of language— before they can pass on the genetic code. They must prove culturally competent before they can reproduce.

If a language needs infants to survive, a culture needs poets to survive. Without poets, Eliot writes, a people's "language will deteriorate, their culture will deteriorate and perhaps become absorbed in a stronger one" (1979, 10). "The word within a word, unable to speak a word, / Swaddled with darkness" is Eliot's description of the infant, the holy animal born to be sacrificed, the potential Word (1970, 29). Through him alone is "immortality," for in him inheres the "divine power to speak words" (Whitman 1973, 383). But the speaking child has to be seduced or "stolen," as Yeats has it (1989, 18), once again—into poetry. And poetic language must also constantly change to seduce, to "earmark," in Charles Wright's term (1981, 15), other "speechless infants" to pass on the tradition of the linguistic code, a communal history of physical and emotional intimacy with the symbolic, not only to perpetuate the code but to reaffirm the symbolic, cultural order.

The Lyric and "The Birth of Tragedy"

> Thy functions are ethereal,
> As if within thee dwelt a glancing mind,
> Organ of vision! And a Spirit aerial
> Informs the cell of Hearing, dark and blind;
> Intricate labyrinth, more dread for thought
> To enter than oracular cave . . .
> —*William Wordsworth*

In the inscription of the erotogenic body, the subject function appears, in Serge Leclaire's terms, as one that tolerates or incites the "vanishing of *jouissance*" in a turn to letters. For *jouissance* is annulment, zero, death, and the letter masks the zero of *jouissance* in order to "*maintain its difference from death*" (1998, 100). The subject alternately engenders its "annulment" and the "effacement of this annulment" in a turn to representation, so that it may come to be known in the only mode it can appear, as representation (97). The subject function "excludes any 'substratum,'" Leclaire writes; it is itself this alternation between the void and the letter, between "the annulment that is *jouissance*" and "the letter that . . . seems to fixate the possibility of the same *jouissance*"—that is, the possibility of its repetition (101). "The repeated affirmation of the letter in the obsessional series or the reiterated affirmation of the void in the hysterical series" attests to the instability of the subject function—the "alternation of affirmation and effacement of the zero that is the subject" (102, 103).[6]

Not only the psychosexual subject—that is, the subject formulated by psychoanalysis as the object of its study—but the subject in language is to be understood as an alternation between the void and representation. Here, I want to engage Nietzsche's reading of the lyric poet in precisely these terms.

Nietzsche's theory of the Apollonian and Dionysian forces operative in human experience and art certainly works on a different scale, but it positions the lyric poet in terms of an alternation between Dionysian annulment and Apollonian representation, which Nietzsche correlates with music and image respectively. Nietzsche's theory thus also addresses poetic "music" and positions the alternation that is an "I" as essentially a synesthetic, rhythmic beat.

The Greek gods "justified human life by living it themselves—the only satisfactory theodicy ever invented," Nietzsche writes (1956, 30). The dismembered god Dionysus lives the "pain of individuation." His dismemberment, "like a separation into air, water, earth, and fire," is the will to creation, the being's will to appear. But individuation is "the source of all suffering," the "root of all evil," and his worshippers' hope for the rebirth of Dionysus is a hope for the redemption of a "ravaged and fragmented world," for the end of "the horror of individual existence" (66, 67, 102). Apollo, on the other hand, is "the marvelous divine image of the *principium individuationis*, whose looks and gestures radiate the full delight, wisdom, and beauty of 'illusion' " (22). He justifies "the ghastly absurdity of existence" (51) as art, redeeming the world of forms by reproducing it in and as a beautiful illusion. For "only as an esthetic product can the world be justified to all eternity" (42).

If art is "a triumph over subjectivity, deliverance from the self, the silencing of every personal will and desire," Nietzsche asks, "how is the lyrical poet at all possible as artist—he who, according to the experience of all times, always says 'I' and recites to us the entire chromatic scale of his passions and appetites?" (1956, 37). The answer is that the lyric poet begins with a Dionysian experience; he surrenders his subjectivity in "a Lethean element in which everything that has been experienced by the individual is drowned" and becomes "wholly identified with the original Oneness, its pain and contradiction" (38, 51). The poet risks annihilation in the "Dionysiac vortex," but on the brink of annulment, the Apollonian power asserts itself and "the poet's spirit feels a whole world of images and similitudes arise" (35, 39). On the verge of Dionysiac shattering, the Appollonian principle "reconstitutes" the individual, "proffering the balm of a delightful illusion." And we are "rescued" from "the Dionysiac universality" into representation, to attend "to individual forms" (128). When empirical reality returns from "this chasm of oblivion," it must return as figure, for unless so transformed, the return—"after the apprehension of truth and its terror"—can only be an experience of "nausea" and "loathing" (51–52). The "I" that returns with this "world of images" is no longer a subjective "I." And it is "No longer the *artist*," who, in this transport, "has himself become a *work of art*" (24).[7] The lyric "I," then, is an illusion, an appearance of a disappeared self; the lyric poet's "'subjectivity' is a mere figment."

Dionysian and Apollonian forces are expressed as music and image. Music sounds the "primordial" pain of "a sphere which is both earlier than appearance and beyond it," and language is "the organ and symbol of appearance"

(Nietzsche 1956, 46). The Dionysian artist begins with a "*musical mood*," "before" words and figures (38). When "the music becomes visible to him again, as in a dream similitude, through the Apollonian dream influence," the original pain is "redeemed"—saved and cashed in, preserved and spent—and the "unselved" "I" returns in the illusion of an "I." The subjectivity of the lyric "I," the reinstituted illusion of individuation after the Dionysian dissolution, is like a "luminous afterimage" of a vision of "the abyss" (61). The lyrical poet allows us to behold the "ground of being" as appearing. Yet through the reinstituted illusion of appearances and individuation, we can still hear the original pain in the "reverberation of the image" (39). In lyric poetry, the words and images that rise from a "musical mood" "reverberate" back into sounds and music.

This rhythmic alternation between sound and word, between sensation and representation, is not "inside" poetry; it *is* poetry. Lyric language is a transmodal, synesthetic process of images dissolving into music and music becoming visible. The lyric "I" is the medium of this transport, an alternation between the specular and the acoustic, sense and sound, cognition and sensation.[8] And its native tongue is neither music nor image but a "voice" and uttered sounds. Nietzsche speaks of "ecstatic sounds," a "clamor" of "delight, grief, knowledge," and even a "most piercing cry" (1956, 34–35), the Dionysian animal sound of the human or the sound of the human animal. It expresses terror, pain and joy, triumph and anguish, all at once; it is a cry of "Woe!" both a "lament over an irrecoverable loss" *and* a cry of birth (35, 27). "Out of nature's womb," out of "the maternal womb of being" (52, 97), one is born—as words. One can henceforth never know oneself but in a second language, in the words of exile. The cry marks the point where "Oneness" is perceived as it is lost, where individuation and representation are perceived as one's fate. Poetry resounds that cry of the "original Oneness" *and* its will to appearance, its "eternal goal" of "redemption through illusion" (33), as—to borrow Stevens's terms—the "cry of *its* occasion." *Its* appearance repeats the loss of sounds to words that makes it possible for us to hear what is lost, to hear ourselves *as* that loss.

The primal duality of the two gods Apollo and Dionysus is a divine justification of the passage from body language into verbal language that makes for the human. While the experience of original Oneness and of "the ghastly absurdity of existence" is utterable only in an inarticulate cry, the poetic word sounds the threshold between the body and representation, between a music that affects the ear and the order that is restored in images and through the eye. While the ear is "the organ of fear," the eye ensures the world of appearances and rational order. If, in tragedy, "myth shields us from music while at the same time giving music its maximum freedom" (Nietzsche 1956, 126), we could say that in the lyric, discourse shields us from the sounds of the body while giving them maximum audibility. Without the body there would be no discourse; without the discourse, there would be no body. Music and figure, sound and sense, auditory sensation and representation are each other's grounding on the shifting stage of an "I." The lyric "I" is a rhythmic pulse "between" music and figure; it is neither music nor figure, and without it there is neither music nor figure.

The lyric "I" is the divide it inhabits; it lives the history of the passage from a cry to a shifter, the entry into language to become "human." Elizabeth Bishop's "In the Waiting Room" (1979, 159–61) narrates this experience. The child in the dentist's waiting room is reading the *National Geographic* when

> Suddenly, from inside,
> came an *oh!* of pain
> —Aunt Consuelo's voice—
> not very loud or long.
> I wasn't at all surprised;
> even then I knew she was
> a foolish, timid woman.
>
> . . . .
>
>   What took me
> completely by surprise
> was that it was *me:*
> my voice, in my mouth.
> Without thinking at all
> I was my foolish aunt,
> I—we—were falling, falling,
> our eyes glued to the cover
> of the *National Geographic*,
> February, 1918.

Immediately following this Dionysian experience is the attempt to restitute order:

> I said to myself: three days
> and you'll be seven years old.
> I was saying it to stop
> the sensation of falling off
> the round, turning world
> into cold, blue-black space.
> But I felt: you are an *I*,
> you are an *Elizabeth*,
> you are one of *them*.
> *Why* should you be one, too?

The unindividuated yet recognized cry—one can and cannot tell whose mouth it comes from—is resolved into the "You are an *I*, / you are an *Elizabeth*," an individuated, gendered, solitary subject and a name, scripted in lines that break.

Bishop recounts a return, from within framing borders, to a Dionysian experience and the subsequent reinstitution of borders—now illusory—of the phenomenal world, both of the immediate surroundings of the waiting room and the whole "world" of the *National Geographic*. The frame and the "inside" make each other visible and audible. The frames are symbolic systems governing social and cultural practices, but the "primal" frame, so to speak, is the system of language.

In all cases it is a question of what is inside and what is outside the borders of a system. In language, it is the body and its cry that are outside; one's "inside" and the sounds from the inside place outside the system, on the inside of which are pronouns and names and men and women in their proper clothes. Yet without the system of language, the cry—not of the aunt but of "Elizabeth"—would be inaudible. It could not have happened; the history—of an "I" and of wars—would not be. Lyric poetry is the one medium that can stage the formation/formulation of an "I" in the passage into language. The uncanniness of the experience—"I knew that nothing stranger / had ever happened, that nothing / stranger could ever happen. / Why should I be my aunt, / or me, or anyone?"—is the recognition, as in a dream, of a dissolution into a cry and an emergence of sense at the brink of the abyss: "I was saying" "you are an *I*."

Dismemberment

Leclaire proposes an alternation between the void and the letter as formative of the psychosexual subject; Nietzsche addresses, on a different scale, an alternation between a Dionysian void and the Apollonian formulation of the text of the world of appearances to locate the lyric subject. In this section, I will focus on the operations of poetic language itself to read the subject function as, again, an alternation between the void and the letter, between the annulment of the subject and the effacement of this annulment.

In terms of poetic operations, this alternation or vibration should be understood as a rhythmic beat between the articulation and disarticulation of words. Poetic language alternates between a phonemic annulment of the coherent word unit and its reinstitution in an effacement of that voiding—between a Dionysian dismemberment of the word and an Apollonian reinstitution of the illusion of discrete, "individual" words with their clear lexical borders. I will approach this topic through Saussure's work on anagrams in Latin verse, which also implicitly confirms the essentially rhythmic character of the subject. Saussure proposes that a complex anagrammatic micro-structure organizes the verse at the phonemic level; the text "imitates" a theme word, usually a sacred name, by obsessively repeating its phonemic components. The phonemes of key words are dispersed in anagrams, "paragrams" (a dispersal over a larger space than that of one or two words), and "hypograms" (a kind of "under-writing" of the theme word across the whole text). If we bracket the mandate to name, which positions this procedure as mimesis or as the "imitation" of a sacred name, the kinds of analyses Saussure performs can also be performed on modern texts, for which a connection to the sacred cannot be assumed. Thus it is best to consider Saussure's proposal of a phonemic system in its broader applicability to the operations of poetic language.

While Saussure uses the suffix "-gram," he insists that he is talking about "combinations of phonemes not letters" (Starobinski 1979, 15): "Neither anagram nor paragram mean that the figures of poetry are directed by way of written signs; but to replace -gram by -phone in one or each of these words would probably lead one to think that some unheard of, monstrous species of things are involved."[9] De Man comments on this passage:

> The "chose inouie[s]" would precisely be that the phonic, sensory, phenomenal ground of poetic diction has been unsettled, for the laws for the dispersal of the key word in the text, be it as ana-, para-, or hypogram, are not phenomenally . . . perceivable. Since the key word is the proper name in all its originary integrity, its subdivision into discrete parts and groups resembles, on the level of meaning, the worst phantasms of dismemberment . . . we would then have witnessed, in effect, the undoing of the phenomenality of language which always entails (since the phenomenal and the noumenal are binary poles within the same system) the undoing of cognition and its replacement by the uncontrollable power of the letter as inscription. By choosing the word *hypogram*, yet making it function as a voiceable name rather than as an inscription, Saussure shelters language from a cognitive dismemberment . . . (1989, 37)

This reading, which actually would shelter us from the radical implications of Saussure's work, is based on the assumption that the phenomena of phonemic dispersal that Saussure addresses are not perceivable. But according to Jean Starobinski, who edited and published the excerpts from Saussure's notebooks, "listening to one or two Saturnian Latin lines, Ferdinand de Saussure could hear, gradually declaring themselves, the principal phonemes of a proper name, separated from one another by neutral phonetic elements" (1979, 15). It is possible that some listeners hear at this level. The laws for the dispersal of phonemes of a key word throughout the text, across lexical units, may not be phenomenally perceivable by the rest of us, but it is in principle perceivable, for, after all, this is precisely what the infant *has* to perceive, via the ear, to learn language—the laws of phonemic recurrence and differentiation in a total phonemic system unto which lexical units will come to be mapped.

Some poets may continue to hear at this level; indeed, according to Starobinski, Saussure ascribes to poets "an acute attention to the phonetic substance of words" and suggests that the craft of ancient poetry was "closer to the ritual of obsession than to the motivating power of an inspired word" (Starobinski 1979,

26). He also speaks of this *"phonic* preoccupation" as a "science of the vocal form of words" (21, 22). Or perhaps—since Saussure is reading ancient poetry—language was at some point heard differently, at the level of the operations of the code, which precisely position the spoken, "phenomenal" word as conceptual. In any case, without indulging in speculation, we can say that this kind of hearing is part of the history of the subject in language.

The kind of patterning Saussure finds is so pervasive that it raises the issue of intention. He claims that the poet starts with the intention, the mandate to imitate a theme word or a name, which is a kind of "title" entitling his text. Thus he starts with a deliberate "procedure" (Starobinski 1979, 11–13), but the anagramming takes over: "one cannot speak of anagrams as of a game which is accessory to the versification. They become the foundation of that versification, whether the poet wishes it or not" (17). The intentions of the poet are taken over by the mechanisms of the reproduction of significant phonemic clusters. This marks a painful crux, compelling the poet's surrender to the binding necessities of arbitrary mechanisms. This is also a metaleptic crux, for the initial, authorizing word is never used. It is dismembered across a text, as the act of adhering to the given word undoes the "given" word, which disintegrates in the ritual, phonemic observation of its laws. Only a phonemic reading can retroactively "discover" or articulate the word that authorizes the phonemic dispersal.

Saussure insists that the dispersal of the phonemes of the key words has no regard for lexical borders, which divide the phonemic stream into meaningful units. Words are lexical or "written" units and punctuate the continuous phonemic flow. Thus the language of a poem requires two kinds of hearing—one of the acoustic and phonemic series and one of "written" or lexical series. Saussure also insists that this phonemic repetition is independent of poetic functions like alliteration, rhyme, and rhythm. It has to do with the flow of the text as a whole and does not privilege initial or final sounds or stresses, which make for rhythmic emphases; such devices also, of course, make for sense stresses. Saussure proposes a dismemberment of both poetic sense and form into phonemic relations following a kind of "linguistic legality" independent of lexical units, semantic considerations, or formal schemes of phonemic and syllabic organization.

The "unheard of, monstrous species of things" involves, then, a return to hearing the code per se, hearing *only* phonemic differentiation. Here a buried history—the one we buried—threatens to come back. This is, indeed, a threat, for what is a "phantasm" of dismemberment on the "level of meaning" is, on the phonemic level, a quite real threat of dismemberment for one who continues to hear on that level. Not only the cognitive function and meaning but the symbolic integrity of a coherent body is at stake. To hear at the level of phonemic relations is to return to the prehistory of the subject, the concurrent processes of the articulation of both language and a body. The "anagramming" is a "backward-writing" dissolution and jeopardizes a stable subject and the "written"—by which I mean the coherent—word. What is dismembered in letters is always only a word; this would be an "Oedipal phase" issue—to use a convenient shorthand—and such undoing of cognition is within the game.

The figure of dismemberment, however, is a real issue with the phonemic breakdown of verbal integrities: phonemic dissolution of a word over a space of other words is a disarticulation of symbolic units and, therefore, a threat of disarticulation of the symbolic body. Here we are on the verge of psychopathology: this is regression, outside the game, to a history that *must* stay buried—the emergence of surfaces, the "memberment" of a body. If the linguistic code must stay buried for rational discourse, phonemic hearing must stay buried for "sanity," the stability of the ego—the mental projection, in Freud's terms, of the surfaces of the body (1989, 636–37). The ego function, which depends on a coherent body separate from others and objects, is most vulnerable to—most permeable by—auditory stimuli. The ear is a passive organ. The infant can close his eyes but not his ears; it will take him years to develop the proper muscle coordination to do that. He must learn language before he has the ability to plug his ears. The process of separation that secures a coherent body (and ego) is a slow process in the case of auditory experience; it is more difficult to separate a "self" from voices in one's head, so to speak—voices one cannot shut out—than from one's images in mirrors. The borders of the ego are more porous when it comes to the sounds of words than they are in specular experience, and they continue to remain more vulnerable to voices.

Writing secures the word against phonemic dissolution, just as eroticization secures an articulate body. In both cases, the "written" or coherent word protects against dismemberment. The graphic inscription of the word further secures the spoken word in visual elements; it effects a passage from aural to visual processing of words, from an audial to a specular relationship to language. The literal dismemberment of the spoken word into visual signs wards off the threat of a dismemberment of the word into bodily depths. Writing draws borderlines, producing oral auditory sensations of words as a text, the way eroticization produces the body as a text.

Yet only a phonemic disturbance of the "written" text can remember the history that we are. A phonemic dissolution into a chaos of obsessive, inhuman, systemic orders "deviates" from the orders of meaningful language. But just such hearing is the norm of the language-acquiring animal, an order from which it "deviates" into symbolic language. Such phonemic hearing is also a facet of poetic language, which keeps in view the history and the imminence, the ever-present threat, of the disarticulation of the word unit into the phonemic elements of a code. At the same time, however, that the text offers a vision of a Dionysian dismemberment of the individual corpse/word into sounds— all the way back to the inarticulate cry—it also reinstitutes them as "art," an afterimage of the void, the illusion of a coherent body and language. In other words, of all that we can know. The Apollonian inscription of a word is a funerary script, the epitaph of the infant buried in a coherent "textual" body and speech. It erects the monument of a corpse as well as meaningful language, and covers up the Dionysian language of the mouth-ear circuit with the language of representation.

I have stressed very specific points in Saussure to situate the function of poetic form and to support one of the larger claims of my study—my argument that the formality of poetry remembers the history of language acquisition. Poetic forms mediate the mechanisms of the linguistic code and symbolic language, as they organize the materials of the code. Meter, for example, measures and regulates the phonemic flow, and alliteration and rhyme consent to word units. Formal devices dismantle the "bad" illusion of lexical integrities, which they reinstitute as Apollonian "beautiful" illusions.

For Saussure, phonemic hearing across a text—hypogrammic hearing—also makes for a disturbance in the experience of time, because it is independent of the consecutive order in which the phonemes of the text are heard—the order that makes for the sequence of heard words. One hears these "anagrams" at variable, unmeasured intervals. This, too, is a regression to a time before the hearing of a word—to the passage between hearing acoustic phenomena and a word that coheres acoustic phenomena as a set of meaningful phonemes. Poetic forms both acknowledge the "linguistic legality" of phonemic procedures and *socialize* these procedures, as they regulate and measure the phonemic flow. We still hear nonconsecutively, but in relation to a system of measured intervals of repetition that protects from annulment. We still hear in terms of repetitions and echoes of phonemic clusters independent of word units, but these repetitions are also within a measured, formal system of sounds and make for sense stresses—as in rhyme, for example—as well as sound stresses. Poetic form mediates the phonemic system and the sense system; this is a social mediation, and it is audible in a rhythmic alternation between sound and sense, phonemic flow and lexical segmentation. Saussure is right to insist that the phonemic system is independent of rhythm, and his theory in effect argues the necessity of rhythm for meaning. Rhythm intentionalizes and regathers the dismembered language, just as meter both necessitates and facilitates this operation.

On the historical register as well, there is a passage from a phonemic to a lexical hearing. Greek lyric poetry, which begins the history of the genre in the West, is intimately connected with the history of alphabetical writing.[10] Breath is primary in an oral culture, but in the transformation to literacy the senses are reorganized to establish the primacy and control of the visual over the aural. In an oral culture, Anne Carson writes, the individual is closely linked to the world outside, because survival depends on keeping open the "conduits of the senses," especially the sense of sound, to register continuous information from outside (1998, 43). To process information in written form, however, the individual learns to control and block the input of the other senses—especially that of hearing—and inhibit bodily responses. Writing and reading demand that one isolate the body from the environment. Thus the sense of the body itself changes to one dependent on separation, self-control, and self-possession. Writing separates words from the environment, from the reader and the writer, and from one another.

While, orally, words come in a continuous stream, the discrete word rather than the phrase becomes the unit of composition in writing (Carson 1998, 43). Orally, lexical borders are fluid, and epigraphic evidence shows that it took a long time to "systematize word-division in writing, indicating the novelty and difficulty of this concept" (50). Moreover, the Greeks' adoption of the Phoenician alphabet introduced a unique kind of symbolization and a further division, for the Greeks assigned letters to both consonants and vowels, breaking units of pronounced sounds into their components. K. Robb writes that, unlike the Phoenician sign that stood for a consonant *plus any vowel*, which the reader would supply from context, the Greek consonant sign, "and this for the first time in the history of writing, stands for an abstraction, an isolated consonant."[11] A consonant is "unpronounceable without adding to it some suggestion of vocalic breath"; it marks the borders, the edges of sounds, the points of contact and distinction. With literacy, "sounds, letters, words, emotions, events in time, selves" become distinct, each with its clear edges (51).[12]

In an oral culture, language would be heard differently, but a phonemic hearing is always possible even in verse that has lost all connection to an oral context, because each person's passage from the "oral culture" of childhood into lexical "writing" in a sense reenacts a similar process, and a phonemic memory may always be reactivated. And in the poetic passage to graphic writing, a second zoning—now of spoken language into visual signs—repeats the reduction of the passage from sounds to words in the initial acquisition of language. Complex oral-auditory phenomena, with a range of tones, pitches, and voice qualities that cannot be represented visually, are now zoned into a graphic medium.

In poetry, this visual medium must institute different kinds of excess texture, affects, and rhythms to compensate for the excess auditory material that cannot be transcribed. Thus visual patterns of letters and spacing would also be operative in a written text, apart from the patterns of phonemes in sound devices such as alliteration and rhymes. In this sense, writing recreates a synesthetic experience, where patterns of visual units may make for auditory measures. William Carlos Williams's "triadic lines," for example, seem to work this way. Williams assigns one beat per line, regardless of the number of stresses or syllables (1957, 327). The visual equivalence of these lines is to be apprehended as an audial equivalence of duration, so that we hear a "a new measure":

Once
    at El Paso
        toward evening,
I saw—and heard!—
        ten thousand sparrows
           who had come in from
the desert
        to roost. They filled the trees
           of a small park. Men fled
(with ears ringing!) (1988, 292)

The look of a page is important for Williams's poetry in general; as Henry Sayre has argued (1983), Williams's visual arrangements on the page defend against auditory chaos. Here the visual order performs the function of meter—a measuring system that segments and punctuates the phonemic flow and institutes a synesthetic rhythm, foreclosing dismemberment.

NOTES

1. A passage from Freud is central to his argument: "An essential component of [the] experience of satisfaction is a particular perception the mnemic image of which remains associated thenceforward with the memory trace of the excitation produced by the need" (Freud, qtd. in Leclaire 1998, 147). What will put desire into play is not the object that satisfies the need but a mnemic image of a perception of satisfaction (Leclaire 1998, 43). While the objects that may satisfy the need are substitutable, the mnemic image is the constant, and the mnemic trace is inscribed on the body, making for its surfaces.

2. The letters of the secret name function as fixations of the original loss of bliss, which enables the variability of the objects of desire whose function is to conceal the fixation (Leclaire 1998, 53ff.). "Psychoanalysis, therefore, proves to be a practice of the letter" (70); the unconscious chain "breaks down into a play of letters" (79), and the analyst must try to hear "the literal trait" that is singular to the individual, the "essence of each individual in his or her most intimate self" (81).

3. 1990, 243; also see 247. Deleuze's theory of the relation of language and sexuality, which alludes to Leclaire, maps the concurrent processes of the emergence and organization of bodily and linguistic surfaces out of depths as follows:

noises (internal sounds of bodily depths)	Voice (from above, of the preexisting language system)	speech (formation of surfaces and words)
sounds	phonemes, morphemes, semantemes	words and sense
oral phase (oral-anal depths)	phallic phase (phallus of organization)	Oedipal phase (phallus of castration)
schizophrenic position	depressive position	sexual organization of the body surface

These concurrent movements, out of material depths to semiotic surfaces to symbolic, "metaphysical" surfaces, are co-implicated, which accounts for the concurrence of linguistic and sexual disturbances in psychopathological disorders (224–33; 240–41).

4. The mother's ear would later get its substitute objects, for the poet, in readers—first oneself, then others. And the written page is another substitute object for the mother's ear. These objects enable the repetition of what gave pleasure—being heard.

5. The widely encountered figure of the "mother tongue" registers the mother's reproduction-production of the subject as well as of the body. But the tongue also has other, masculine associations. Fonagy wries: "The study of neurotic symptoms and of dreams has taught us that a faint resemblance or a certain functional analogy are sufficient for an unconscious identification of one sexual organ with another. It is no coincidence, for example, that it is the phallic period during which children learn to master the rolled [r], a sound that presupposes a strong erection of the tongue" (qtd. in Tsur 1992, 137–38). Via this unconscious identification of the tongue with the penis, the tongue's hardness in the articulatory gestures of certain phonemes make for perceived masculine qualities. One such case is the rolled /r/, and in certain linguistic communities in Russia, Tsur reports, it is taboo for women to roll their /r/s (1992, 140–41).

Hearing Pound read provides supporting evidence. Also, interestingly, /l/, which the "soft" tongue might gender feminine, and /r/ are easily substitutable liquids. According to Jakobson, "The number of languages with a single liquid (whether /l/ or /r/) is extraordinarily large. . . . The child has only a single liquid for a long time and acquires the other liquid only as one of his latest speech sounds" (qtd. in Tsur 1992, 65).

Rita Dove's "Parsley" engages the phallic /r/ and its figural significance in representing racial and sexual anxieties. "El General" (Rafael Trujillo), who orders "many" to be killed—twenty thousand, to be exact—for failing to roll their r's, fixates on that trait to distinguish his mother, who "could roll her r's like a queen," from the Haitian field workers (1993, 133–35).

6. Poetry is the proper discourse of that subject, the alternation between the two series.

7. Thus in the production of the lyric "I" lies the origin of tragedy (Nietzsche 1956, 39, 104). Whereas the epic poet is purely Apollonian, the lyric singer is the union of "Apollonian and Dionysiac intentions" (42). Eventually, we get tragedy, the "Apollonian embodiment of Dionysiac insights and powers" (56–57).

8. The Dionysiac rupture of proper cognitive functioning involves the body. It is brought on by intoxication and arousal of the sexual body that connects to natural sexual powers. The destruction of an individuated subject and empirical reality and their reinstitution as illusion entail the dissolution of cognitive processes into bodily rhythms and their subsequent reinstitution as dream.

Nietzsche writes, "Art owes its continuous evolution to the Apollonian-Dionysiac duality, even as the propagation of the species depends on the duality of the sexes" (1956, 19). The marriage metaphor, the gendering of Apollo as male and Dionysus as female and their alignment with the visual and the aural respectively, places their generative agon at a crux between the body and representation, which is in turn represented as a sensory-modal crossing.

9. Qtd. in de Man 1989, 37. In Olivia Emmet's translation, "Neither anagram nor paragram intends to suggest that poetry is arranged for these figures in accordance with

written signs, but to replace *gram* by *phone* in either of these words would result precisely in a suggestion of something extraordinary" (Saussure 1979, 18). "Precisely" would suggest that the phenomenon is not extraordinary.

10. Lyric poetry develops, Anne Carson writes, concurrently with a number of changes in forms of representation and symbolization that take place in the archaic age: "In politics with the rise of the *polis*, in economics with the invention of coinage, in poetics with the study by lyric poets of precise moments in personal life, and in communications technology with the introduction of the Phoenician alphabet to Greece" (1998, 42).

11. Qtd. in Carson 1998, 54.

12. This separation creates different kinds of symbolic, textual spaces between letters, between words, and between the written word and the writer-reader. Carson argues that these are new kinds of erotic spaces, spaces of desire born of difference and absence. Thus the lyric poet's subject matter, eros, is also operative both in the workings of the textual medium itself and the poet's relation to the text.

Williams's recurrent association of edges, letters, and the deployment of the page space with eros—"The Botticellian Trees," "The Rose," "The Attic Which Is Desire," and many others—exhibits this configuration. Edges, separation, and letters create the graphic spaces of desire. In "The Botticellian Trees," the covered "limbs" of the woman instigate desire for what is under the clothing, the limbs, which, in the poem's conceit, correlate with the bare branches of the trees (under the leaves) and with letters (under the words and sentences).

Chapter 4

⚜

THE BODY OF WORDS

Hysteria

Hysteria, with its four-thousand-year history, is the oldest and most widespread psychological disorder. More accurately, it comprises a set of psychosomatic phenomena considered a disorder in some cultures and assimilated in others in ritual practices of individuation/socialization. The definitions of hysteria change through its long history, as do its manifestations or "symptoms." Although the symptoms are historically and culturally specific, certain syndromes recur, including amnesias, arrhythmic movements, eating disorders, and, most important for my purposes, body "language" and linguistic disturbances.

My question remains "Why is there lyric poetry?" and hysteria with its linguistic problems offers a different perspective on the social function of the formality of poetry. The hysterical body, a body that can be reconfigured by following rhetorical and linguistic procedures, is placed inside language, and my excursion into hysteria and a range of associated phenomena is intended to refocus on the articulation of the subject in language from the perspective offered by its disarticulation into the affectively charged, bodily produced materials of language. I necessarily draw on psychoanalytic literature on hysteria and Freud's work—which, of course, read the linguistic disorders of hysteria as symptomatic of psychosexual disturbances. But my essentially different argument is that hysterical procedures in fact confirm the priority of language in the formulation of the subject and the sexual body. In hysteria, the erotogenically inscribed body itself becomes a linguistic medium and "speaks" by following poetic procedures of figural and phonemic substitutions.

The sexual and the ego instincts are Freud's two "great instincts," and he proposes that "pathological consequences" ensue when these two fundamental instincts are in conflict (1963, 54, 55). Hysteria is the particular pathological consequence of such a conflict in the oral zone. According to Freud, the erotogenic significance of the oral zone is intensified in hysteria and the libidinal impulses focus on the labial area (1975, 48). If repression ensues, the zone too intimate with the sexual instinct will "refuse itself" to the other great instinct, for "the more intimate the relation of an organ possessing . . . a duality of function with one of the great instincts, the more it will refuse itself to the other" (1963, 55). Thus the "common possession" of the labial zone by the sexual and alimentary functions, which accounts for the reason "sexual satisfaction arises during the taking of nourishment," also accounts for the nutritional disorders that arise when the erotogenic functions of the shared zone are "disturbed" (1975, 71–72). Hence the range of alimentary disorders in hysteria: constrictions of the throat, hysterical vomiting, refusal of food, anorexia, intestinal problems, and so on.

Remarkably, Freud does not address the topic of speech, the *third* and socially vital function of the oral zone. The mouth also comprises the organs of speech; *the* distinction of human language is its concentration in the oral cavity. Given the multiple functions of the mouth, the "borders" between somatic, erotogenic, and linguistic formations are permeable in the oral zone, for they are drawn only in a rhythmic intercourse of distinct functions, each of which is, therefore, implicated in the others. These formulations that give us, in turn, the ego (a mental projection of the body),[1] the erotogenic body (the text inscribed on the physiological body), and the subject (one who can say "I") thus may be confused in the oral zone, and the paths of their articulation may remain open for regression to earlier formations and "confusions" of the somatic and the symbolic.[2] If we think in terms of three rather than two oral functions, unsuccessful sublimation of the alimentary and the sexual mouth opens the borders to traffic and affectively charges the phonemes of the mother tongue, so that words come to do more, or less, than signify, as shown in the linguistic disturbances in neuroses and psychoses. In poetic language, the same "confusions" formally reappear as civilized currency—as a formal and public "script." Poetic form ensures the audibility of a somatically produced language in a socially, culturally, and historically legible "script."

Regression to an alimentary language characterizes the linguistic disturbances in psychotic disorders, where words disintegrate into the mouth and bodily depths. The mother tongue now becomes "essentially alimentary and excremental," Deleuze writes about Artaud's language.[3] As language and the body blur, the word "bursts into pieces; it is decomposed into syllables, letters, and above all into consonants which act directly on the body, penetrating and bruising it" (1990, 87). Phonemes now have immediate physical effects on the body, for what also disintegrates is that other "metaphysical" surface, the surface of the body. Sense disappears along with these surfaces. In the primary order of schizophrenia, language is reabsorbed into the body's depths and is indistinguishable from the passions and actions of the body: "There is no longer anything to prevent propositions from falling back onto bodies and from mingling their sonorous elements with the body's olfactory, gustatory, or digestive affects. Not only is there no longer any sense, but there is no longer any grammar or syntax either—nor, at the limit, are there any articulated syllabic, literal, or phonetic elements" (91). But before that limit, "the moment that the maternal language is stripped of its sense, its *phonetic elements* become singularly wounding" (88). Here we descend to the phonemic threshold and the pain of language.

Hysteria, standing at that limit of the inscription of the linguistic and the erotogenic body, makes clear the relationship of speech to the two "great instincts." The linguistic procedures of hysterical symptom-formation attest to the coincidence of the passages from the organic to the symbolic body and from somatic to symbolic language. For the configuration of the hysteric's body and the problems that affect it conform to "everyday language," David-Menard writes, not to the anatomy of the nervous system, and "for a part of the body to be affected as popular speech would have it, and not as anatomy requires, the body must in some sense belong to the order of language" (1989, 2–3).[4]

The body that belongs to the order of language is not the physiological but the represented, erotogenic body, and hysteria displays the intimacy of erotogenic and linguistic representations. In the domain of representations, tropological substitutions, translations, or transcriptions of desires and fantasies into somatic symptoms become possible following the logic of language—specifically, that of the mother tongue, which the texts of the unconscious and the erotogenic body share.[5] If, as Freudian theory has it, psychic life and repression operate on verbal representations of drives, then the transcriptions of unconscious impulses into somatic symptoms would have to substitute along verbal and literal linkages. Ideas and impulses are repressed only after achieving verbal representations, and symptoms embody metaphors for these predications, as well as "the more primitive versions from which the metaphoric replacements themselves are derived." Thus, for example, the symptom of a bent back may express through the body or somatize the metaphor "spineless," which itself rests on a more "primary" substitution of a body part (spine) for another body part (phallus) (Abse 1966, 180–83).

But Wilfred Abse is citing an English case, and who is to say that the *spine-penis* anagram does not motivate the metaphoric linkage? For hysterical "transcriptions" of libidinal impulses into somatic symptoms work not only with figural substitutions but with substitutions through literal and phonemic links. They function at the level of the primary process and exhibit the same techniques of distortion that operate in manifest dream-formation.[6] Like poetic language and dreams, symptoms show, in Ella Sharpe's words, the "fact that the bridges of thought are crossed and recrossed by names" and "that we all learned our mother tongue phonetically." And hysterical symptom-formation, like dreams and poetic language, has at its disposal a "store house of memory and experience," including "all experiences from infancy."[7]

The storehouse of linguistic memory and experience includes the individual's phonetic acquisition of language, which allows for one path of regression. While words come to convey abstract ideas, Sharpe writes, "they do not lose the concrete significance experienced in their first hearing and use in the unconscious storehouse of the individual's past. . . . [T]he word is always connected with the speaker's historical past."[8] Thus phonetic or clang associations, for example, will play a role in symbolization. Sharpe cites a case of phonetic substitution based on sound memories: a symptom becomes intelligible to the analyst when she sees that the past-tense "read" is substituting for the repressed "red." Such substitution is possible because the word was first *heard* as "red" (qtd. in Abse 1966, 179). This is also one way poetic language moves; Stevens's "Large Red Man Reading," for example, plays with the same confusion of *red-read*, which is likely rooted in the personal memory of the man from Reading, Pennsylvania.

The storehouse of linguistic memory also holds the shared, public past of the language. Thus words with imitative origins and naturalized metaphors, for example, may be literalized on the body in hysterical symptom-formation. Since repression operates within the linguistic system, the confusion of symbolic and somatic phenomena in the formation of symptoms is traceable along the figural and literal paths that draw their common border. If an "instinct" appears as a "concept on the frontier between the mental and the somatic" (Freud 1989, 566), it can only appear in words, which occupy that frontier and thus, in effect, put the "concept" itself in question. While the instinct is a "concept" that must be posited as a "third thing" to get from the body to the mind, language and its history—personal and communal—already occupy that passage, and have no need for the "concept" of an "instinct."

The symptoms produced through a verbal logic—whether they act out or literalize metaphoric linkages or substitute along literal and phonemic linkages—signal a regression from abstract language.[9] Freud provides many examples of the genesis of hysterical symptoms by means of verbal expressions. An insult that feels like "a slap in the face" will give rise to facial neuralgia; a "piercing look" will trigger a sharp head pain; a sensation of nails being driven into the head will act out "[s]omething's come into my head," symbolizing a painful thought (Breuer and Freud 1955, 178–79). Such symbolization, which takes "a verbal expression literally," Freud concludes, is not "taking liberties with words, but is simply reviving once more the sensations to which the verbal expression owes its justification" (180–81).[10]

Hysteria also entails speech disturbances as distinct from symbolization disorders; both disorders negotiate the internal divide of a physiological-symbolic language. In conversion reactions, the body is re-figured by language, as if it had replaced speech organs. In speech disorders, on the other hand, language is dis-figured by the body in a regression to the presymbolic, as articulate words disintegrate into phonemes, sounds, and eventually noises. Somatic symptoms in conversion reactions may be "explained" by linkages among signifiers and their material elements, whereas the "refusal" of speech is a refusal of the symbolic altogether.

Speech aligns with ego instincts, since it clearly has survival value. It also aligns with sexual instincts, for just as clearly it gives pleasure; especially in the mother tongue, it is linked to the pleasure body. Speech appears to be the threshold where the two "great instincts" are socially negotiated. Thus it is susceptible to pressure from both sexual disturbances and disturbances of the ego function. Psychiatric literature contains many examples of both. A speech disturbance may be a denial of sexual instincts or ego instincts or *both*. It may be either a denial of both or an attempt to accommodate the concurrent claims of each in the oral zone in an eroticized/alimentary "speech." In discursive terms, the "aims" of the two "great instincts" become "audible" in and as linguistic disturbances—as interferences with symbolic discourse. Language cannot "recover" an intimacy with the body, however, without damage to the symbolizations that give us the erotogenic body and the ego. By somatizing language, by refusing the symbolic, the hysteric in effect bears inadvertent testimony to an erotogenic body that is only a script—a currency, a signifier. And he bears witness to an ego that is only a representation, an "I."[11]

Poetic language, like hysterical "language," also displays its somatic materiality. While the hysteric "speaks" a private language that would reduce the symbolic to the body, however, the message of the poet's formal and public medium is that one can never recover a not-already-symbolic language, a not-already-textualized body, a not-already-represented physiology; these figures of "origins" become conceivable only in their vanishing into words. For both poetry and hysteria, the crucial point seems to be the end of childhood, the period of language acquisition. If a child is not exposed to language during a certain phase of brain development, linguistic capacity is lost, and this period has its limit at around age twelve and the full development of the cerebral hemispheres.[12] The acquisition of new languages becomes more difficult after this age, which also coincides with puberty and the onset of adult sexual life. Freud points out that "most psychoneurotics only fall ill after the age of puberty as a result of the demands made upon them by normal sexual life" (1975, 36).[13] The age of puberty is also when "most" poets begin writing, which may not be unrelated to the same demands, for most of Freud's cases also write poetry. Poetry is a way of remembering or retrieving the emotional and erotic resonances of the materials of language on the verge of their disappearance—or, rather, as the wake or trace of their disappearance in referential, "adult" language.

Seamus Heaney's "Death of a Naturalist" presents a moment in adolescence when a Dionysian experience threatens to absorb the speaker in an undifferentiated, infantile matrix. As the schoolroom boundaries maintained by "Miss Walls" and her labels dissolve, so do the distinctions between the alimentary functions, sexuality, and speech. The stability of referential language is now in jeopardy, as it threatens to dissolve into bodily depths that would swallow speech and speaker both. This dissolution of identity is a sickening, a swoon, out of which emerges a poet—one for whom words are both affectively charged physiological phenomena and symbolic units. The bodily "depths" are presented in an "eruption" of the materiality of language, and the threat of annulment of the subject occurs in the context of the "croaking" animal sounds of reproductive activity, which the echoic "coarse croaking" of the second stanza reproduces:

The air was thick with a bass chorus.
Right down the dam gross-bellied frogs were cocked
On sods; their loose necks pulsed like sails. Some hopped:
The slap and plop were obscene threats. Some sat
Poised like mud grenades, their blunt heads farting.
I sickened, turned, and ran. The great slime kings
Were gathered there for vengeance and I knew
That if I dipped my hand the spawn would clutch it. (1990, 5–6)

This passage is a staged poetic performance of what predates—and remains the "underbelly"—of referential language itself. The "poetic" conventions of rhymes, alliteration, and consonance, together with the exploitation of the tonal, expressive qualities of different phonemes, render audible the imbrication of the alimentary, sexual, and speech functions in the oral zone. The birth of a poet is at once a relearning of language, a reliving of what infantile amnesia forgets, and a "turning" away from it again, now into poetic language.[14] This sequential history is remembered in the simultaneous annulment and reinscription of the subject in poetry, of the dissolution of the subject and its return as illusion. Poetic language, with its culturally sanctioned rules licensing a licentiousness with words, writes and rights the initial passage into language. This is poetic justice, evening the score:

Now, to pry into roots, to finger slime,
To stare, big-eyed Narcissus, into some spring
Is beneath all adult dignity. I rhyme
To see myself, to set the darkness echoing. (Heaney 1990, 11)

"Rhyme" discursively sublimates the "slime" but acoustically reinforces it; it marks the poetic threshold. For poetry draws the borderline between the somatic and the social, the material and the referential aspects of language. Rhyming ensures the audibility of the somatic materiality of language as it discursively articulates a natural-biological "darkness." There is no outside or inside "dark" nature available to us; on this side of pathology, "the darkness" is only a reverberation, a linguistic echo off of the material medium of language, an auditory illusion that poetic forms guarantee.

The poet accepts the intimacy of the symbolic and recalls, in the sounds of words, a prehistoric intimacy of the body and language, both dissolving and reinstituting symbolic language as "beautiful illusion." The poet's vocation, Agamben writes, is a "reverse embrace of memory and forgetting which holds intact the identity of the unrecalled and the unforgettable" (1995, 45). Mnemosyne, the mother of the Muses, bids the poet at once to remember and forget again.

Poetic vocation is a remembering that is a form of forgetting. For the affectively charged bodily language is officially re-membered in a formal discourse that displays the "inhumanity" of the system of language—its mechanical nature. The social function of poetic discourse—by the very fact of its existence, apart from any local functions it may serve—is to maintain the fragile, "beautiful illusion" of the "human," to hold that precarious figure of the choice of an "inhuman" language against the claims of the rational "mind" and the biological "body." Poetry will not reduce to bodily language any more than it will reduce to rational language. While there would not be much disagreement on the latter point, a slew of poetic theories attempt to ground poetry in the body, but poetry counters a hysterical somatizing of language as much as it counters a rational reduction of language to an instrument of thought. Indeed, the bodily language of hysteria is best understood as the "other" of rational language. In poetry no such mind/body opposition exists. Language is certainly somatically produced—even silent language is produced by memories of somatic articulation of sounds—but the body that produces language is a body of both personal and cultural linguistic memory. Poetry keeps intact the emotionally charged linguistic histories of the mind and the body—abstractions that get carved out of poetic language. In poetry, the mechanisms of language—the Doppelgänger of the Dionysian—puts in question the status of both a mind and a body outside language, its procedures, and its social and cultural history.

To reduce poetry to bodily language is to reduce it to hysteria. Poetry formally hosts bodily language, just as it hosts referential language. Any theory of poetry has to admit the somatic interference of poetic language with the referential function, but to read such interference as signifying a bodily challenge to the symbolic order is to consent to the priority of rational language and, thus, to reduce poetry to hysteria. Kristeva's elaborate theory, for example, is a hysterical theory. The difference of poetry is that the "body" in poetry interferes formally—through conventionally sanctioned rules and procedures based on the givens of a language. The cultural function of poetry lies in the fact that its interference with the symbolic is socially and historically sanctioned;[15] it lies in what sets it apart from the alimentary/sexual mouth, even as it acknowledges all that rational language-use suppresses.

Poetry is a threat to reason precisely because it is *not* hysterical. What is at peril is more than the repressive social and political institutions of a given time and place; indeed, in many cultures poetry functions explicitly to reaffirm the orders in place. What is at stake is the entire Apollonian show of the "real." The universality and long history of lyric poetry tells us that cultures may need to be reminded of the arbitrariness and relativity of their "rational" and "natural" systems and their attendant values. Precisely because so much is at stake, however, poetry can only be regarded as culturally conservative. If we would grant poetry as such any cultural power, we would have to understand it as a practice that conserves what it most radically calls in question. The social power of poetry lies in the concurrent annulment and reinstitution of the symbolic—however and to whatever local ideological ends it may choose to wield that power.

ANNA O.

"Hysterics suffer mainly from reminiscences," write Breuer and Freud; a hysterical symptom disappears when the memory of the event that provoked it is brought *"clearly to light,"* *"when the patient had described that event in the greatest possible detail and had put the affect into words"* (1955, 7, 6). This "curable" amnesia rests, however, on another kind of "peculiar amnesia" that accounts for most adults' forgetting the experience of their childhood up to their "sixth or eighth year" (Freud 1989, 259). Infantile amnesia, which has "hitherto eluded explanation," Freud writes, is "astonishing," because

> the very same impressions that we have forgotten have none the less left the deepest traces on our minds and have had a determining effect upon the whole of our later development. There can, therefore, be no question of any real abolition of the impressions of childhood, but rather of an amnesia similar to that which neurotics exhibit for later events, and of which the essence consists in a simple withholding of these impressions from consciousness, viz., in their repression. But what are the forces that bring about this repression of the impressions of childhood? Whoever could solve this riddle would, I think, have explained *hysterical* amnesia as well. (260)

The connection between hysterical and infantile amnesia is more than just a "play upon words," he adds, for hysterical amnesia is explicable only if the subject already possesses a storehouse of memory-traces that are not available to consciousness but are now "attracting to themselves the material which the forces of repression are engaged in repelling from consciousness." Thus, "[i]t may be said that without infantile amnesia there would be no hysterical amnesia."

In Freud's reading, of course, infantile amnesia, "which turns everyone's childhood into something like a prehistoric epoch," is a concealment of the beginnings of one's sexual life (1989, 260). This repressed material "speaks" in symptoms, and the anemnestic work of the therapist is comparable to an archeologist's excavation of an ancient ruin: "Imagine that an explorer arrives in a little-known region where his interest is aroused by an expanse of ruins, with remains of walls, fragments of columns, and tablets with half-effaced and unreadable inscriptions." If the digger's work of uncovering what is "buried" is "crowned with success," he discovers that "the ruined walls are part of the ramparts of a palace or a treasure-house; the fragments of columns can be filled out into a temple; the numerous inscriptions, which, by good luck, may be bilingual, reveal an alphabet and a language, and, when they have been deciphered and translated, yield undreamed-of information about the events of the remote past, to commemorate which the monuments were built" (97–98). In other words, the archeologist must crack a code to decipher the language of the buried past.

Yet the linguistic character of hysterical symptoms brings into question the order of precedence or, at least, the separability of the beginnings of one's sexual life and the beginnings of one's life in language. Hysteria is as old and as widely encountered as lyric poetry, and both appear in societies very different from late-nineteenth-, early-twentieth-century European societies in their understanding of sexuality and what, if any, sexual experiences must be repressed. Since sexuality is a relative matter, it would not seem unfeasible that the *real* childhood trauma is the universal, constitutive human experience of the historicizing entry into language. The ruin left of that history is referential language itself, which is precisely what must be deciphered for "information about the events of the remote past." Freud's uncanny figure is the return of the repressed of his theory. What is buried is an "alphabet," a primitive language now lying in ruins and forgotten below the stratum of referential, rational language. Freud simply evades the history of language acquisition and the implications of its concurrency with the history of sexualization. The passage into language needs to be buried and consigned to oblivion—and universally—so that referential language and the symbolic order can remain stable.

A return to the story of Anna O.—at the origin of the "science" of psychoanalysis—might be justified at this point, since the case involves not only somatization but speech disturbances, linguistic regression, and flight from the mother tongue. The patient develops numerous classic symptoms in the course of caring for her sick father—arrhythmic muscular contractions, rigidity,[16] somnambulism, dissociation, hallucinations, "absences," amnesias, and so on (Breuer 1955, 22–24). Alongside these, she also develops "a deep-going functional disorganization of her speech," progressing from being "at a loss to find words" to losing her command of grammar and syntax. In time, "she became almost completely deprived of words. She put them together laboriously out of four or five languages and became almost unintelligible." Finally, she was "unable to say a syllable."

Breuer interprets this literal silence as enacting a figurative silence: she was "determined not to speak about" something that had deeply offended her. When he encourages her to speak about the event, the inhibition disappears, and her ability to talk about it coincides with a return of muscular movement, a recession of her paraphasia. *But*: "But thenceforward she spoke only in English—apparently, however, without knowing that she was doing so" (25). She is no longer somatizing; she is able to speak, but she "refuses" the mother tongue. A trinity—not a duality—seems to be at work here, for the mother tongue is very much in the game of the two "great instincts." English delivers her from both the "body language" of somatization and from the affective power of the mother tongue. It "sanitizes" both the body and the mother tongue, which confirms their intimacy, their affective contagion in her "insanity."

She can still understand German, though, and "when she was at her very best and most free, she talked French and Italian. There was complete amnesia between these times and those at which she talked English" (25). Following the psychic trauma of her father's death, she enters a new stage: she speaks only English and cannot "understand what was said to her in German." She is still able to read French and Italian, but if asked to read aloud, she produces extempore English translations. And at the time of the switch to English, "she refused nourishment altogether" (26). This course of events suggests the importance of the affect of the sounds of words. Some pleasure of a sexual nature is being denied in "forgetting" German and, again, in the refusal to sound out French or Italian, in which she seems to have been more at home. If English is denying some form of oral pleasure, according to Freud's logic, this denial would lead to a refusal of the other great instinct at work in the oral zone: a refusal of "nourishment altogether."

Then the "talking cure"—her term and her contribution to psychoanalysis—begins. Relating her hallucinations under hypnosis and verbalizing the psychic events triggering the appearance of some of her symptoms remove these symptoms (34–35). She retranslates the body language of hysterical symptoms into a verbal language. If, as Freud holds, sexual repression causes the hysterical reversion into body language, talking would be a "cure," because it would be like learning verbal language all over again. Learning to narrativize and verbalize affects, in a referential language addressed to an other, the therapist, represses the body in language all over again until, "finally," her speech disturbances are "talked away" (35). The "talking" cures a linguistic problem; it sanitizes words, cleansing them of affect, so that they can perform their referential offices.

The recovered traumatic origin of her illness is a frightening "waking dream" of snakes at her father's bedside; she tries to keep them off, but "it was as though she was paralysed" (38). When the hallucination disappears, "in her terror she tried to pray. But language failed her: she could find no tongue in which to speak, till at last she thought of some children's verses in English and then found herself able to think and pray in that language" (39). Immediately after the reproduction of her terrifying hallucination she is "able to speak German" (40). The symptom had arisen—as had "each of her hysterical symptoms"—in an "affect" (39). The "affect of anxiety" led to inhibition of speech, "which found a chance discharge in the English verses," accompanied by the "loss of her mother-tongue" (42).

The origin of her speech disturbance, however, is not quite the hallucination, which "explains" her paralyses, but the attempt to *pray*, which has to do with a linguistic crisis—a faith in language. When she comes up with an English nursery rhyme instead, she has regressed to a different, rhythmic, ritualistic language, outside the mother tongue with its affective contaminations and its effectively failing her. The inability to pray and the refusal of the mother tongue concur in the substitution of English children's verses for her dilemma. Whether T. S. Eliot read Breuer's text or not,[17] "The Hollow Men" tells the same story, moving from "lips that would kiss" to lips that "form prayers to broken stones," to paralysis, to the inability to pray, and finally to children's rhymes. The psychic drama is played on a moral and religious stage, to be sure, but sexuality is a strong factor in the poem, and its displacements are part of the problem presented. The difference is that the poet stays in the mother tongue as he confronts the hollowness of the "I" in a publicly sanctioned discourse.

The hysteric and the poet bear witness, in their different languages, to the intimacy of the relationship between linguistic, psychosexual, and social representational processes. The hysterical scripting of verbal language onto the body reverses the socializing/individuating scripting of the body into language. Poetic language rescripts the body into verbal language once again, and the language that keeps the pleasures of sound in play courts—explicitly, in incantatory or hypnotic verse—a hysterical regression, jeopardizing the "I," the linguistic construct of a psychosocial subject. Both "languages" expose the abysmal representational grounds of the subject and the erotogenic body itself. The "ground" is *not* a ground: it is only a symbolic system sutured by pain and pleasure to a phonemic-literal system. An "I" is that suture, a syncope of pain and pleasure. The hysteric and the poet both register the losses attendant to the articulation of sexuality and subjectivity. While the hysteric says no, however, the poet says both no and yes, at once dissolving and reinstituting the representational in a rhythmic alternation between the void and the letter. The difference of the poet rests on rhythm and its function in constructing a "space" for the history of the subject in the mother tongue in order to ensure the divergence, as well as the convergence, of somatic materials and signifying elements.

POSSESSION

> I can recall clearly enough the moment when, at the age of
> fourteen or so, I happened to pick up a copy of Fitzgerald's
> *Omar* which was lying about, and the almost overwhelming
> introduction to a new world of feeling which this poem was
> the occasion of giving me. . . . [T]he world appeared anew,
> painted with bright, delicious and painful colours.
> —*T. S. Eliot*

"I may be generalizing my own history unwarrantably," T. S. Eliot writes, "or on the other hand I may be uttering what is already a commonplace amongst teachers and psychologists, when I put forward the conjecture that the majority of children, up to say twelve or fourteen, are capable of a certain enjoyment of poetry; that at or about puberty the majority of these find little further use for it, but that a small minority then find themselves possessed of a craving for poetry which is wholly different from any enjoyment experienced before" (1986, 24). He describes this new craving as an experience of "complete possession," even a "daemonic possession," and compares it to falling in love (25, 26). The relationship between the onset of adult sexuality and poetic possession is obviously beyond the scope of this project; I only wish to emphasize once more the concurrence of the histories of sexuality and language and the priority of language. For the child ensures that the linguistic—and, therefore, the cultural—code is passed on before he is capable of passing on the genetic code. The confluence of the onset of poetic "possession" with sexual maturation singles out the poet: he "remembers" his history in language and is "elected" to culturally transmit the history of one who will not give up his emotional life in language.

I have approached hysteria in Freudian terms. Since the individuated subject in language is a social construction, hysteria also has social manifestations. Altered states of consciousness and even dissociation are involved, for example, in communal religious experiences.[18] Glossolalia (ecstatic utterances during religious ceremonies) and "verbigeration" ("xenoglossia," "speaking in tongues") are hysteriform conditions that are met with in early Egyptian, ancient Greek, and early Christian religious practices and are periodically revived by certain Christian sects. Glossolalia is a way station, as are hypnoid states in general, "between the loss of valid word language and motor automatisms" (Abse 1966, 151–52, 154). The process of hearing sounds as meaningful words is reversed, and one hears words as sounds linking to other words only through sounds: glossolalia is a "degradation of word language," ending, usually, with complete reversion to body language and "a release of motor automatisms in an ecstatic crisis."[19] This is a Dionysian dismemberment—an annulment of individuation and coherent language.

Jean-Michel Oughourlian's anti-Freudian reading of hysteria links it more specifically to the phenomenon of possession. Certain cultures practice possession rites that display hysterical behavior but serve socially to integrate the possessed, as rituals serve to maintain cultural order. The trances experienced in possession have the character of hysterical attacks marked by the loss of motor control, convulsions, and, finally, loss of consciousness (1991, 109). In this "imaginary coalescence" with the other, language disappears, replaced by cries of pain and pleasure, "tears, howls or growling, and sometimes barking" (111). The cry especially is a shared feature of possession and hysteria and is described by anthropologists as "resembling the howl of an animal more than a human cry" and as "bordering on music" (181). Possession and hysteria, then, are two expressions of the radically social—or "interdividual," in the terminology of René Girard and Oughourlian—nature of the subject (Oughourlian 1991, 101). The hysteric, Oughourlian writes, is the negative of the possessed, who "gains himself" by "giving himself over": "by letting himself become other, he preserves himself; by yielding himself, he discovers himself" (182).

Possession rites are often also rites of initiation. The candidate descends into disorder and undifferentiation, gives himself over to violence, and is then reintegrated into the cultural order by way of "a new identification that establishes him as an individual" (Oughourlian 1991, 98). These rites involve an identity crisis, an initial dispossession that manifests itself as a loss of consciousness and a kind of death, followed by a ritual resurrection in a "new state of consciousness." In Girard's terms, this would be an " 'immersion in the undifferentiated' (loss of identity) and 'differentiation' (in this case identification), or to put it still another way, disorder followed by a new order" (Oughourlian 1991, 105). To put it yet another way, this is a Dionysian dissolution and an Apollonian individuation; an "individual" is now explicitly a socially conferred status.

Insofar as poetry is not a "talking cure" and does not narrate a cohering history but enacts the temporalizing in-coherence of the subject in language, it aligns with hysteria. While the hysteric and the poet share the same knowledge about the subject, they differ, because poetry entails a submission to the other, which renders its language a publicly receivable discourse of the radically social subject in language. The lyric "I" becomes an "I" by submission to the other. Before all else, this is a submission to the otherness of language and the alienation of the subject in language. "I" do not speak my words; "I" am spoken by the materials of the language that speaks through me. As Anne Sexton keeps reiterating, "I" am empty; someone else writes "my" words.

But the poetic subject also submits to a communal other and is audible precisely in proportion to the intimacy of his conversation with the collective of other speakers and, particularly, other poets. The poet finds his individuating voice through what he hears in another poet's voice. One recognizes oneself in others' sounds, to which one yields in order to be oneself. The poet, one who will not give up his personal life in language, is socialized in submission to poetic language, whereby he "gains" his voice. Seamus Heaney affirms the "connection between the core of a poet's speaking voice and the core of his poetic voice, between his original accent and his discovered style." One finds one's poetic voice, however, through someone else: "In practice, you hear it coming from somebody else, you hear something in another writer's sounds that flows in through your ear and enters the echo-chamber of your head. . . . This other writer, in fact, has spoken something essential to you, something you recognize instinctively as a true sounding of aspects of yourself and your experience. And your first steps as a writer will be to imitate, consciously or unconsciously, those sounds that flowed in, that in-fluence" (1980, 43, 44). The poet begins acquiring his poetic voice by repetition; he learns a second language in the mother tongue to socialize his emotional life in language.

Textual audibility rests on repetition and revision of a discursive and formal tradition. Pound presents this process explicitly as a "dissociation," a "borrowing" of personality, an assumption of a mask to be an "I." The "live tradition" lives through possession. "Histrion" (1908) presents this process:

> No man hath dared to write this thing as yet,
> And yet I know, how that the souls of all men great
> At times pass through us,
> And we are melted into them, and are not
> Save reflexions of their souls.
>
> . . . .
>
> So cease we from all being for the time,
> And these, the Masters of the Soul, live on. (1976, 71)

The "I" that is the "midmost us" is a "histrion"; it exists in surrender to the "Masters" over the self. The possessed poet, thus initiated into a cult, passes on what he has received.

"The Tree" presents the process of such transmission:

> I stood still and was a tree amid the wood,
> Knowing the truth of things unseen before;
> Of Daphne and the laurel bow
> And that god-feasting couple old
> That grew elm-oak amid the wold.
> 'Twas not until the gods had been
> Kindly entreated, and been brought within
> Unto the hearth of their heart's home
> That they might do this wonder thing;
> Nathless I have been a tree amid the wood
> And many a new thing understood
> That was rank folly to my head before. (1990, 3)

A psychological experience of undifferentiation is validated by, and validates, other poets who have written of such experiences in a reciprocal motivating. This is, properly, an initiation rite, whereby the initiate acquires "a state of *belonging* (that is to the cult)" and "a *status* (that of a possessed person)" by abrogating individual identity.[20] The Dionysian experience of becoming a tree is followed by an Apollonian return to myths of metamorphoses and a public tradition of their telling and retelling. The poet submits to or "under-stands" the truth of the "laurel bow," the process of identification and metamorphosis, and thereby joins the "laureled" company, the cult of Apollo.

NOTES

1. For Freud, "The ego is first and foremost a bodily ego"; it is "the projection of a surface." A 1927 footnote adds: "I.e. the ego is ultimately derived from bodily sensations, chiefly from those springing from the surface of the body. It may thus be regarded as a mental projection of the surface of the body" (1989, 636–37). The representation of the body evolves as part of the maturation process of the infant, whereby the body is separated from the outer world and objects and is figured as a coherent whole. Wilfred Abse cites a number of studies of the process the infant undergoes to build a sense of his separate self out of "kinaesthetic, motor, and visceral data" and the coordination of "optic, tactile, and other sensations with motoric body experience" (1966, 141). But there is a "nucleus of the body image from the beginning," and this focuses on organs that "obey the needs of the body": "This beginning nucleus represents especially the oral zone of the body" (142). See pp. 146–47 for further discussion of the oral nucleus.

2. Freud writes that "all the connecting pathways that lead from other functions to sexuality must also be traversable in the reverse direction" (1975, 71).

3. Such regression may also instigate a flight into foreign languages, as in the case of Louis Wolfson, whom Deleuze cites.

4. Indeed, the hysteric's body exhibits the same duality as the linguistic sign that configures it: it both has a physical, material reality and functions as a signifier. Even in cases where hysterical pain has a physiological basis, it also serves as a signifier. In general, the hysteric's body is a sign or a system of signs, and this overlap is possible because the physical materials of the linguistic signs can themselves produce strong somatic innervations, which may then function as signifiers. See David-Menard 1989, 19–20.

5. David-Menard, working with Freud's case study of Elisabeth von R. and her leg pains, writes that the hysteric's attention to her body is selective: not her entire body but certain "movements, states, or positions" are affected (1989, 40). What sets limits and "configures" the hysterical body is language—more specifically, wordplays. "Standing alone," unable to "take a single step forward," "spellbound" to the spot, "not having anything to lean on"—these terms will configure the patient's pains, limiting them to her legs. "All these expressions that assign the symptom its form bear witness to the fact that the orientation of Elisabeth's attention toward her bodily positions, the very terrain of conversion, consists in a discourse that determines the scenario of which her body is at once the theater and the instrument" (42).

6. Freud reads symptoms as "transcriptions" of the sexual life of the neurotic. But the "choice" of a particular symptom involves literal and verbal paths of substitution (1975, 29–30). "The hysterical symptom reveals the structure of a language," Lacan writes, and "the dream has the structure of a sentence," which, "in the adult, reproduces the simultaneously phonetic and symbolic use of signifying elements" (1977, 50, 57). In translating the dream text, one deciphers its "rhetoric": "Ellipsis and pleonasm, hyperbaton or syllepsis, regression, repetition, opposition—these are the syntactical

displacements; metaphor, catachresis, autonomasis, allegory, metonymy, and synecdoche—these are the semantic condensations in which Freud teaches us to read the intentions . . . out of which the subject modulates his oneiric discourse" (58). From a perspective outside the psychoanalytical, however, it seems that it is the "reading" procedure that intentionalizes the syntactic and semantic substitutions in order to project a subject.

7. Qtd. in Abse 1966, 173.

8. The unconscious, Lacan writes, is in "the stock of words and acceptations of *my own* particular vocabulary" (1977, 50; emphasis mine).

9. Other kinds of regression from abstract language include the experience of verbal signs as physical sensations and the "*pseudo-naming*" of objects, using words not for their abstract meaning but as "properties of objects," on the order of color or size (Abse 1966, 108–9).

10. "All these sensations and innervations," Freud writes, "belong to the field of 'The Expression of the Emotions,' which, as Darwin [1872] has taught us, consists of actions which originally had a meaning and served a purpose. These may now for the most part have become so much weakened that the expression of them in words seems to us only to be a figurative picture of them, whereas in all probability the description was once meant literally" (Breuer and Freud 1955, 181). Yet the possibility of a physical recall of a past on a Darwinian scale would attest to a repetition or duplication of the "common source" of "hysteria and linguistic usgage" in "early sensorimotor experience" (Abse 1966, 246).

11. "Histrionic Personality Disorder," the diagnostic term that has replaced "Hysteria," accurately names the truth of the subject—its constitutive "pathology."

12. Lenneberg, qtd. in Agamben 1993, 57.

13. Freud writes: "The ultimate traumatic experiences" share "the two characteristics of being sexual and of occurring at puberty" (1989, 101). But, again, there is a third factor—of the end of a certain phase of the subject in language, of a certain kind of personal relationship to words.

14. In "Hysteria" T. S. Eliot presents the horror of the oral cavity, where sexual, alimentary, and linguistic functions merge (1970, 24). The sensible language of the waiter would cover up—just as his pink and white tablecloth would cover the "rusty" table—the abysmal somatic depths of sounds; but it is barely heard. That the piece is in prose is telling; breaking it into lines and a pattern of sound relations would sanitize the body of language.

15. This is the case with poetry as such, not just with formalist poetry. Certainly, even the most radically experimental poetry signifies against, and reinscribes the authority of, convention in order to authorize its revisions of convention and render them significant.

16. "Epileptiform convulsions" and "cataleptic rigidity" (Breuer and Freud 1955, 14, 15) are common rhythmic disturbances in hysteria, which lends support to the argument that rhythm is formative of the subject; arrhythmia is symptomatic of a crisis of the subject function.

17. *Studies in Hysteria* was originally published in 1895.

18. Dissociation, a characteristic of hysteria, is the separation from the personality of one or more systems of ideas, which then develop outside the control of the personality (Abse 1966, 137). Extreme cases of dissociation make for double or multiple person-

alities; more common are somnambulisms. Somatic conversions illustrate the dissociation of the "mental representation of a specific physical area" from consciousness and conscious control (140).

19. The phenomenon of reversion to body language, Abse writes, takes us to the "heart" of "hysterical symptom formation, and, indeed, to the origins of the science of psychoanalysis" (1966, 153). In conversion reactions, body language—a "language more primitive than speech"—"substitutes for word language," and its meaning is "dissociated from the awareness of the communicant." Gestural language has preceded speech in both phylogenetic and ontogenetic development (154).

20. This is Oughourlian's description of possession (1991, 106).

PART TWO

Lyric Practice

Chapter 5

※

FOUR QUARTETS: RHETORIC REDEEMED

"The Natural Sin of Language"

It is impossible to say just what I mean!
—*T. S. Eliot*

la la
—*T. S. Eliot*

T. S. Eliot's early work poses the generic double question of the lyric: what can ensure that the subject does not reduce to a set of "lyric" gestures, postures, and rhetorics, and what is to guarantee that the sounds of words do not reduce to meaningless acoustic events or, at another level, to formal mannerisms? The overdone rhymes of multisyllabic Latinate words in "Prufrock," for instance, are formal mannerisms that mock their author even as they serve him to ridicule the social conventions, mannerisms, and "measures" of his speaker's milieu. Eliot speaks of a "great simplicity" that would ensure the subject in language; but it is "only won," he writes, "by an intense moment or by years of intelligent effort, or by both. It represents one of the most arduous conquests of the human spirit: the triumph of feeling and thought over the natural sin of language."[1]

For Eliot, Ronald Bush suggests, the "natural sin of language" meant rhetoric: words cannot express feelings without reducing them to rhetorical gestures in ready-made formulas.[2] Eliot certainly engages rhetoric in this sense; his dramatic personae, histrionic performers watching themselves act, present just this problem. But "sin" is a big word, and Eliot is speaking of a struggle of the "human spirit." Further, "natural sin" suggests something other than rhetoric or even a postlapsarian language of exile: it suggests a sin that is innate, of the very body of words. The association of sin with the flesh thematically pervades Eliot's work in general, and if we keep in mind this sense of sin, we can better engage the question of lyric poetry in early Eliot.

The "failure" of language in the dramatic poems is sometimes a matter of the slipperiness of meaning. In "Portrait of a Lady," for example, "friend" can mean an acquaintance, a soul mate, or a lover; it is an empty social counter. This knowledge about the social currency keeps Prufrock from "saying" what he "knows": "Would it have been worth it, after all," to "say" "I am Lazarus

. . . / Come back to tell you all, I shall tell you all," if "one" "should say" in response, " 'that is not what I meant at all. / That is not it, at all' " (1970, 6). "All" can mean "everything" or "nothing"; it is just a manner of speaking that fails to mean or de-means, and this literal draining of the word's meaning reduces all to rhetoric. But, *at the same time*, "all" works formally to compose the text as *a poem*, providing rhymes and other types of sound repeats: "all" is repeated thirteen times and provides end-rhymes for "I know the voices dying with a dying fall"; "When I am pinned and wriggling on the wall"; "Arms that lie along a table, or wrap about a shawl"; "To have squeezed the universe into a ball"—all thematically significant lines. It also structures syntactic "refrains" such as "I have known them all already, known them all," and "that is not what I meant at all." The hollowness of the word does poetic work, which effects a further formal "emptying" of sense and reconfirms the empty rhetoric. On both counts, it is no more possible to say "what I mean" in a poem than it is in a drawing room.

The specific problem of the irreducible materiality of language also shows up in certain kinds of significant word play. In the "Preludes," for example, the subject is presented as constituted by external phenomena: "You dozed, and watched the night revealing / The thousand sordid images / Of which your soul was constituted" (1970, 14). The inside, the "soul," has no innerness. And a series of wordplays plays out this theme literally, moving from "your soul," to yellow "soles" of feet, to "soiled" hands, to "His soul" of the fourth Prelude. The homophony of "soul" and "sole" itself negates an inner core: language has no soul.

In "The Hollow Men," the speaker is a socially and historically unlocatable voice. While the rhetoric of lyric innerness and formal devices, such as various kinds of insistent repetitions and rhymes, shape the poem, the theme of the poem is the hollowness of forms and the "meaningless" "voices" of the hollow men. The forms emptied of meaning include not only the effigies of men but poetic forms and the very words. The poem presents only the markers of "lyric" poetry and covers a variety of lyric modes—song, supplication, pronouncement, prayer, and so forth. Not only do the incantatory rhythms resist a clear articulation of argument but the words themselves are used in an incantatory fashion. Each repetition further drains them of precise referential meaning, and they become participants in a ritual of sounds; the "natural sin" of language holds full sway.

In early Eliot moral, psychological, and spiritual issues and crises are difficult to tell apart from poetic problems. The indeterminacy of language and reference in "The Hollow Men" is an expression of the despair of a poet without authority outside the "deception" of the word, which is emphasized by the semantic instability and the lyric devices of the poem. The lyric cannot survive its own gestures: the formal devices and repetitions exploiting the sounds of the words cannot also articulate a subject with a will to mean, an intending

"I." The divide between the material fact and meaning, between the motion and the act, is the divide between sounds and sense.

"The Shadow" falls just here, as it intervenes in all translations that involve human agency, motivation, and will—ranging from the aesthetic and the moral to the sexual and the theological. And the failure of will is represented by a syntactic formula—"between x and y falls z"—the stability and reiteration of which compromise and may even preclude the possibility of meaningful intervention, of choice or intention. Falling between the "conception" and the "creation," the "idea" and the "reality," the "desire" and "the spasm," the "Shadow" will not let us get from "motion" to "act," "emotion" to "response," and so on. And *yet it does*, of course, and *that* is the problem. The word itself, capitalized and repeated, links by not linking. It links *formally*, ritualistically going through the motions, just as the grammatical form of these stanzas goes through repetitive motions that fall short of "action." This is not the hollowness of the social currency but of poetic language itself. The difference between "hallowed" or "hollowed," for example, is all the difference in the world, and it turns on one letter, an accident. Hence the logic that the Shadow and not the Lord be the ruler of the Kingdom. Plus, "Shadow" rhymes with "hollow."

The Shadow cast by the disappearance of God opens up a gap that will not close except through the moral intervention of an intending subject. But on what ground can an "I" stand? As Prufrock asks, how can "I presume"? In simplest terms, the issue is whether poetry is possible without metaphysics. If an authoritative subject and an authorized language must go when God goes, can we speak of who we are and recognize our human selves in the words we speak? There is no I without a you; there is no I or you without speech, the possibility of meaning; and there is no assurance of a meaningful language without the Word within the word.

Questions of will and desire also inform *The Waste Land*, which has a number of passages where language disarticulates into sounds. The most significant instance of "noise" is the severance of sound and sense in the "DA DA DA" of the concluding section. In Eliot's source in the *Upanishads*, various auditors articulate different words to draw different lessons out of Prajapati's initial syllable "DA." What the auditors seem to agree on is the imperative to interpret the sound—even perhaps to interpret it *as* an imperative. There is a will to meaning: the auditors motivate the sound because they desire knowledge, and their readings are all correct because each group hears what only it can hear. The auditors read by intentionalizing the sound as a syllable and thus recognize and own up to themselves in choosing their words, their meanings out of sounds.

In Eliot's text, the thunder resounds Prajapati's syllable. "What the Thunder Said" is a very noisy section: "After the frosty silence in the gardens," there is "shouting," "crying," "reverberation / Of thunder," the "cicada / And dry grass singing," "sound[s]" of "murmur of maternal lamentation," "cracks" and "bursts," "fiddled whisper music," bats' "whistle," "tolling . . . bells," more "voices singing" and "grass . . . singing," and a final "Co co rico co co rico." "Then spoke the thunder." The "speech" we finally get is only a sound among other sounds, a "DA" that we are to *hear as* speech, which means we must attribute to it an intention to mean.

The speaker proceeds to draw moral lessons for conduct from the three words DA generates, reinterpreting the words from the *Upanishads*. This procedure, however, is problematic, for when the god is not on the scene, interpreting thunder sounds becomes a suspect activity. The obvious figure of personification emphasizes the rhetorical moment and the issue of choice—of how to assign meanings to natural sounds, how to read, or whether to read at all. And the reader of the text has choices, just as the auditor of the thunder does. *We* don't hear the thunder; we "hear" a repeated "DA," and we can, for example, choose to hear "Dada"—a nihilistic denial of all super-structures of meaning, all "dadas." Since Eliot's note refers the reader to a German translation of the text, although an English translation was available, he may want us to hear the German "da." "Now" the DA would be a shifter, indicating only that discourse is taking place, and this reading might work best, given the instability of DA. If DA only indicates a discursive situation, the question is not how to read the god or nature but how to read letters, the nature of represented sounds, and how to assign sense to sounds. It has become a question of language.

The arbitrariness of the signifier—or more precisely, the language-specific nature of "meaningful sounds"—is patent. What the thunder says in a "foreign" language may be wisdom or pure sound without meaning. The referent of the "DA" is an acoustic event—the thunder—that must be heard as intending to mean. It is an onomatopoeic formation, but even a mimetic or onomatopoeic use is language-specific. How the thunder would sound in English and what lessons its different sounds would yield in English are not idle questions, because just preceding the thunder we heard a cock crow in French. An onomatopoeic word refers to an acoustic event, a nonhuman sound. It is a verbal reproduction of a sound without intention and it intentionalizes not the original sound but our "transcription" of it, and thus our particular system of "transcriptions" of sounds into words. In the original fable, though, the auditors' "Teach us, sir!" has already intentionalized the "DA" before the fact.

The distance between natural sounds, God's word or syllable, which we cannot hear except as it resounds in nature, and meaningful human language is absolute. At least in English. And this too undermines the thunder's message. The three imperative words that can be derived from DA, the syllabic "transcription" of a sound, link to the thunder only in Sanskrit. Any necessary connection among and between *these particular* imperatives—"give," "sympathize," "control"—and the original, root syllable is lost in translation. The English words are not intentionalizable by an appeal to roots via etymology or by like sounds. It seems that Eliot's invoking a text where God-nature speaks but in Sanskrit, in effect dismantles an authorized language. A Logos outside the game of fragments and exchanges of fragments is indistinguishable from non-sense: the "DA" that is to anchor language and moral values embodies the very "sin" of language, its resistant materiality, its "la la" (1970, 64). And this materiality is the very substance of lyric language, where sounds must both make sense and remain distinct from sense, so that we can apprehend *the event* of sense in a groundless desire and intention to mean.

The Lyric Subject: It Is Possible to Mean Just What "I" Say

> . . . yet the words sufficed
> To compel the recognition they preceded.
> —*T. S. Eliot*

Four Quartets both yields to the seductions of words and affirms an intending subject. Incantatory rhythms and syntax; compulsive repetitions of sounds, words, and syntactic phrases; and a limited vocabulary that brings into play the multiple meanings of a given word all emphasize the material medium at the expense of stable reference. The marked stress on the sounds of the conceptual terms and the sonic links and repetitions steering the articulation of abstract, theoretical statements make for a material force that steadily interferes with the propositional content and renders the abstract meanings highly precarious. It is impossible to ignore the materiality of language in reading *Four Quartets*, for it is directly pitted against philosophical abstractions. To read the poem for its content, we would have to, in Nietzsche's words, put our "ears away in the drawer."[3] The insistence on the materiality of the language of the poem in effect positions its ideological content as a pretext for the poem. *Four Quartets* rests on the poetic ground of the natural sin of language that is "my" beginning and "my" end. It is a confidently lyric-meditative poem; Eliot has outgrown an expressionist model of poetic language. *And*, I will argue, it is also a post-metaphysical poem, despite the Christian subject matter and Eliot's pronounced faith, for here Eliot has set his poetic "lands in order." The possibility of a subject, of freedom, moral agency, and responsibility, rests on the secular words, on the deceptive, seductive, sinful words as they articulate the coeval emergence of the subject and meaning. The "I" who motivates or wills the code to mean puts himself on the line, at risk, but the risk is not aesthetic, for the issue is not whether or not one is a "poet" or a "good poet" of "talent." Rather, the issue is ethical: the choice to be human, without metaphysical back-up.

Eliot insists that a man's beliefs and his poetry should be kept distinct: "Poetry is not a substitute for philosophy or theology or religion . . . ; it has its own function. But as this function is not intellectual but emotional, it cannot be defined adequately in intellectual terms. We can say that it provides 'conso-lation': strange consolation, which is provided equally by writers so different as Dante and Shakespeare." Belief has "different meanings . . . in different minds according to the activity for which they are oriented. I doubt whether belief proper enters into the activity of a great poet, *qua* poet. That is, Dante, *qua* poet, did not believe or disbelieve the Thomist cosmology or theory of the soul: he merely made use of it, or a fusion took place between his initial emo-tional impulses and a theory, *for the purpose of making poetry.* The poet makes poetry, the metaphysician makes metaphysics, the bee makes honey, the spider secretes a filament; you can hardly say that any of these agents believes: he merely does."[4] While Eliot's figure naturalizes poetic production, *Four Quartets* clearly shows that this does not entail a naturalization of the operations of poetic language and hence of the product. The poet may be, in some compli-cated way, "programmed" to produce poetry (the way a child is programmed to produce language) but what he produces—and thus produces *himself as*—is no more natural than the "metaphysics" that the "metaphysician makes." The poet produces the unnatural, the "human."

And the poet's "making" is impelled by personal emotion: "Dante's railings, his personal spleen—sometimes thinly disguised under Old Testamental pro-phetic denunciations—his nostalgia, his bitter regrets for past happiness—or for what seems happiness when it is past—and his brave attempts to fabricate something permanent and holy out of his *personal animal feelings* . . . can all be matched out of Shakespeare. Shakespeare, too, was occupied with the strug-gle—which alone constitutes life for a poet—to transmute his personal and private agonies into something rich and strange, something universal and im-personal" (Eliot 1932, 117; emphases mine).

To approach *Four Quartets* as a poem, I want to look closely at the opening section of "Burnt Norton" and work through its language rather than the con-cepts presented or the beliefs of the man.[5] The poem certainly has ideological content; what is significant, however, is how its propositional content is posi-tioned in relation to the language that accommodates it. For the poem unfolds by generating the very terms its discourse depends on. And a language that generates discourse by explicit, emphasized reliance on certain linguistic, rhe-torical, and formal devices is not best approached in terms of the concepts presented or the beliefs of the poet. The action of the poem is the emergence, in the lyric language of sounds that introduces the time it measures, of some-thing as rich and strange as a human speaker making sense in the time he is measured by.

The poem begins:

Time present and time past
Are both perhaps present in time future,
And time future contained in time past. (BN, 1–3)[6]

The first sentence raises a question: what kind of speaker would have the authority for such sweeping abstractions and generalizations? Clearly, this is not yet an individuated speaker; indeed the lines do not require that we assign an individuated speaker to them. We take these lines as somehow "given," because the sentence presents a recognizable view of time. Far from sounding like a "bewildered seminar,"[7] the first sentence recites a coherent, Christian model of history—a closed, Messianic history, where all time is present in a future Telos or Judgment, which is already preordained by a past Incarnation; the whole statement might as well be in quotation marks. "Contained" signals both a determinism of sequence and the enclosure of the whole historical and temporal bubble in one eternal moment: history is illusion; time is not.[8]

Perhaps. For two things disturb the self-sufficient closure of the propositional content of the lines. First, the "perhaps," the pivotal word in the first sentence, interferes with the closure of the statement. And "perhaps" may be functioning not only as a speculative "may be" or "could be" but in a way closer to its root meaning, to introduce a sense of "by chance." The very semantic indeterminacy of "perhaps" introduces "chanciness" into the deterministic model of history. It renders the opening statement hypothetical and interjects a more specific voice and motivation. At the same time, the word "perhaps" is generated literally out of "present" and "past," as a variation on sounds already in play, and it is metrically the strongest word in the sentence.[9] It picks up the sentence rhythmically and calls attention to the verse form. The word that enters a phonemic pattern already in play, sounds the rhythmic base, and metrically solidifies the line also wobbles the statement, casts it as speculation, and introduces doubt and, therefore, a specific speaking subject.

Second, the fact of verse disturbs the proposition: lineation breaks up the sentence, and the measured temporal and literal unfolding of the verse interferes with the conceptual closure or "stasis" that the sentence proposes. The fact of verse puts the authority of the sentence structure and the validity of the statement in question. Indeed, the proposition requires a good deal of metrical strain, which oddly foregrounds time: the proposition goes against the grain of the verse. The language is highly stylized and repetitious: in three lines, "time past," "time future," and "present" are all used twice, and "time" is used five times. We register the emphasis on the formality of the language before we proceed to read the "meaning" of the sentence. The lines read slowly, and the reader is conscious of the articulation of a sentence, the disclosure, in a temporal sequence of words and lines, of the proposition of transcendent unity, the *indifference*, of all time. Not only repetition but the high number of strong stresses slow down the lines making for a dissonance between semantic and syntactic stress and the verse form—the norm of measured time that the second line invokes with its briefest passage of metrical regularity. In all, the lines highlight their formal performance and the material presence of the words, even as they deal with huge abstractions.

The opening sentence, then, is less of a pronouncement by an omniscient speaker and more of a rhetorical beginning, a hypothesis about the unity of time, presented in a temporal form that itself challenges the hypothesis it presents. The poem is positioned as a discourse generated by a rhetorical statement that is already challenged by the verse form. Measured time is the ground on which hypotheses and speculations about time and timelessness may be entertained.

The following passage speculates on the initial proposal and elaborates its implications:

> If all time is eternally present
> All time is unredeemable.
> What might have been is an abstraction
> Remaining a perpetual possibility
> Only in a world of speculation. (BN, 4–8)

The language adheres to logical and grammatical procedures and maintains an air of high seriousness. But the passage is semantically unstable and difficult to read, because words like "unredeemable," "abstraction," and "speculation" have clear economic resonances that also place the poem's language in its specific historical moment.

I want to approach the opening passage first through its economics. A hypothesis, Marc Shell writes, is "logical correspondent to a hypothec." " 'Hypothec' derives from *hypotheke* ('deposit,' 'pledge,' or 'mortgage'; literally 'a putting down'). . . . Hence, a hypothec is directly related to the problem of symbolization and deposition." The word *hypotheke* is associated with "both economic and intellectual deposition": "Plato suggests that the dialectic is informed by the act of depositing money and drawing interest on the principal." Like the hypothec, the hypothesis is a deposition kept out of play: "Not itself subject to questioning, it is that principle from which knowledge can be drawn" (1978, 45). A hypothesis kept out of play as the ground of dialectics is a kind of gold bullion.

By contrast to Plato, Heraclitus of Ephesus "incorporated the money form into his thought" (Shell 1978, 62), and the "lack of a concept of metaphysical stillness" is "what Plato dislikes in Heraclitus's philosophy" (50). Shell discusses Heraclitus's understanding of money and symbolization, citing the same fragment that Eliot uses as one of the two epigraphs to *Four Quartets*: "The way up and the way down are one and the same." Heraclitus refers, Shell writes, "not only to the transformations of fire . . . but also to its monetary exchanges. . . . The way up and the way down refer to sale and purchase. Ephesus, a port on the Mediterranean, was a trading center between Sardis (the capital of Lydia, where gold was minted) and major trading nations (such as Phonecia). The way to which Heraclitus refers is (in part) a road like that between Sardis and its port, Ephesus. The road between Lydia and Ephesus was one, but the goods moved in both directions. Many commodities moved from Ephesus to Sardis. From Sardis to Ephesus, gold moved. There was no movement in one direction unless there was also movement in the other. One direction is the way of sale, the other is the way of purchase" (60–61). The only solid here is the path of exchange, the "road" that is the event of exchange.

Eliot appears to be working with a Heraclitean concept of language and symbolization here, and the economic backdrop of the poem would seem to shape his understanding of language and his vocabulary. The Great Depression, I would suggest, is more of a factor in this poem than Eliot's personal history of conversion. The economic crisis entails going off the gold standard and affects the economy of language and representation. The decade of the 1930s has not received attention in discussions of the postmodern "divide"; yet I would argue that the market crash and the crisis of economic representation, specifically representation on paper, dates the postmodern turn. The 1930s certainly date a decisive change in the work of Eliot; it marks the divide between the modern Eliot of *The Waste Land* and the Eliot of "Burnt Norton," which presents us with a medium that generates abstract values, a language without the concept of "gold bullion" backing up its exchanges.[10] The economic crisis also challenges the ideology of progress, for with the Crash, progress bottoms out and the future, even the secular version of the deferred paradise, on which the present had speculated, vanishes.[11] After this point, "the past is all deception, / The future futureless" (DS, 43–44). The past, the future, an authorized language, and Tradition all go:

Had they deceived us
Or deceived themselves, the quiet-voiced elders,
Bequeathing us merely a receipt for deceit? (EC, 75–81)

The "receipt for deceit" is the unredeemable paper, the "withered stumps of time" (1970, 56) that the past bequeaths the present, thus foreclosing *its* future redeemability.

If we keep the economic context and subtext in mind in reading the opening passage, "unredeemable" may mean not only unrecoverable, unatonable, or unalterable, but also a fixed value kept out of circulation, out of the economy of language, or an inconvertible sign, or even an empty, worthless sign. When we place the economic meanings of "unredeemable" in circulation, the "argument" seems to shape thus: if the above hypothesis is true and all time is eternally present and unredeemable, the power of memory and of poetry is in jeopardy. But if this *hypothesis* about time must itself be thus kept out of play (unredeemable), it also becomes worthless (unredeemable). Here the poetic anxiety and the metaphysical anxiety are pitted against each other: poetic language can have a function only if the metaphysical premise—the premise *of* a metaphysical premise, the hypothesis of a metaphysical ground—is let go. While for the early, modern Eliot, poetry without metaphysics was in danger of disintegrating into nonsense, here poetry and metaphysics are enabled at each other's expense.

The third sentence, then, both articulates this double anxiety and overcomes it by an indeterminacy of the meanings that proliferate around its discrete words, partly because we are unable to fix who is speaking; we have a rhetoric as yet without a rhetor, the one motivated to interject the "perhaps." "Only in a world of speculation" is the key line. If a specific individual were the speaker, "only" would mean "merely," and "speculation" would be a sad substitute for "what might have been," hinting at opportunities missed, regrets. But if a poet were speaking *as* poet, "only" would mean "solely," and the statement would be a defense of temporality, which opens up the space of memory and speculation—the space of imagining and imaging, or making visible as in the root sense of the word, what was not but might have been. Moreover, "what might have been" could also mean what has been, what actually has happened but cannot be retrieved or recalled except as speculation; in other words, memory might be imagination, the past might have to be imagined. In either case, the statement is one of metaphysical diminishment and lyric power.

The world of speculation is the world of thought, conjecture, reflection, meditation, imagination, and figuration or a making visible. Etymologically, the word is an echoic garden: Latin *speculari* (to view); *speculum* (mirror), from *specere* (to look). But the world of speculation is also the world of economics. The economic undercurrent runs from "unredeemable" to "speculation" via "abstraction" and "perpetual possibility," as in speculation on paper, which turned out to be unredeemable. The insolidity of a language or a currency not redeemable for hard bullion is its speculative freedom, its redemption from the referential economy (the currency of communication value), its ability to revise and alter the unredeemability (now in a noneconomic sense) of a deterministic, Christian time overseen by Logos, the Author of History. The world of speculation is indeed unredeemable, for it is a world of signifiers, a permanent exile from a root and center to one's discourse. The cost of freedom is exile, an old story "East Coker" will retell, playing the theme on autobiographical and historical registers.

Reading this poem, we actively motivate it, assigning meanings to the words by articulating various contexts for them. Reading *The Waste Land*, say, one might ask what an image, symbol, or figure means or how it functions in the poem, and Eliot very helpfully provides us with an instruction manual. Eliot's "Notes" propose a narrative scaffold, an authoritative structure external to the text.[12] Reading "Burnt Norton," however, one has the task of stabilizing reference by *choosing* in which sense a key word is being used. The reader has to decide how and what a word "now" means. Such a poem is not a figure on the ground of something else: postwar London or Europe, social history, "personal grouse," biography, Tradition, philosophy, or whatever. Such a poem is the ground of a language in which all of the above may be figures, insofar as this language is formulating the necessary conditions for discourse. For, beginning only with repeated sounds and words, one has to choose their *operative* meanings to construct a context and an "I" who speaks. One has to assign the values governing the exchange and ensure that the way up and the way down are one—that the sounds of the words match up with the meanings operative *in a given instance* of circulation.

The lines immediately following move into the world of speculation. The poet's language creates a disturbance in time to allow for a disturbance of time. The language here does what theology and philosophy cannot do: it allows for the interference of motivation, of a subject made by the choices that he did and did not make:

Footfalls echo in the memory
Down the passage which we did not take
Towards the door we never opened
Into the rose-garden. My words echo
Thus, in your mind.
                              But to what purpose
Disturbing the dust on a bowl of rose-leaves
I do not know.
                    Other echoes
Inhabit the garden. Shall we follow?
Quick, said the bird, find them, find them,
Round the corner. Through the first gate,
Into our first world, shall we follow
The deception of the thrush? (BN, 11–24)

As "footfalls echo in the memory" of what did *not* happen, "my words" echo in "your mind." A tightly woven text of sound patterns and echoes leads the "argument" from an impersonal, generic "the memory," to "we," to "my words," and "your mind." The echoing is both a trope and a literal device; it writes the page as an echoic space of returning sounds. The very devices that articulate this textual passage also allow a "passage" or an "opening" in/out to a speculative garden. The auditory and literal presence of the words on the page carry the reader "down the passage which we did not take" into a "garden."

"My words echo / Thus, in your mind" may mean that they echo in the way just stated (the way footfalls echo in memory), *or* in the way that follows (the way echoes inhabit the garden). *Or* "in your mind" is the only way "my words" *can* echo. "Thus" is the pivotal word here, linking before and after, as well as "my words" and "your mind." "Memory," "your mind," and the "garden" are analogous spaces inhabited by echoes of "footfalls," of rhythms, of words, of sounds. The garden opens in "your mind" where "my words" echo.

There has to be a "you" for "my words" to echo. *And* there have to be echoes for there to be an "I" and a "you." Not identity but the difference of echoing or speculation *centers* "my words" and "your mind." The reader is at liberty to take this "you" personally, which would place her in the garden "we" never entered. "My words" and "your mind" enter the poem in the same sentence, articulating the components of the "we," the only anchor of the poem. This sentence has greater certainty and authority than the preceding, for there *must* be certainty here: for a rhetorical model of poetry, there must be the possibility of contact through words, prior to specific meanings, or there is nothing. And that contact already places us in a world of speculation or reflection, the auditory equivalent of which is "echo."

Finally, an "I" enters the poem. After a hypothesis has initiated a poem, after the hypothesis has been poetically questioned, a world of speculation opened, a rose garden specified, and a connection between "my words" and "your mind" established, we hear an "I" who does not know *why* all this, "to what purpose" or end the world of speculation and the garden of memory have been proposed. This "I"—the author of "my words"—does not know why the exercise of words, why memory, why poetry. Thus the "I" motivated to set in motion the whole apparatus of the poem is positioned by that apparatus as also subject to a motivation other than personal.

The sentence spoken by the "I" is an aside, typographically set off by the spacing, which visually punctuates it as bracketed; the aside also departs from the trochaic thrust of the preceding lines. It contains the first (and only) rhetorical question and a note of uncertainty in a passage that has moved with grammatical and rhetorical certainty. It is not indispensable to the "argument" of the passage and may indeed "interfere" with it, since "other echoes" follows directly from "My words echo / Thus, in your mind." The lines spatially interrupt the temporal flow of the argument and the look of the page. The "I" as distinct from "my words" breaks the flow of "my words" and their "purpose."

The world of speculation that opens is a rose garden, and the garden scene is generally read as presenting a transcendent experience—what Donoghue calls the union of "existence and essence" (1993, 7). Even if we assume that the poem represents such an experience, we have to recognize that it "places" that experience not as a psychological or religious but as a speculative experience. The representation is heavily mediated: "my words," echoes, apostrophes to the reader, talking thrushes, memory, the abstraction of what might have been, and so on all render the experience clearly speculative. "Echoes" is used three times, and other words and phrases like "reflection," "invisible," "unheard music," "unseen eyebeam," and "hidden" (used twice) stress that there is no one in the "garden." These purely speculative presences are posited by our choosing to follow the repeated invitation: "Shall we follow?" "Shall we follow / The deception of the thrush?"—the deception of a poetic device, giving voice to the voiceless. The thrush calls "in response to / The unheard music"; and the poet calls the thrush in response to the echoes in memory. "Follow" echoes "know," incorporating the parenthetical lines into the question: shall we follow although we do not know to what end?

The outrageous speaking thrush renders the Romantic figure of poetic inspiration the most threadbare of conventions by speaking in words. Eliot's thrush is an allusive thrush. It is a North American bird that gets one of the odder footnotes in *The Waste Land*, providing the much-needed Latin name of the genus: "This is *Turdus aonalaschkae pallasii*, the hermit-thrush which I have heard in Quebec Province." Another thing Eliot may have heard is the "solitary" thrush—the "hermit bird" and his "song of the bleeding throat"—that calls Whitman into the "deep secluded recesses" of the woods (1973, 330).[13] Eliot's thrush is much more social: it speaks English and calls to the "heart of light" and laughter (BN, 37). Eliot does not appeal to the American sublime or Fate; his thrush does not lament, and the space of Eliot's poem is not deep nature; it is a discursive space, a lyric topos, a rose garden of echoes. And Eliot relies on such commonplaces throughout *Four Quartets*.

Eliot's thrush is so seductive, its words so lively and urgent—"find them, find them"—that Eliot seems to be investing power in the figure *as* figure. In other words, personification has power as such, without having to invoke natural power. The conventional rhetorical gesture poses no problem for Eliot here. We know there are no speaking thrushes, and there are no such rose gardens as they usher us into. But "I" say *these words* and they "echo / Thus, in your mind": "Shall we follow?" Not only the poet's but the reader's will is a factor in making the poem be a poem. We choose: Shall we follow the poet's daring? Shall we consent to enter a rose garden, speculate on first gates and first worlds, on origins at once personal, tribal, national, and literary? There are no first gardens unless opened up by figures of, say, speaking thrushes, and there is no one in these gardens. "They" that inhabit them are "echoes."[14] The aesthetic lure is so transparent, so consciously a ruse, that we are not in any Platonic danger. Our challenge is to choose whether or not to follow; this choice is the ground of the community between the poet and his reader, and it is an ethical choice. Shall we follow what we know to be deception, a call in a language we are told outright is deceptive, into "our first world"?

Clearly, "Burnt Norton" is beyond the modern problematic of "The Hollow Man" or *The Waste Land*, but *not* because of Eliot's faith. Rather, Eliot seems to affirm that "we" *are* hollow; we inhabit and are inhabited by echoes. We are made of words and make our echoic inner worlds—"my" world, "your" world. The presences in the garden are "our guests," visitations gathered by "I," "you," and the hosting discourse, the "words" that echo. "So we moved, and they, in a formal pattern": this was the end, the purpose of "Disturbing the dust on a bowl of rose-leaves."[15] The vision in the garden is literally a mirage: the "drained pool. / Dry the pool, dry concrete" is "filled with water out of sunlight." "Then a cloud passed, and the pool was empty." As the garden itself is an auditory hallucination, the transcendent vision is an optical illusion. Yet "we" have only to consent to the deception, and it will be "reality." The reader is invited to consent to deception, to speculate a space of "freedom" and "laughter," a space of "echoed ecstasy" (EC, 131), and dare to call it "reality."

The garden of echoes and reflections is a subjective space "we" enter;[16] it opens up with the explicit collaboration of the reader, and it is not a private space. The enclosed garden is a public figure of a subjective space and has a long and wide-ranging history as a lyric topos. This space offers

> The inner freedom from the practical desire,
> The release from action and suffering, release from the inner
> And outer compulsion, yet surrounded
> By a grace of sense . . . (BN, 70–73)

The slight pause of the line break after the "inner," the brief formal suspension of the syntax before the word is reabsorbed into the argument, again confirms that this is not a private space in any psychological or biographical sense. The biographical person of the poet and Emily Hale are among "our" guests. They are echoes in the poem's garden, "our first world," as Eliot insists (BN, 20–21). They are ghosts, "invisible, / Moving without pressure, over the dead leaves"—the literal page, the ground cover of the garden—"surrounded / By a grace of sense." Eliot reverses the expected "a sense of grace": the figures are graced with meaning.

The poem ends with an echoic return of its beginning:

> Time past and time future
> What might have been and what has been
> Point to one end, which is always present. (BN, 44–46)

The tone is one of deflation, and the "end" suggests less of purpose and more of finality. While the closing lines reconfirm the opening frame, the tone suggests something has changed by our experience of the words. Between the conceptual propositions and the logical grammar of the opening sequence of sentences and the closing lines, we have taken the chancy excursion into speculation, illusion, and reality. We have experienced the lyrical disturbance of an "I," a "you," and echoing words in time.

In the microcosm of the first section, the rhetoric of logical propositions encloses and hosts the rhetoric of figural language and *its* enclosed garden, which hosts sounds and echoes. The former is a written language; tropes of echoes and speech enter with the second garden. The verse form hosts both rhetorics: it makes for a disturbance in time—disturbing both the logic and the vision, which correspond in their speculative evasions of measured time.[17] The epistemological claims of propositional rhetoric to greater truth value are challenged by the patently speculative experience and language, but neither the logical nor the figurative procedures can claim authority. They are equally groundless, equally rhetorical. And they are equally entertainable in a form of measured sequences of sounds of words that "keep time" and will a disturbance of time.

Eliot points out that the meaning of poetry is distinct from the argument a poem might present. That poetry must give pleasure is a given, but we can get pleasure from reading poets whose ideas may be historically or politically distant from our experience and values. For "real poetry survives . . . the complete extinction of interest in the issues with which the poet was passionately concerned" (1979, 6). It outlasts ideologies. Eliot also distinguishes poetry from meters, for "the music of poetry is not something which exists apart from the meaning" (21). Conversely, the meaning of poetry does not exist apart from the music (22); it is not a stable meaning that can be abstracted from the poem. Eliot's criterion for meaning is emotion: "If we are moved by a poem, it has meant something, perhaps something important, to us. If we are not moved, then it is, as poetry, meaningless." The meaning of poetry is neither its sense nor its sounds but its ability to move a reader; "meaning" is a movement, a moving, an emotion.[18]

The "music of a word," Eliot proposes, is "a point of intersection" of two sets of relationships: first, the relationship of the word to those "immediately preceding and following it, and indefinitely to the rest of its context" and, second, the relationship of the word's "immediate meaning in that context to all the other meanings which it has had in other contexts"—to its "wealth of association"—both intratextual and intertextual (1979, 25). The intersection of sound relations (syntagmatic relations of sequence) and of meaning (paradigmatic relations to other meanings and contexts) is the "music": "a 'musical poem' is a poem which has a musical pattern of sound and a musical pattern of the secondary meanings of the words which compose it, and that these two *patterns* are indissoluble and one" (26; emphasis mine). There is no music without sense: "The sound of a poem is as much an abstraction from the poem as is the sense" (26). Sound patterns and the referential, "paraphrasable" sense of the poem are equally abstractions. What is concrete is their "intersection" as a "music." Music moves sequentially (even as such motion accrues paradigmatic associations, links, and echoes and becomes a pattern of sounds), and music is moving (affective). The meaning of the poem is its moving us and motivating us to "follow," to move with the sounds of its words.

The meaning of Eliot's poem does not depend on the central Christian paradox of the Word, "The point of intersection of the timeless / With time" (DS, 201–2). Rather, the "intersection" that is the Word is a projection, on a theological register, of the precondition of meaningful language that poetry-as-poetry spells out. Eliot's explicit ideological commitment enables him to keep the category of poetry as poetry distinct. In "Second Thoughts on Humanism," he criticizes the general tendency of humanist critics to make litera-

ture do the job of philosophy and theology: their "approach to every other field
of study is through literature. . . . The trouble is that, for a modern humanist,
literature thus becomes itself merely a means of approach to something else."
The "game" of literature and "the games of philosophy and theology," are
played by different "rules," Eliot insists, and the "trick of making literature do
the work of philosophy, ethics and theology tends to vitiate one's judgment
and sensibility in literature" (1932, 397–98).

The poet's direct "duty," Eliot writes, "is to his *language*, first to preserve,
and second to extend and improve" (1979, 9); and what that improves is our
"sensibility," safeguarding "our own ability, not merely to express, but even to
feel any but the crudest emotions" (10). "Burnt Norton" (1935) poses most
radically the question that Stevens is also articulating at about the same time:
what is "the function of poetry as poetry" (Eliot 1979, 4). This is a post-
Romantic question, inaugurating a poetics we might call postmodern. Eliot's
faith and Stevens's resistance to faith worked, in the end, to the same end: to
dissociate poetry from the burden of metaphysics and the pressures of social
obligation, to distrust all utopian schemes, all plotted earthly paradises, and to
take the risk that it may have no tangible purpose or use. We choose—by
whether we are moved or not; or whether we are movable or not chooses for
us. The moment is ethical—to choose to move to the *call* of words, at the risk
of "everything":

Quick now, here, now, always—
A condition of complete simplicity
(Costing not less than everything). (LG, 252–54)

NOTES

1. Qtd. in Bush 1983, 6.
2. Bush takes rhetoric in a rather narrow sense and attributes this sense to Eliot as
well: the "dramatization of the soul's eternal imprisonment in the rhetorical conventions
of its own gestures" became Eliot's subject matter (1983, 21).
3. *Beyond Good and Evil*, no. 247.
4. Eliot 1932, 118; emphasis mine. Marx's comments on Milton make the same
point: "Milton produced *Paradise Lost* for the same reason that a silk worm produces
silk. It was an activity of *his* nature" (in Solomon 1979, 75). The crucial issue is the
"value" of poetry: whether or not poetry is a pretext for producing capital—economic
or ideological.
5. Writing about "Burnt Norton," Denis Donoghue points out that we have not yet
developed the critical procedures to respond properly to this kind of poem, for we still
work with a limited set of terms, such as image, symbol, and structure: "No critical
method has arisen which proposes to show the poetic character and potentiality of
discourse" (1993, 18). After the publication of *Notes Toward a Supreme Fiction*, at least,
"it might have been expected," Donoghue continues, that "a critical method sensitive

to poetry as a work in the creation of new concepts might have been developed. It has not happened." And "[r]eaders are still encouraged to believe that a poem is an action (or a structure) of words chiefly concerned with the development of the resources of imagery and symbolism within the fiction of a dramatic monologue" (19). I agree that we do not have a poetics of discourse and do not quite know what to do with poems like *Four Quartets* or *Notes*. For to read *Four Quartets* as a religious poem—or to read *Notes* as a philosophical poem—is to misread them. What such readings leave out are the poems themselves, which keep evading just such grounds and insist on their self-articulative procedures.

6. References to *Four Quartets* will be cited in the text as BN, EC, DS, and LG, followed by line number.

7. Donoghue 1993, 4.

8. This Christian model is also the model of "modern" history—a continuous, progressive, teleological history oriented to the future. The model also has an "organic" sequence: the past is a seed containing all that grows out of it. Eliot here encapsulates the continuity of several models of Western history and how they figure the relationship between past, present, and future.

9. Bush notes this in his metrical analysis of the opening passage (1983, 196).

10. Pound's poetry is also affected by the same crisis. His interest in economics certainly predates the market crash and the Depression, events that confirmed his economic theories. At the same time, however, they presented him with a poetic crisis as his organicist poetics, resting on metaphysical bullion, threatened to collapse. At this point, the ideological hardening sets in; the usury canto (canto 45) dates from 1936, the year after Eliot's poem.

11. Economic terminology dominates the discussion of poetry, knowledge, deceit, and value, as militaristic terminology later comes to dominate the discussions of language—from "wrestle" to "conquest" to "venture," "raid," "equipment," "squads of emotion," "competition," "fight" (EC, 178–86).

12. Of course, the problem is more complicated, because the "Notes" are part of the text before us, but the argument still holds: we are directed to a narrative authority that would stabilize the text, authorizing its "decompositional" procedures.

13. Robert Frost's "Come In" (1942) is also in dialog with Whitman—and probably Eliot as well. Frost imagines how he would respond were he to be called by thrush music, as Whitman was, "to come in / To the dark and lament" (1979, 127). Whereas Whitman's space is the "dark recesses," the deep night woods, and Frost's is liminal, pastoral nature, "at the edge of the woods" at "dusk," Eliot's discursive space is a sunlit, formal rose garden.

14. Bush offers an extended discussion of the "they" in the garden, and lists possible biographical referents for the pronoun (1983, 190–92). Nowhere does he note that the plural subject preceding the first use of "they" is "echoes":

> Other echoes
> Inhabit the garden. Shall we follow?
> Quick, said the bird, find them, find them (BN, 19–21)

And the earlier "footfalls" that "echo" in memory (l. 11) are echoes of rhythms, not people, as the trochaic emphasis calls attention to the "footfalls" of the passage.

15. The figure of the dusty bowl of rose-leaves is hopelessly passé: it belongs in the furnishings of "Portrait of a Lady." Again, Eliot relies on commonplaces to mark a nostalgia for a future that no longer exists. In "The Dry Salvages," Eliot spells out the cliché: "the future is a faded song, a Royal Rose or a lavender spray / Of wistful regret for those who are not yet here to regret, / Pressed between yellow leaves of a book that has never been opened" (DS, 126–28). The rose-leaves are a faded song, a future already past, a future necessarily of regret. But Eliot's roses do not recuperate a past either:

> It is not to ring the bell backward
> Nor is it an incantation
> To summon the spectre of a Rose. (LC, 182–84)

When the dust on the bowl of rose-leaves is disturbed, we have a disturbance in teleological and sequential time and "move" "over the dead leaves," "through the vibrant air." Thus

> Sudden in a shaft of sunlight
> Even while the dust moves
> There rises the hidden laughter
> Of children in the foliage
> Quick now, here, now, always—
> Ridiculous the waste sad time
> Stretching before and after. (BN, 69–75)

This dust moves "through the vibrant air" reflecting light and making audible

> The laughter in the garden, echoed ecstasy
> Not lost, but requiring, pointing to the agony
> Of death and birth. (EC, 131–33)

16. "I" is used very sparingly throughout *Four Quartets*, and most often it refers to the scribal self, confessing his limited knowledge, or lack of knowledge, or criticizing his wording (EC, 172 ff., for example). Twice, it represents a dramatic character (EC, 112 and the Dantean "I" of LG, 85 ff.).

17. This disturbance "rhymes" with the "disturbance" of the seasonal order of natural time in Indian summer: "What is late November doing / With the disturbance of the spring" (EC, 51–52). There's a similar figure of mid-winter spring in LG, 1–3.

18. There is an interesting turn in Eliot's argument: since the meaning of poetry is not paraphrasable, and a poem may mean different things to different readers, its content—what it communicates as its content—is not its social dimension. The music of poetry, though, is social because it is a "music latent in the common speech of its time" (1979, 24).

Chapter 6

⚜

WALLACE STEVENS AND "THE LESS LEGIBLE

MEANINGS OF SOUNDS"

The comedy of hollow sounds derives
From truth and not from satire on our lives.
—*Wallace Stevens*

. . . a new aspect, say the spirit's sex,
Its attitudes, its answers to attitudes
And the sex of its voices, as the voice of one
Meets nakedly another's naked voice.
—*Wallace Stevens*

The Sound of Words

Wallace Stevens is not equivocal about the "social, that is to say sociological or political obligation of the poet": "He has none" (1951, 27). He writes Hi Simons: "It is simply a question of whether poetry is a thing in itself, or whether it is not. I think it is."[1] If poetry is a "thing in itself," it has no social obligation, any more than a social or political practice or discourse has a poetic obligation.[2] And if poetry is itself a social practice, which it clearly is, it must have a function in itself. Stevens proposes that its function is "to help people to live their lives" (29). In "The Noble Rider and the Sound of Words" he places "our lives" in the broadest context of Western philosophy and history of ideas, changing representations of human nobility, the ongoing European war, the "war-like" social, economic, and political conditions "at home," the life of the individual psyche that such pervasive violence threatens, and the survival instinct of the human species. Against this backdrop, he famously defines "nobility" as "a violence from within that protects us from a violence without": "It seems, in the last analysis, to have something to do with our self-preservation; and that, no doubt, is why the expression of it, the sound of its words, helps us to live our lives" (36).

"Nobility" has to do with how we represent ourselves to ourselves. Thus, to imagine human nobility at any time is to articulate a specific historical reality. Stevens's extended discussion of Plato's chariot proves the point: we do not feel "free to yield ourselves" to its fiction (1951, 4). Our very different historical experience constrains us. Since the types of fiction or the "unreal" to which we feel "free to yield ourselves" in poetry are historically variable, what we experience in the work of the imagination is precisely our current reality. And to imagine an "unsponsored" *and* posthumanist self has become imperative at a time that witnessed the Enlightenment man join the beasts.

Yet it is not the imagined human hero who will help us to live our lives but the sounds of the imagining words. How can the sounds of words do this? In poetry the sounds of words give pleasure, of course, but clearly Stevens is speaking about something other than aesthetic pleasure here. And it would seem that he is speaking about something other than poetic form, the sum of the schemes for organizing the sounds of words, what he calls elsewhere a "banal" topos (1951, 168).[3] Thus the claims for poetry as the sound of words do not contradict the claim that the interest of a poet finally rests on what he has to say (168). The sound schemes and the sense of the poem organize the sounds of words for the ear or for the mind, according to different, sometimes overlapping, syntaxes. The sounds of words are not to be opposed to what the poem says; they are the ground of both form and meaning in poetry. "Above everything else, poetry is words; and . . . words, above everything else, are, in poetry, sounds" (32).

"The subject matter of poetry," for Stevens, "is not that 'collection of solid, static objects extended in space' but the life that is lived in the scene that it composes." And that life is one of flux:[4] "Every body, every quality of a body resolves itself into an enormous number of vibrations, movements, changes" (1951, 25). If material reality is unstable, so is nobility: "As in the case of an external thing, nobility resolves itself into an enormous number of vibrations, movements, changes. To fix it is to put an end to it"; "if it is defined, it will be fixed and it must not be fixed" (34). Hence, the radically metaphoric language of poetry, which insures that neither the object nor the subject is self-identical by a constant evasion of definitions and names that would "fix" what "must change."

"And what about the sound of words?" Stevens asks, and answers: "The deepening need for words to express our thoughts and feelings which, we are sure, are all the truth that we shall ever experience, having no illusions, makes us listen to words when we hear them, loving them and feeling them, makes us search the sound of them, for a finality, a perfection, an *unalterable vibration*" (1951, 32; emphasis mine). The sounds of words, which literally exist in perceptible vibrations, movements, and changes, instigate a desire and a *search* for an "unalterable vibration," a "finality" that cannot and must not be, since it would silence the words themselves.[5]

Thus words are not only articulated in time but they articulate time by initiating a search for a finality. They motivate time itself in awakening and perpetuating a desire that must not be fulfilled, so that *their* self-perpetuation is ensured:

If ever the search for a tranquil belief should end,
The future might stop emerging out of the past,
Out of what is full of us; yet the search
And the future emerging out of us seem to be one. (1954, 151)[6]

This passage links the search for a timeless "tranquil belief" with memory, a past that is "full of us," and desire, which makes the future emerge "out of us." The search for a finality or a supreme fiction instigated and driven by the sounds of words articulates "our" history, both personal and collective.

The sounds of words are acoustic phenomena that become distinguished from other acoustic phenomena. All kinds of sounds impact the ear, and Stevens's poetry is full of the cacophony of "non-sense" sounds and onomatopoeic effects. "Meaningless" sounds often represent "mindless" natural sounds, like the sounds of the waves that "never formed to mind or voice" (1954, 129). "Nonsense" sounds may be used in poetry to represent natural acoustic phenomena. But, like the "locust's wings, // That do not beat by pain, but calender, / Nor meditate the world as it goes round" (286), the sounds of the waves do not "help us to live our lives." And neither do the "nonsense" sounds that represent them in poems.

But Stevens also uses "meaningless" sounds to represent the purely musical element in poetry, an equally mindless word use—"mere sound . . . to stuff the ear" (1954, 144). For "meaningless" sounds in Stevens's poems are so jarring that they work as defenses against rather than calls for surrender to the seductions of sounds:

The physical world is meaningless tonight
And there is no other. There is Ha-eé-me, who sits
And plays his guitar. Ha-eé-me is a beast.

.   .   .   .

Ha-eé-me is the male beast . . . an imbecile,

Who knocks out a noise. The guitar is another beast
Beneath his tip-tap-tap. It is she that responds. (337; first ellipses mine)[7]

The "noise" of such music is part of the "physical world," meaningless in itself. And there is no other world.

The sounds of words, though, eke out something from the physical, something that is other than physical but less than metaphysical. They mark a zone where we seem to hear something in or through the sound of words, something as distinct from the acoustic phenomena a musical poetry might exploit as it is from the referential work words may perform. In that excess or otherness that the "acutest" poet can make audible, we hear not the "hoobla-hoobla-hoobla-how" (1954, 383) of the body, nor "reason's click-clack" (387), nor their poetic analogs, but a voice, speaking "thoughtfully the words of a line," saying, perhaps, "Stay here. Speak of familiar things for a while" (338).

This speech is "a speech only a little of the tongue" (1954, 397); it is heard in the "delicatest ear of the mind" and it resounds a history. It is heard in sounds that return, as in an echo, through time. And they return through history, echoing off of other poets' words, which also makes for a more than physical, a more "familiar" hearing. Words are distinguished not by the physiological auditory sensation but by a *version* of it in the voiced and heard sounds of words. In the sounds of words, we hear that difference of the voice troping auditory sensation as a signifying event. For "It is never the thing but the version of the thing":

> The day in its color not perpending time,
> Time in its weather, our most sovereign lord,
> The weather in words and words in sounds of sound. (332)

"Sounds of sound" are voiced and heard sounds of words, and the conscious and unconscious memories that cluster around the sounds of words shape our mental speaking and hearing and define who we are.[8] Each speaker/hearer's troping of sensation into sense is unique because it reverberates a history. An act that is also an echo, this turn is heard by the ear and again by the ear of the mind; it is "spoken twice, / Once by the lips, once by the services of central sense" (317).

Stevens's alarm at the "war-like whole" of twentieth-century experience (1951, 21) and its threat to the existence of the "self" underlies his huge claim that the sounds of words help us to live our lives. They help us live our lives *as* our lives. The subject in language is an individuated sensibility produced by and resounding a personal and communal history in words. But she is never self-identical because she is an echoic medium. What the "pressure" of reality threatens and what other, contemporaneous discourses may bracket is the audibility of that subject. Poetry ensures the audibility of the echoic personal/communal subject—not in what is said but what is heard in the sounds of what is said.[9]

The sounds of words do not make for a metaphysical third thing, a bridging that perpetuates the gap between sound and sense. Rather, the location of poetic "speech" in a history it remembers without remembering and transmits *as* itself marks a moral crux of character. "The Search for Sound Free from Motion" explicitly links natural and musical sounds and distinguishes speech on moral grounds:

> All afternoon the gramophone
> Parl-parled the West-Indian weather.
> The zebra leaves, the sea
> And it all spoke together.

The many-stanzaed sea, the leaves
And it all spoke together.
But you, you used the word,
Your self its honor. (1954, 268)

Natural sounds, and the "poetic" wordplay of "parl-parle" and "gramaphoon" rhyme. But "your" word is distinct, not only because its sounds form to mind and voice but because it sounds the moral presence of an intending speaker: "Your self its honor." The word's honor is your word of honor: "You" stand by your word.

"The Region November" similarly distinguishes the sound of the wind from speech: the "treetops" "sway, deeply and loudly, in an effort, / So much less than feeling, so much less than speech, // Saying and saying, the way things say / On the level of that which is not yet knowledge: // A revelation not yet intended" (1982, 115). Material sounds come to mean when there is an intending speaker and a hearer to grant sounds their intention, ratifying the act of "the inhuman making choice of a human self" in speech (1951, 89).

What makes for the human is the event of the "speech / Of the self that must sustain itself on speech" (1954, 247). Stevens's focus on the sound of words defines this self as other than the man of reason. Just as "There are things in a man besides his reason" (351), "there is a sense in sounds beyond their meaning" (352), and poetry offers "the pleasure of powers that create a truth that cannot be arrived at by reason alone, a truth that the poet recognizes by sensation. The morality of the poet's radiant and productive atmosphere is the morality of the right sensation" (1951, 58). The aesthetic-moral truth rests on the *rightness* of the sensation.

At the same time, the profoundly irrational event of "sensation-as-discourse" precludes the reduction of the lyric to subjective or inner experience, for the lyric subject comes to be in between acoustic sensation and reference, where the history of the poet and the reader are in play. The lyric subject stands on the "meta-phoring" ground of history, between and against the two facets of language, and thus helps us to hear "our" history. If Stevens wants to refigure the human as other than a beast and other than a spokesman for the "gaunt world of reason" (1951, 58), he also wants to refigure him as other than a self-identical subject. Poetry is personal, he insists, but the person *in* the poem is not prior to or distinct from the "meaning" of the sounds of his words, and the person of the poet is not distinct from his power to "recognize" that "meaning" of the "right sensation." The right sensation is "meaning" as sense and intention—"sound's substance and executant." It is

The particular tingle in a proclamation
That makes it say the little thing it says,

Below the prerogative jumble. (84)

The Mother Tongue

To say more than human things with human voice,
That cannot be; to say human things with more
Than human voice, that, also, cannot be;
To speak humanly from the height or from the depth
Of human things, that is acutest speech.
—*Wallace Stevens*

More than physical and less than metaphysical, the sound of words in the mother tongue marks the historical threshold of the human, a threshold of memory and desire:

The self is a cloister full of remembered sounds
And of sounds so far forgotten, like her voice,
That they return unrecognized. The self
Detects the sound of a voice that doubles its own,
In the images of desire, the forms that speak,
The ideas that come to it with a sense of speech.
The old men, the philosophers, are haunted by that
Maternal voice, the explanation at night. (1982, 82)

Remembered sounds make the "Children and old men and philosophers"—"Bald heads with their mother's voice still in their ears"—"more than parts" of the "universal machine," the "merely revolving wheel" that "Returns and returns, along the dry, salt shore." The haunting "maternal voice" ensures that they will "need more than that," and the poet "satisfies" that "need / The desire for the fiery lullaby," born of the memory of "her voice."[10]

The acquisition of language is a loss of "innocence," a "fall" from a deathless infancy that, after the fall, can only be imagined as a maternal voice. "In the Carolinas," the third poem in *Harmonium*, cites the fateful history: "Already the new-born children" have lost the "timeless mother" and are consigned "to interpret love / In the voices of mothers" (1954, 4). The "fall" into language, time, sexuality, and death, constitutes the human as a desire born of an irrecoverable memory, a memory necessarily consigned to oblivion. This "eccentric" fate of desire—the poet's "fated eccentricity" (443)—instigates "mumblings" about "large-sculptured, platonic person[s]," "azury centre[s] of time," and other such paternal "propositions." But the sounds of the words that express such desires carry a history and run on another frequency of "keener sounds,"[11] and may make audible a more native experience in the strange intimacy of poetic language:

Our breath is like a desperate element
That we must calm, the origin of a mother tongue

With which to speak to her, the capable
In the midst of foreignness, the syllable
Of recognition, avowal, impassioned cry,

The cry that contains its converse in itself,
In which looks and feelings mingle and are part
As a quick answer modifies a question,

Not wholly spoken in a conversation between
Two bodies disembodied in their talk,
Too fragile, two immediate for any speech. (470–71)

What we hear in the mother tongue, what we imagine through the words, is the end of "foreignness." In this intimate conversation "not wholly spoken," we are neither bodies nor minds, and our words are neither sounds nor do they represent. In this conversation, "calming" breath itself, we are ourselves "in the midst of foreignness." Something like the "spirit's sex," this conversation is not audible in brute sounds but makes audible who we are:[12]

I hear the motions of the spirit and the sound
Of what is secret becomes, for me, a voice
That is my own voice speaking in my ear. (298)

And this is the answer to the final question—not the "Mother, what is that" of the "grandson," "the expert aetat. 2," but the "Mother, my mother, who are you?" of "drowsy, infant, old men" (462–63). It is heard in the echo chamber, the reverberated voice, of the lyric "I." The "virile poet"—not "aetat. 2" and not an "old man" or "philosopher" (1982, 81–82)—has the answer, for he holds a more intimate conversation with the mother, the earth mother of death and the father of language, "In that distant chamber, a bearded queen, wicked in her dead light" (507).

SAYING OURSELVES

My own voice cheered me, and, far more, the mind's
Internal echo of the imperfect sound;
To both I listened . . .
—*William Wordsworth*

"We have grown weary of the man that thinks," Stevens writes: "He thinks and it is not true. The man below / Imagines and it is true." The "man below" is not a musician, and he was not "born in another land":

He was born within us as a second self,
A self of parents who have never died,
Whose lives return, simply, upon our lips,
Their words and ours . . . (1982, 67)

The man below "dwells below," "in less / Than body and in less than mind" and he is heard in the sounds of words that are other than mind and other than body. In his words we are no longer prisoners of representation or of the body—the "beasts" and the "incommunicable mass" from which the human "demands his speech" (1954, 328). Given its context in the poem, "incommunicable mass" has a religious as well as a material resonance. For the metaphysical and the physical are equally alien; the beasts make noise, and the god must be silent: "If there must be a god in the house," he must not be in our image; "He must dwell quietly. // He must be incapable of speaking" (327). We are the language we learned from "parents who have never died"—parents both personal and communal. In this language we can be and know ourself, but only as an other, second self, for the truth of the "subject" in poetic language is the experience of being a speaking animal, amplified through the communal history that it reverberates.

"The Creations of Sound" defines the poet figure against an "X" who is "an obstruction, a man / Too exactly himself." A self-identical ego in power over his words, "X" clarifies silences, produces "imitations for the ear" or "expresses" himself. He does not know "that there are words / Better without an author, without a poet," words of "a secondary expositor, / A being of sound," words that make the "visible a little hard / To see" and

> . . . reverberating, eke out the mind
> On peculiar horns, themselves eked out
> By the spontaneous particulars of sound. (1954, 310–11)

A mind thus "eked out" is neither a subjective nor a rational origin of words; although "peculiar," or individuated, it is a creation of sound. The "author" of such poems in which "we say ourselves . . . in speech we do not speak," in "syllables that rise / From the floor," is not an authority over his words; he is "a separate author" of words without an author, returning the father's language to the mother's voice.

A speaker that does not express a prior ego sounds the generic discourse of lyric poetry. Yet the words that articulate this discursive subject have a dimension other than discursive, since the mother tongue, and the physiological mouth-ear circuit and memory, render lyric poetry less than a discourse.[13] The lyric subject is one who negotiates—or who is negotiated as—a historical and historicizing passage between physiology and discourse. Thus, the words that "say" us "rise from the floor." They do not rise from a primal ground but from the foundation of an "architectural" structure that separates humans from primal grounds. Physiological experience can signify only within a structure, and sounds of words ground a discourse that posits them as "ground."

Hence "we" do not speak the syllables that nevertheless "say ourselves." We are alien to the language that produces us as subjects *and* unspeakably intimate with it. It speaks in our mouths. This intimacy is not a matter of an inner, subjective dimension. We can *only* say *ourselves* in what *we* do not speak, in an alien medium that we also physically produce and process. The history of a passage from sounds to syllables to speech is our innermost self, where a personal and cultural memory is encoded. And we hear that "excess," the memory that encodes the code over again and defines us; it is audible.

"A Page from a Tale" is a complex sounding of that double history:

> In the hard brightness of that winter day
> The sea was frozen solid and Hans heard,
> By his drift-fire, on the shore, the difference
> Between loud water and loud wind, between that
> Which has no accurate syllables and that
> Which cries *so blau* and cries again *so lind*
> *Und so lau*, between sound without meaning and speech,
> *Of clay and wattles made* as it ascends
> And *hear it* as it falls *in the deep heart's core*. (1954, 421)[14]

The difference between "loud water," "Which has no accurate syllables," and the "loud wind" that "cries *so blau* and cries again *so lind*," is audible to Hans, whose mother tongue is presumably German. I might not hear those particular syllables, but I might hear others that link and separate natural sounds and words. Figuring the German of Hans as a mother tongue, Stevens can mark the difference of the poetic word, which activates another ear and memory in a tongue partly derived from, yet also "foreign" to, the mother tongue, as English is to German. Hans hears the differences between not only the "loud wind" and "*blau*" and "*lind*" but between those syllables and a "speech, / *Of clay and wattles made*." Poetic speech goes beyond the German, the mother tongue, which is represented as close to a natural source—"loud," "wind," "*blau*," and "*lind*" have sonic links. But poetic language, an "English" derived from the "German," does not just echo the sounds of nature; it sounds a historical memory and a desire for another kind of sound. The quoted English words, though "foreign" to Hans, are heard "*in the deep heart's core*," as a kind of "home," the way "lake water lapping with low sounds by the shore" might be heard "in the deep heart's core" (Yeats 1989, 39) on a sea "frozen solid." The echoing difference Hans hears between the "loud wind," the "*blau*" and "*lind*," and the "*bee-loud glade*" is who he is—that's his "cabin," his "home" in exile, his exile at home. Hans is an echoic medium of tradition: he is composed of sound devices, such as rhymes and alliterations, that also remember a "speech, / *Of clay and wattles made*."

"Of Modern Poetry" also proposes that sounds heard in the mind's ear contain the mind—not the other way around. In such sounds we listen to and converse with ourselves, but always as if with another. The truth the sounds tell is that we are not self-identical, and it is heard in the

                    words that in the ear,
In the delicatest ear of the mind, repeat,
Exactly, that which it wants to hear, at the sound
Of which, an invisible audience listens,
Not to the play, but to itself, expressed
In an emotion as of two people, as of two
Emotions becoming one. (1954, 240)

The audience "listens" to itself, not to the play or to what the words say. And it hears itself in the sounds of the words spoken "slowly and / With meditation." Each one in the audience would hear differently, articulating its self and history in the words in which the "acutest" poet has articulated his personal history and feeling for words. "I" listen to "myself" *as if* to an other, an actor, by listening to an other *as if* to "myself." In that *as if* I recognize myself as "myself": I experience the intimate otherness of an "I" in words. The poet communicates through words something other than what words say and other than mere sounds. But this private affair is carried on in public, at a theater: Stevens's metaphor stresses a community of discrete listeners and hearers. One listens and hears oneself in a public medium and forum. The "audience" is a plural, made up of members with different "ears"; but an audience listens "to itself" and coheres around varying, individual responses to sounds of words. A community of those who have feelings for words coheres "as of" two or more "emotions becoming one." This is a figurative community grounded in the personal and communal histories encoded in the sounds of words.

The "metaphysician in the dark" offers no final solutions or perfections, no metaphysical solace; he is only "twanging a wiry string that gives / Sounds passing through sudden rightnesses, wholly / Containing the mind, below which it cannot descend, / Beyond which it has no will to rise" (1954, 240). The mind cannot descend to pure physiological sounds of the body. And to will to rise above the sounds of words is to aspire to be a "large-sculptured, platonic person," a master mind, thinking "the mighty thought" of "the mighty man" (55). "Abysmal instruments make sounds like pips / Of the sweeping meanings that we add to them" (384), Stevens writes. The "sweeping meanings" and the "pips" of the "abysmal instruments" are equally alien.

With the "right" sounds of words, where their "wrongness" becomes audible, we recognize the human as other than body-nature and other than mind-reason. The human is realized in the "otherness" of poetic language to meaning and to the mind that it objectifies as sounds of words.[15] Neither nature nor mind, neither sounds nor sense, but the "sound of words" make for the lyric subject, for in the word is coded the personal—a particular, unique ratio of individual and collective history—which both sounds and reference would efface. Hence the necessity for poetry. "There is so little that is close and warm. / It is as if we were never children," Stevens writes (338).

The "threat" of words reducing to sounds/body is disarmed everywhere in Stevens. It poses no real danger and can be indulged for comic relief. Nonsense sounds are never non-sense, for they always signify the body of language; non-sense, to be perceived as such, depends on the linguistic code as much as sense does. The real danger is that our words and our selves reduce to merely discursive entities. Only the sounds of words—their violence from within—can disrupt the discursive and resist the violent reduction of the human to discourse. They have to do with our "self-preservation," because in them we hear ourselves in and as our otherness to our discourse.

The "planet" is a book "on the table," and it is "a world of words to the end of it" (1954, 345): "The catbird's gobble in the morning half-awake— // These are real only if I make them so." But this is the pyrrhic victory of the "rabbit as the king of the ghosts" (209). Except, even as I make them "real," in the words with which I "realize" them, "I" have a sensation: "I taste at the root of the tongue the unreal of what is real" (313). I have a real sensation of the unreal, a real experience of the otherness of words. Discourse exercises power over the world of things; but poetry allows words to exercise power over discourse. This is a violence from within—not from within an "inner" subject, but from within the discursive medium, to counter *its* violence. And without that counterviolence, we are prisoners of representation, with no hope of freedom, no parole. Our only freedom is to "*taste*" the unreality of all the discursive "real" in the sound of its words. Hence, Stevens insists words must be stubborn and flawed. They must violate the discourse that violates the world of things, *and* they must violate their own discourse. They must dismantle what they mantle. "It is with strange malice / That I distort the world" (61), he writes. To counter the violence of representation, sounds must be "stubborn" (194);[16] their wrongness and their opacity must be maintained so that the "evilly compounded, vital I" may be heard (193). "Personally, I like words to sound wrong," Stevens writes (1966, 340).

THE IRRATIONAL

> . . . interest in the imagination and its work is to be regarded
> not as a phase of humanism but as a vital self-assertion in a
> world in which nothing but the self remains, if that remains.
> —*Wallace Stevens*

In the final canto of "Notes toward a Supreme Fiction," Stevens speaks of "The irrational // Distortion / . . . the more than rational distortion, / The fiction that results from feeling. Yes, that." Instigated by feeling, this is a special kind of

fiction, "yes, that," among other fictions, and it is neither antithetical nor assimi-
lable to reason. Stevens's stress on the irrational is part of his project of envi-
sioning a postenlightenment human hero, an accountable subject who is other
than a central power of Reason, or Man in the image of God, a master-man:
"There are those who, having never yet been convinced that the rational has
quite made us divine, are willing to assume the efficacy of the irrational in that
respect" (1982, 228). While "[i]t is easy to brush aside the irrational with the
statement that we are rational beings, Aristotelians and not brutes," Stevens
writes, it is "becoming easier every day to say that we are irrational beings" (218).

But "all irrationality is not of a piece" and Stevens's irrationality is distinct
from any consciously cultivated irrationality, any local, historically contingent,
programmatic or methodological irrationality that depends on and reaffirms
the norm of reason, or any mystical or psychological phenomenon:[17] "What I
have in mind when I speak of the irrational element in poetry is the transaction
between reality and the sensibility of the poet" (1982, 218, 217). Stevens
admits: "Clearly, I use the word irrational more or less indifferently, as between
its several senses. It will be time enough to adapt a more systematic usage,
when the critique of the irrational comes to be written, by whomever it may
be that this potent subject ultimately engages" (229). For Stevens, the irrational, which is manifested in "the individuality of the poet" (217), includes feelings, emotions, taste, unaccountable impressions and responses to stimuli, individual sensibilities, desires, and choices. The irrational includes all that makes
for our history and who we are, all that we do and feel that cannot be explained
by reason.

Stevens thus places irrationality at the core of what human beings do when
they *choose* to do something—such as write a poem, for example. The source
of poetry is an irrational impression—"a particular process in the rational mind
which we recognize as irrational in the sense that it takes place unaccountably"
(1982, 218). The unaccountable irrational process distinguishes individual sensibilities' transactions with "reality." Since these terms are somewhat abstract,
I will cite his example of such a transaction, to show how literally he means it:

> A day or two before Thanksgiving we had a light fall of snow in Hartford.
> It melted a little by day and then froze again at night, forming a thin,
> bright crust over the grass. At the same time, the moon was almost full.
> I awoke once several hours before daylight and as I lay in bed I heard the
> steps of a cat running over the snow under my window almost inaudibly.
> The faintness and strangeness of the sound made on me one of those
> impressions which one so often seizes as pretexts for poetry. I suppose
> that in such a case one is merely expressing one's sensibility and that the
> reason why this expression takes the form of poetry is that it takes what-
> ever form one is able to give it. The poet is able to give it the form of
> poetry because poetry is the medium of his personal sensibility. (217)

The poet irrationally responds to a sound, which moves him to words, the medium of his "sensibility": "He hears the cat on the snow. The running feet set the rhythm. There is no subject beyond the cat running on the snow in the moonlight. He grows completely tired of the thing, wants a subject, thought, feeling, his whole manner changes. All these things enter into the choice of subject" (1982, 221). The individuality of the poet is the irrational element at the core of poetry: he makes irrational choices because he has irrationally responded to a sound and rhythm and irrationally grown tired of it. The desire for change is irrational. But Stevens notes: "it does not follow that poetry that is irrational in origin is not communicable poetry" (222). It is simply not rationally accountable for.

The irrational entails both an automatism and freedom: "If each of us is a biological mechanism, each poet is a poetic mechanism. To the extent that what he produces is mechanical: that is to say, beyond his power to change, it is irrational," and "I think, too, that the choice of subject matter is a completely irrational thing, provided a poet leaves himself any freedom of choice. . . . [I]f you elect to remain free and to go about in the world experiencing whatever you happen to experience, as most people do, . . . either your choice of subjects is fortuitous or the identity of the circumstances under which the choice is made is imperceptible" (1982, 220). This nice qualification seems to say, either your choice is irrational or something or someone else is choosing for you. The irrational processes of the poet's sensibility make for his freedom and account-ability: "You can compose poetry in whatever form you like. . . . It is not that nobody cares. It matters immensely. The slightest sound matters. The most momentary rhythm matters. You can do so as you please, yet everything mat-ters. . . . You have somehow to know the sound that is the exact sound; and you do in fact know, without knowing how. Your knowledge is irrational" (226–27).

If irrational emotions and desires motivate poetry, so do they motivate the turn to poetry:

> There were ghosts that returned to earth to hear his phrases,
> As he sat there reading, aloud, the great blue tabulae.
>
> . . . .
>
> They were those that would have wept to step barefoot into reality,
>
> That would have wept and been happy, have shivered in the frost
> And cried out to feel it again, have run fingers over leaves
> And against the most coiled thorn, have seized on what was ugly
>
> And laughed, as he sat there reading, from out of the purple tabulae
>   (1954, 423–24)

Disappointed with the final poverty of life and death, the ghosts come back to hear sounds. Their desire to feel, to have physical sensations, returns them to hear the "large red man reading." And the subject matter—the concrete pots and pans and tulips and the abstract "being and its expressings"—is indifferent to those who have returned to hear the man "reading, aloud," to "hear his phrases." Poetry is not the literal characters nor the vatic lines but their realization as physical sensations in sounds that touch the hearers and take on, for them, the shape of "things as they are."

NOTES

1. "February 18, 1942" (Stevens 1966, 403).

2. James Longenbach (1991) has shown how closely Stevens's thought on poetry was engaged with social, political, and economic issues. But Stevens insists on the social function of poetry *as* poetry, not as substitute religion, philosophy, sociology, or politics. He would agree with I. A. Richards: "The poem is no ticket to the Fortunate Isles, or even to Purgatory, or even to Moscow. The journey is its own end, and it will not, by having no destination, any less assist the world to become what Moscow should be" (Richards 1949, 303).

3. Stevens distinguishes poetry "that is modern in respect to what it says" from poetry "that is modern in respect to form": "The first kind is not interested primarily in form. The second is. The first kind is interested in form but it accepts a banality of form as incidental to its language." Of course, he goes on to qualify: "What I have said of both classes of modern poetry is inadequate as to both. As to the first, which permits a banality of form, it is even harmful, as suggesting that it possesses less of the artifice of the poet than the second" (1951, 168).

4. As much of Stevens's poetry reiterates, memories, desires, feelings all make for different perceptions, even if the object were stable, which it is not: the "solid, static object" is as much an abstraction as a stable subject.

5. "The Search for Sound Free from Motion" is another way of phrasing this search for the impossible that is poetry. Certain "balances" of "The syllable of a syllable" are possible, however, and "A few sounds of meaning, a momentary end / To the complication, is good, is a good" (1954, 268, 303).

6. In "The Pure Good of Theory," he writes:

> . . . If we propose
> A large-sculptured, platonic person, free from time,
> And imagine for him the speech he cannot speak
>
> A form, then, protected from the battering, may
> Mature: A capable being may replace
> Dark horse and walker walking rapidly.
>
> Felicity, ah! (1954, 329–30)

The mind, hearing the "horse that runs in the heart" and "batters against the mind," is prompted to imagine "large-sculptured, platonic person[s]" and various "azury centre[s] of time" (425), which Stevens dismisses: "Felicity, ah!"

7. The gross sexuality of pure sounds threaten to unman the "virile *poet*." In "The Plot Against the Giant," other senses cannot compete with sound. The "first girl" and her "civilest odors" will "check him"; the "second girl" and her "colors" "Will abash

him"; but the "third girl," "With a curious puffing," will "whisper / Heavenly labials in a world of gutturals": "It will undo him" (1954, 6–7).

8. The speakers and hearers of voiced and heard sounds are absolutely individuated. No two people will read a poem the same, as any reading aloud shows; more, the poem we hear read aloud is never the poem in our mind's ear—even if we are the ones voicing it.

9. The audibility of what is not said in what is said cannot be imitated or represented or theorized. Stevens repeatedly addresses this phenomenon, which eludes definition. Nietzsche wrote "Only that which has no history is definable" (qtd. in Calinescu 1987, 310). Or, perhaps, only what can be distinguished from its history is definable.

10. See also section 23 of "An Ordinary Evening in New Haven," "And the goodness of lying in a maternal sound, // Unfretted by day's separate, several selves, / Being part of everything come together as one" (1954, 482).

11. The "keener sounds" in "The Idea of Order at Key West" (1954, 130–31) are distinct from the sounds of the sea, the song, and the discourse with Ramon Fernandez. They are words of "ourselves" and "our origins." They are heard only in the "ear of the mind," not in sounds but through sounds, in a different frequency than what the ear can register.

12. Stevens consistently sexualizes nonsense sounds. See, for example, 1954, 155, 337, 383. But "sex" is not "all" (17).

13. The ear and the "throat" are the mother's organs; the eye is the father's (1954, 317). Knowing is associated with seeing, and feeling with hearing (518). On another register, the mother is time, as the father is space (413–14), and time is heard (329–30), as space is seen. Ultimately, the image-making faculty links to the father's powers, and the sounds to the mother's. "We" are the synesthetic conceits of these parents as they are "conceived" by the poet "parent" (195).

14. The poem dates from 1948, and would seem to have in its background the transport of Yeats's body on September 6, 1948 from France, where he had died in 1939 and been buried because of the war, to Galway to be brought to Sligo for burial. Stevens refers in a letter to this event and its affirmation of "the meaning of the poet as a figure in society" (1966, 617–18).

15. "Thirteen Ways of Looking at a Blackbird" presents a subject encountering itself in the mirror of word-objects. Looking at a blackbird is an encounter with the self as an object as seen by the eye of a blackbird. But the I's very words are also objects, his "others" that shape his subjectivity. The speaker who is moved to say "I" by the "eye" of the blackbird resolves itself into letters and sounds and their mechanisms and possibilities of combination:

> II
> I was of *three* minds,
> Like a *tree*
> In which *there* are *three* blackbirds. (1954, 92; emphases mine)

The letters, the literal objects of the code and their anagrammatic procedures, visibly and audibly shape the figures that articulate the "mind," or rather "minds," in relation to the blackbird. The poet is concurrently arranging the sounds of words and articulating a natural object/scene and a speaking subject in relation to it. In this triangular relationship, the subject and the object are termini written by the words. The word-objects shape the subject himself in the same way that the word "blackbird" shapes the parameters of his discourse. The word "blackbird," repeated in each section, is as impenetrable and irreducible as the blackbird that it keeps failing to fix. The stubborn opacity of its sounds must be "involved" in the "noble accents / And lucid, inescapable rhythms"—not so that "I" can see the blackbird but so that "I" can see myself.

16. Georges Bataille writes that poetry is "the sacrifice in which words are victims." We use words, make them "instruments of useful acts." But we would not have "anything of the human about us if the language had to be entirely servile within us." So we "tear" words away, "in a delirium," from their useful functions (1988, 135).

17. Stevens distinguishes his project from "the din made by the surrealists and surrationalists" (1982, 216), whom he calls "romantic scholars" (217); from the "irrational in a pathological sense"; from the "irrationality provoked by prayer, whisky, fasting, opium, or the hope of publicity"; and from the stylistic conventions of a local practice, a given time and place ("The Gothic novels of the eighteenth-century England are no longer irrational. They are merely boring" [218]). "The poet cannot profess the irrational as the priest professes the unknown" (229).

Chapter 7

POUND'S SOUNDTRACK: "READING CANTOS

FOR WHAT IS *ON THE PAGE*"

> You begin with the yeowl and the bark, and you develop into
> the dance and into music, and into music with words, and
> finally into words with music, and finally into words with a
> vague adumbration of music, words suggestive of music,
> words measured, or words in a rhythm that preserves some
> accurate trait of the emotive impression, or of the sheer char-
> acter of the fostering or parental emotion.
>
> When this rhythm, or when the vowel and consonantal
> melody or sequence seems truly to bear the trace of emotion
> which the poem (for we have come at last to the poem) is
> intended to communicate, we say that this part of the work
> is good.
>
> —*Ezra Pound*

THE CANTOS is the tale of the tales of the tribe. The action of the poem is the construction of "Ezra Pound of the Cantos" in and as an intimate conversation with written and spoken language. Pound's tale includes both living and dead languages; diverse kinds of printed texts; various writing systems; different dialects of languages, individuating accents, tones, rhythms, inflections, and pronunciations; heard or remembered speech that has "carved" its "trace" in the ear or the mind; typographical transcriptions of speech sounds and rhythms on the page space. His interest is in the physical presence and the history of the material medium.

Different genres are chapters of this story, and if the first canto opens by resounding the epic tradition, it ends by invoking lyric poems. Pound interrupts the Homeric narrative, and, in a sense the tradition of oral narration, with a switch to his "I," a translator addressing his predecessor: "Lie quiet Divus. I mean, that is Andreas Divus."[1] He thus signals not only the "present" of his English text but, figuratively, the end of the oral and scribal traditions with the coming of print. "In officina Wecheli, 1538" that marks the medium of print also gives us the first non-English phrase used in the *Cantos*—Latin, a dead language circulating *only* on paper. If the ear remembers "The Seafarer," the script of letters remembers Latin. Both the oral tradition that travels in the air and the written tradition that passes through books are communal creations, changing with tellers and retellers, scribes and printers, translators and translators of translators. "This is not a work of fiction / nor yet of one man" (99: 728).

Throughout, we are within one man's mind and memory—personal, historical, literary, visual, auditory. We read what he reads, thinks, remembers, picks and chooses, and how he puts his and others' words down on the page. But because the speaker is constructed as a conversation, he is not at all a subjective entity. Indeed, in the most emotionally charged, personal moments in the text—especially in the Pisan Cantos—Pound characteristically switches out of English or cites other poets. Although we are in an inner world of mind and memory, this is "a world of words to the end of it"[2]—others' and his—and this speaker's voice, which is unmistakably his, is heard when he gets others' voices right. Who else but Pound could have written these lines, where we hear not Yeats but Pound:

> sun rises lop-sided over the mountain
> > so that I recalled the noise in the chimney
> as it were the wind in the chimney
> > but was in reality Uncle William
> downstairs composing
> that had made a great Peeeeacock
> > in the proide ov his oiye
> > had made a great peeeeeeecock in the . . .
> made a great peacock
> > in the proide of his oyyee
>
> proide ov his oy-ee
> as indeed he had, and perdurable
>
> a great peacock aere perennius (83: 553–54)

The action of this passage is not in the narrative but in the transcription of the voice, the accent, and intonation accurately into a visual print medium. If he gets Yeats's "eye" right, Yeats gets an "I," making a poem out of "a mouthful of air" (Pound 1970, 152), as does the one who "recalled the noise." In fact, Yeats gets Pound's "I." For Pound's transmission changes the text itself; "The Peacock" reads differently when we return to it after Pound. This individuating abrogation of the individual is the logic behind Pound's masks and translations.

The medium for this kind of language is the air and the mouth-ear path. Poems are made out of "a mouthful of air," and they travel in the air; Pound's page aims for an accurate transcription of this language for transmission on paper. In two of his comments on the *Cantos*, Pound presents his page as a score for reading. First, "[a]ll typographic disposition, placings of words on the page, is intended to facilitate the reader's intonation, whether he be reading silently to self or aloud to friends. Given time and technique I might even put down the musical notation of passages or 'breaks into song.' " Second, "The order of words and sounds ought to induce proper reading; proper tone of voice, etc., but can *not* redeem fools from idiocy, etc. If the goddam violin string is not tense, no amount of bowing will help the player" (1971, 322, 323).

The assumption here is that sense depends on the proper tone of voice, on intonation. "There aren't any *rules*" when it comes to rhythm: "Thing is to cut a shape in time. Sounds that stop the flow, and durations either of syllables, or implied between them, 'forced onto the voice' of the reader by nature of the 'verse' " (1971, 254). Unless the text "forces" itself " 'onto the voice' of the reader," it is dead matter, adding to the "piles of stone books" (14: 63). Pound points out the "descent to the shades," the "metamorphoses," and "parallels" in the *Cantos* and concludes: "All of which is mere matter for little . . . rs and Harvud instructors *unless* I pull it off as reading matter, singing matter, shouting matter, the tale of the tribe" (1971, 294). Pound's epic purpose to pass on the tradition depends on a reader's voice sounding his script: the tradition lives through the voice, whether it is transmitted in the air or on paper.

The reader is to process the visual, typographical material as a shape "cut" in time for proper "intonation" of lines, which may or may not be pronounced aloud. They may be experienced as "acoustic and motor images" of sounds,[3] in the same way that, in another register, the sounds of words may provoke visual images. "The eye catches" the "cadence" of the words on the page layout (1971, 142). The act of reading is a sounding, and the silent Chinese script, where the eye cannot connect to the mouth-ear, works to remind the reader of this fact. However "transitive" ideograms may be in theory, in practice, they block the eye's access to the mouth-ear circuit and serve to render perceptible how the words *around* them are transitive.[4]

My thesis is that the *Cantos* are organized by lyric procedures and that Pound's sounds, fraught with dangers ideograms would keep at bay, motivate the larger arguments, narratives, and organizational patterns such as subject rhymes. The second canto introduces "What is there—permanent—the sea,"[5] the medium of unchanging change, where things "become other things by swift and unanalysable process" (1968a, 431). In the poem *as* verbal artifact, the permanent "sea" is the physical medium of language, the physiological phenomena of sounds, on which are borne the narratives of recurrent ship voyages, metaphors, and myths of metamorphoses. These conveyances and "crafts," the syntax of sentences and of stories, are figures on the ground of the physical medium and its movement, its unchanging change, its "unstillness" (2: 10). Thus the second canto tells as much about the material medium of language—the sounds composing their sequences, with little regard for proper names or for individual identities—as about psychological-mythic metamorphoses:

Hang it all, Robert Browning,
there can be but the one "Sordello."
But Sordello, and my Sordello?
Lo Sordels si fo di Mantovana.
So-shu churned in the sea.
Seal sports in the spray-whited circles of cliff-wash,
Sleek head, daughter of Lir,
    eyes of Picasso
Under black fur-hood, lithe daughter of Ocean;
And the wave runs in the beach-groove:
"Eleanor, ελεναυσ and ελεπτολισ!" (2: 6)

There are too many Sordellos: different readers, writers, and times make for different Sordellos. Underlying the stability of a consistent persona and the repeats in history are sounds of words, and Pound begins again by dissolving the name into its constituent elements. Along with the logic of "So that" must go "Sordello." Stable identities—of speakers, names, and words—dissolve in the Dionysian sea of sounds: "So-shu churned in the sea." The logic that generates "So-shu" is the illogical metamorphoses of the sounds out of "Sordello" and the line in Italian.[6] This is a different aspect of the poet than the story teller: Homer, "blind, blind, as a bat" is also the name for an "ear, ear for the sea-surge."

The erotic and destructive physical medium of sounds and its "craft" compose the canto. It is the wave that "runs" "Eleanor, ελεναυσ and ελεπτολισ!" (Eleanor; Elenaus, Eleptolis: ship destroyer, city destroyer), speaks the subject rhymes of Eleanor and Helen, prewrites history, and prespeaks Aeschylus's puns on "Helen." In the sounds of words, nature writes words and words write nature. The wave's pun, its sound sport, also gives us the "naus" (ship), which will take us to "Naxos" (a place with a name) and the "naviform" rock (likenesses), to generate the narrative about the power of Lyaeus to make "Ship stock fast in sea-swirl." In the beginning were the physical phenomena of sounds and their music; then came words about gods and stories of "god-sleight": "out of nothing, a breathing" is how gods and poems appear and take shape.

Pound repeatedly proposes a three-part scheme for the *Cantos*:

A. A. Live Man goes down into world of Dead
C. B. The "repeat in history"
B. C. The "magic moment" or moment of metamorphosis, bust thru from quotidien into "divine or permanent world." Gods, etc. (1971, 210)

"If the reader wants three categories he can find them . . . in: permanent, recurrent and merely haphazard or casual" (Cookson 1985, xvii). Another passage proposes:

a) What is there—permanent—the sea.
b) What is recurrent—the voyages.
c) What is trivial—the casual—Vasco's troops weary, stupid parts. (xxi)

The lyric is associated with the "permanent" part of his three-part scheme: "Narrative not the same as lyric; different techniques for song and story. 'Would, could,' etcetera" (Pound 1971, 322). Narrative involves sequential events, tenses, "etcetera." It contrasts "breaks into song," as recurrent narrative patterns contrast "The magic moment" or the "bust" into " 'divine or permanent world.' Gods, etc." The divine/permanent sea is always there. Gods do not return, for "they have never left us."

Pound's sounds in this canto do not function as alliterations or rhymes, which normally perform a rhetorical function, directing our attention to tonally, argumentatively, and figurally significant words or sequences of words. Here, however, the sounds function as the ground, and the particular embodiments of the sounds—words, mythic figures and names, seals and sleek-headed Lirs, and so on—are figures on the ground of sounds repeating and transforming themselves. The sounds and their drift are the structural determinants of the poem, audibly enabling the story we are reading. The sound shape of the poem, then, is neither ornamental, nor rhetorical, nor positioned against content but shapes the very drift or movement of the content, determining thematic sequences, writing the story, in this particular way, this time around. For Acoetes' story is told through incantatory repetitions and is of the same texture as the nonnarrative passages that bracket it. It is structured less as a narrative sequence and more as a magical articulation or momentary focussing of repeated sounds into a story:

And, out of nothing, a breathing,
    hot breath on my ankles,
Beasts like shadows in glass,
    a furred tail upon nothingness.
Lynx-purr, and heathery smell of beasts,
    where tar smell had been,
Sniff and pad-foot of beasts,
    eye-glitter out of black air.
The sky overshot, dry, with no tempest,
Sniff and pad-foot of beasts,
    fur brushing my knee-skin,
Rustle of airy sheathes
    dry forms in the *æther*. (2: 8)

The second canto establishes lyric language as the origin; narratives are generated out of its resources and drives and are repeated over and over to make for a "history" of forms, such as the one we hear in the "audible etymology" of the first canto. The ships journey on the sea, and narratives journey on sounds and the changing patterns and associations they can enter and leave, as the poet plies his craft. But we hear outright, "Circe's this craft" (1: 3): sounds are bewitching, erotic, creative, and destructive. To give into their physical lull is to be drugged and turn swine, stop making sense. "In *melopoeia*," Pound writes, "we find . . . a force tending often to lull, or to distract the reader from the exact sense of the language. It is poetry on the borders of music and music is perhaps the bridge between consciousness and the unthinking sentient or even insentient universe" (1968a, 26).[7] To surrender to sounds is to lose identity in a fluid medium where nothing is itself, and this Dionysian danger also inheres in puns, homophony, and homonymy. The sounds must neither be repressed— in set orders and closed forms[8]—nor indulged for their own sake. They must be patterned to make for "character," a standing "firm in the middle."

The canto ends with an homage to the metamorphic powers of language.[9] The scene is distanced, as in a vision; but we are within it, caught in the words and their will, as in an auditory hallucination. In this fluid medium, sentences dissolve into fragments, the functions of parts of speech—nouns, verbs, adjectives—tend to blur, and words freely join with and part from one another. Pound uses metamorphic compounds that are often almost oxymoronic: "rock-slide"; "fish-hawk"; "rock-hollows"; "green-ruddy." He also joins terms that are not compounds and splits what should be single words: "vine-trunk"; "grape-leaves on the rowlocks"; "like a keel in a ship-yard"; "grape-cluster over pin-rack"; "olive-trees"; "out of the olive-grove." These work as mini-metamorphoses and make for a visual confusion; they also seem to be meant to work rhythmically, to guide reading.[10] If we look back from the canto's end to the first line, its dramatic voice and the solidity of "Robert Browning," immune to all we have witnessed, are markers of the illusion of self-identity—of names, poets, and sense. The knowledge of this Dionysian canto is the fragility of the illusion of Apollonian language.

In canto 4, sounds ground the subject rhymes so that they appear neither as mere fanciful tropes nor as typological givens of some master blueprint but as if somehow inherent in the movement of language; they appear to "run in the wind" (5: 20), which seems to be the element of this canto. The opening, "Troy but a heap of smouldering boundary stones," sets the theme of violence, linking sexual transgression and the war that gave us the stories. Line 3 has two apostrophes: "ANAXIFORMINGES! Aurunculeia!" The second is the name of the bride in Catullus's marriage song, which has the refrain "Hymenæus Io! Hymenæe!" that will be recalled on page 15. The first is from Pindar's second Olympian ode. Pound quotes the second part of Pindar's opening apostrophe: "My songs, lords of the lyre / which of the gods, what hero, what mortal shall we celebrate?" (Pindar 1947, 5). This is followed by "Hear me. Cadmus of Golden Prows!" Phoenician letters were supposedly brought to Greece by the legendary

Cadmus—Kadmos—a Phoenician,[11] and this might be why he is invoked here, for the canto also concerns letters—the writing of the animal sounds.[12]

It is not clear whether the speaker is Cadmus or is addressing Cadmus. In any case, he must be "heard":

> Dew-haze *blurs*, in the grass, pale ankles moving.
> Beat, beat, *whirr*, thud, in the soft *turf*
>   under the apple trees,
> Choros nympharum, goat-foot, with the pale foot alternate;
> Crescent of blue-shot waters, green-gold in the shallows,
> A black cock crows in the sea-foam. (emphases mine)

The /ur/ sound harks back to the second canto: it is a Dionysian sound, of the churning sea-surge, the murmur, and the "purr" of furry beasts.[13] What I hear in "Beat, beat, whirr, thud, in the soft turf" is a "blur," "in the grass," of dancing nymphs and satyrs and war calls. What is also audible, in the memory, is what has been driven under with the "thud"—the "Beat! beat! drums! . . . / whirr and pound" of Whitman's drum-taps (1973, 283). The integrity of Whitman's phrases *and* the identity of Pound both resolve themselves into the common "root" and "sap," the Dionysian language the two share. Their shared root undoes individuation and subsumes both identities. Whitman's terrible call to the drums to drown out the voice of the "singer," to silence the poet, is enacted in Pound's own erasure of his name, the deletion of "pound." And yet "beat! beat!" reinscribes the name; Pound's beat is his rhythm and audibly distinguishes his "character."

The Dionysian language generates the subject rhymes of various stories of violence. The stories of sexual transgression, Dionysiac excesses, dismemberments, and cannibalism follow a sound drift, as if the stories were conjured to explain certain phenomena of sounds—such as a swallow's cry:[14]

> And by the curved, carved foot of the couch,
>   claw-foot and lion head, an old man seated
> Speaking in the low drone . . . :
>   Ityn!
> Et ter flebiliter, Ityn, Ityn!
> And she went toward the window and cast her down,
>   "All the while, the while, swallows crying:
> Ityn!
>   "It is Cabestan's heart in the dish."
>   "It is Cabestan's heart in the dish?
>   "No other taste shall change this."
> And she went toward the window,
>   the slim white stone bar
> Making a double arch;
> Firm even fingers held to the firm pale stone;

Swung for a moment,
                    and the wind out of Rhodez
Caught in the full of her sleeve.
       . . . the swallows crying:
'Tis. 'Tis. Ytis!
       Actæon . . .
                    and a valley,
The valley is thick with leaves, with leaves, the trees,
The sunlight glitters, glitters (4: 13–14)

The following description of the valley is an even more markedly incantatory
repetition of words and syntactic phrases and structures:

    Beneath it, beneath it
Not a ray, not a slivver, not a spare disc of sunlight
Flaking the black, soft water;
Bathing the body of nymphs, of nymphs, and Diana,
Nymphs, white-gathered about her, and the air, air,
Shaking, air alight with the goddess,
    fanning their hair in the dark,
Lifting, lifting and waffing:
Ivory dipping in silver,
    Shadow'd, o'ershadow'd
Ivory dipping in silver,
Not a splotch, not a lost shatter of sunlight.
Then Actæon: Vidal,
Vidal. It is old Vidal speaking (4: 14)

Precisely at the point of his appearance, Acteon changes into Vidal: "Then
Actæon: Vidal." The characters are units in a rhythm apprehended in repetition. The lulling repetitions of sounds and syntax *train us* to "see" likenesses,
directly apprehend the rhyme of figures, for we have entered a rhythmic state,
where identities are fluid. "It is old Vidal speaking" circles back to the sounds
that first introduced Acteon: " 'Tis. 'Tis. Ytis!"
    The subject rhymes thus composed—of Procne / Lady Soremonda and
Acteon / Vidal—cross the categories of mythological figures, real women, and
poets. Again, we are on the Dionysian ground of fluid identities, and I want to
stay with the sounds. The droning "old man" first utters "Ityn! / Et ter flebiliter,
Ityn, Ityn!" The Latin phrase ("three times with tears") is from Horace; Procne
is mourning her son, Itys. Ityn, the accusative form of Itys, also "sounds" like
"eaten." A sound link across languages grounds the theme of the canto, the
central violent acts of dismemberment and cannibalism that link the subject
rhymes. "The swallows crying: / Ityn" adds another English pun. And the swallows give the line about Cabestan's heart, which the lady repeats. The lines

echo Itys with "It is . . . It is . . . this." Finally, both stories and the "it is" of English blend in the swallows' final cry: " 'Tis. 'Tis. Ytis!" The metamorphoses of the sounds—Ityn (eaten) / Itys / It is / 'Tis / Ytis—are the grounds of proper names, discrete stories, different languages. And the subject rhymes of the stories of Procne, Cabestan, Acteon, Vidal, and Gyges are not abstract parallelisms but are conjured or confirmed by the ear, as we listen to the generic poet and the persuasions of micro-rhetorical linkages. In this "drone," the alphabet becomes fluid: *i* and *y* are again interchangeable. And the dissolution of identities, the regress to Dionysian ground, is destructive quite literally; it is a kind of cannibalism of the oral zone, of the eating mouth dismembering the words.[15]

Thus the concept of subject rhymes is too limited for the multidimensional links of Pound's vortex(t). Acteon and Vidal link in being hunted by their dogs, and Lady Soremonda rhymes with Procne in her "flight." But she also links to Tereus through unwitting cannibalism, as Cabestan blends with Itys. In the concluding sections of the canto, Diana, the virgin huntress, links to Danaë through letter play, and letter play also gets us from Acteon to Cabestan to Ecbatan (4: 16). And both Diana and Danaë—the "god's bride" and mother of Perseus—link to the Regina. The Virgin, worshipped in the procession along "Adige, thin film of images," is also God's bride, at once Diana and Danaë, and the mother of Christ, the Word, who offers his flesh and blood to be eaten and drunk (Matt. 26:26–28), before he "flies" up to heaven (Luke 24:51). The myths tell and retell in words the primal emergence of words out of the mouthbody. This abysmal Dionysian ground of language is veiled, ply over ply, in Apollonian illusion, the "thin film of images."

The canto is overwhelmingly elegiac. What is being mourned is individuation and its loss. It is a perfect balance of the Apollonian and the Dionysian, where the words sound the Dionysian abyss while the Apollonian principle—after having been destroyed along with Troy—is reinstituted as a "beautiful illusion," to "console mortal men." "The Centaur's heel plants in the earth loam" (4: 16); individual stories and names are transparencies, illusions that hide as they reveal the primitive terror, the ground of the acts of eating flesh and the eating mouth sounding words.

Thus lyric language shapes the poem's development and arguments at a different level than the patterns that subject rhymes or the repeats in history provide. The poem is convincing because these larger patterns, "rhymes," and repeats by which Pound would organize his tale are grounded in another kind of patterning that does not work by argumentation and "proof-bringing." The repetitions, patterns of sounds, rhythms, and syntax, make for the "persuasion" of Pound's form as they train the reader to "see," imagine, desire other kinds of links, in the same way that one is moved to connect the different senses of rhyming words.

In canto 39, the cluster of sounds, rhythm, and eating is again engaged. The canto begins with loss—the looms are now silent. Like the opening passage of canto 4, the opening of the canto is an auditory hallucination—a memory/ imagination of sounds of a weaving loom on the hill above Rapollo/Circe's house: "In hill path: 'thkk, thgk' / of the loom / 'Thgk, thkk' and the sharp sound of a song." Personal memory blends into literary memory in this sound, which has an onomatopoeic "thickness" as well as a suggestion of clock ticks.

The "sharp" sound of a song is distinct from this bass rhythm and consonantal cluster. Circe is singing, but elsewhere "sharp" describes the sirens' song. The lines move along the sounds of the loom—*th*, *t*, *g*, and *k* in a thick alliterative text(ile)—plus *f*-sounds: "Fat panther lay by me / Girls talked there of fucking, beasts talked there of eating, / All heavy with sleep, fucked girls and fat leopards." But we are also prepared for the "fucking" by another route— onomatopoeically the "thgk thkk" gets us there. This thick, fleshly language is all body and tongue—the alimentary mouth. And there is much eating in the canto. The Greek from the *Odyssey*—"Kaka pharmak edoken" (She had given them evil drugs)—fits with the *sound texture*, as does "ptheggometha thasson." We experience the flesh of language, its opacity and its material "foreignness," here oddly represented by Greek and Latin. The canto relies heavily on Greek and Latin, and Circe's animal entourage and its bestial language link her to Dionysus: the panthers and beasts are there, as well as lions "loggy," a word describing Dionysus in canto 2.

Then the sounds shift to another register, *f* giving way to *v*, of which it is a descendent: "wolf to curry favour for food / —born to Helios and Perseis / That had Pasiphae for a twin / Venter venustus, cunni cultrix, of the velvet marge / ver novum, canorum, ver novum / Spring overborne into summer / late spring in the leafy autumn." Again, the Latin is there for the sounds. And we get here an additional pattern that will take us to the repeated acorns and Hathor and orcum, and beyond, to a new kind of language: "To Flora's night, with hyacinthus, / With the crocus (spring / sharp in the grass)."

Spring is "sharp," like the song, not thick. It is new birth, "new" sap. In the modulation of sound textures, we come to new spring at once seasonal and aural. "Unceasing the measure" of the looms, of the lines, and of "fucking": "With one measure, unceasing: / 'Fac deum!' 'Est factus.' / Ver novum! / ver novum! / Thus made the spring," "Beaten from flesh into light." And we end with some goddess: "His rod hath made god in my belly / . . . . I have eaten the flame." "Fac deum" is a bilingual homophony sublimating fucking into making god. In coitus, illumination: "Sacrum, sacrum, inluminatio coitu" (36: 180). Light is made out of flesh; "Fac deum" out of fucking; "ver novum" out of "venter"-"velvet." *Et verbum caro factum est—and* the flesh was made word.[16]

The principle of lyric organization also underpins the cantos with historical and documentary content. I want to look at canto 71 to see how and to what effect the lyric language counterpoints the epical-historical import. John Adams has the floor, and Pound is in charge of Adams's words. The charge of both men is fidelity to the historical record and the distribution of information to make us understand those who made the revolution, for "without knowing their actions / you know not what made our revolution." Adams is a hero—the just, rightful, moral leader. A spokesman for proper distribution of money and knowledge, he stands against all forms of absolute power. He rhymes with Confucius, the figure of an "unwobbling pivot" that stands, firm in the middle, for an order that neither represses nor surrenders to nature but works with it. And clearly both rhyme with Pound: their political and ethical values project and are projected by Pound's poetic values.

In Pound's language we hear the constitution of such a hero. The canto begins with Pound quoting Adams:

A GERMAN ambassador once told me he cdn't bear
                              St Paul
     he was, he said, so hard on *fornication.*
         Dismissed to the joy of both parties, I do not
curse the day I entered public affairs.
         Now in the *first* year *before* congress
         (that is *before '74*)
I was drying my saddlebags and *four* yeomen in the bar room
were talking politics: 'If' says one 'they can take
Mr Hancock's wharf and Mr Rowe's wharf
They can take my house and your barn.' Rebel!
I was disgusted at their saying rebel. I wd/ *meet* rebellion
when British governors and generals should begin it,
that is, their rebellion against principles of the constitution.
         'and in the mean time build *frigates*'
. . . .
in every principal sea port . . . not to *fight* squadrons at sea
but to have *fast* sailing *frigates.*
From England greater injuries
than *from France,*
I am *for fighting* whichever *forces* us *first* into a war.
                    (71: 414; emphases mine except "meet")

In the first sentence, Pound replaces Adams's "severe" with the more colloquial "hard on." The sentence in Adams is part of a different argument; it is followed by "On the same principle these philosophers cannot bear a God, because he is just."[17] Pound picks up Adams's vehicle, not his tenor. Fornication, of course, is a slipperier issue than injustice. Quoting half of Adams's statement makes for a greater interest for the reader, leaves a grayer area in play, and charges Adams's words differently. Against this sentence, "the joy of both parties," and even "affairs," make for a developing sexual subtext. The part Pound leaves out from the second letter (line 3ff.) gives a kind of context for the seemingly gratuitous subtext: "At the close of the 18th c., I was dismissed, to the joy of both parties, to a retirement in which I was never more to see any thing but my plough between me and the grave." Adams's statements are one page apart in the source, *The Works of John Adams, IX* (Terrell 1980). With ploughs and earth and graves, we are on the primal ground of sex and death. Adams is eighty years old (Pound is close to sixty). The point is not just to liven up Adams's talk but to situate his life, actions, and thought on a primal natural ground, and the sexual subtext gets us there.

The sounds of the words and their microrhetorical persuasions constitute the figure for that primal ground. "Fornication"—a bit archaic but jolted into the twentieth century with "hard on"—acoustically and thematically weaves through the text of the twentieth-century reader. Pound's source has "half a dozen, or half a score" or so yeomen "saying rebel," but Pound chooses "four." "Four" acoustically resonates with "fornication," and subliminally we register a rhyme between these two different kinds of danger, or threat of anarchy. Adams is a conservative republican, and he is "disgusted at their saying rebel." The prospect of being "forced" into war adds another rhyme. And the immediate transition to Adams's obsession with "frigates" resonates against that bass note and appears as a convincing, civilization-building sublimation.

Pound's editing Adams's words attributes a lyric language to Adams himself and gives him a kind of "unconscious," which sounds the Dionysian, sexual, anarchic bass note. Pound is steering Adams, by his word choice, clear of the despotic (demagogic) and the Dionysian extremes. He puts in Adams's mouth words that "argue"—subliminally, irrationally—against what Adams represents: hierarchy, morality, both private and public, and principles. And peace. ("Freedom" is the wild card.) Adams's "rectitude" is undermined with a lyric license, letting sounds do their separate subliminal work. Since the subliminal sound associations have a specifically sexual undertone—which is also politicized—the historical record of our "uncorrupted, uncontaminated unadulterated" republic is being adulterated by lyric devices. Such adulteration or corruption of the sources and records is, in the *Cantos, the* evil, a "diabolical" sign of "despotism" (canto 33). Yet the lyric language that adulterates the historical record makes the past audible and "useful" in the present.[18]

The threat of political anarchy sounded by the "four" yeomen and that of the unruly body registered in "fornication" rhyme, and they rhyme with the unruly body of words, a language that has its own "mind." In such a language, Pound's Adams coheres: his words argue for his political and ethical values, without repressing the anarchic bass note. Pound presents a leader who does not practice despotic control over *himself,* one who stands between "aristocratical and democratical fury" (1998, 417), against all forms of despotism.

The *f*-words return in a passage that would make little poetic sense (as to why it is here, that is) unless we keep fornication in mind and ear:

> I am a church-going animal
> but if I inculcate fidelity to the marriage bed

they will say it is from resentment against General Hamilton.
>   and I had *forgot* the story
of the *four* English girls General Pinckney was to hire
in England, two *for* me and two *for* himself.
>   The number of licensed houses
was soon reinstated, you may as well preach against rum to Indians.
>   (71: 415–16; emphases mine)

Pound's language works on the level of sounds, echoes, and acoustic memories and inscribes the lyric principle within the epic history of the revolution to render audible the irrepressible, uncontrollable, anarchic rule of the signifier.

"Fornication" organizes thematic clusters as well as sound movements; in fact the sonic network grounds the thematic network. The subject matter of the canto includes France, frigates, fidelity, fisheries, federal(ism), freedom, funds, forces, fighting, facts, fury, *fabulis* (fabulation). These key words, linked by their initial sound, organize the movement and subject matter of the canto as rhyming words would organize a different kind of poem. Sound links are deployed to argue the political import; they quite literally make for sense connections and subject rhymes. A second string runs along the related consonant *p*: Paul, parties, politics, principles, policy, papers, public, private, people, peace, print, prosody. The poem is "about" these sets of words. And in this kind of patterning, we hear Pound "rhyme" with Adams. For Adams's fears are Pound's fears. The conflict is between sounds and sense; yeoman and republican; body and mind; frigging and frigates; lyric sound and epic narrative sense. The balance of sides gives us representative government, civilization, and the *Cantos*, a sublimation of force to forms, fornication to frigates, "fucking" to "fac deum" (canto 39) that also always allows us to hear the sublimation, to *hear* the "sea" the frigates would rule.

The prevailing defense of the *Cantos* is that its epic openness and polyvocality save the poem from being a totalitarian text, which, in the standard reading, is aligned with "lyric closure." But we always only hear other voices as edited by Pound. My argument is that *lyric* language, which is "open" to a different history, keeps the poem ideologically fluid. The text has a kind of negative capability because it allows language to organize itself in a fashion that undoes tendentious messages. To motivate the signifier, the lyric listens to the words otherwise, and if we listen to words otherwise, we hear a different Adams—or, more accurately, different Adamses—than the one he would like to leave for the record:

> JOHN ADAMS
> FOR PEACE
> 1800

And we also hear different Pounds. Canto 74 provides a most remarkable instance of poetic procedures interfering with and countering Pound's political message:

> but poison, veleno
> in all the veins of the commonweal
> if on high, will flow downward all through them
> if on the forge at Predappio? sd/ old Upward (74: 457)

Predappio is the birthplace of Mussolini—a blacksmith's son, a man of the people. The anaphora "if on" leads us to expect a statement in some symmetrical relation to the preceding line, but the question mark disappoints our expectation. The switch to "Upward" (Allen) is micro-motivated by the "downward." The way poetic language moves among words by generating rhymes here seriously compromises, and may even negate, the presumed message—Mussolini as the antidote to the poison, the man who, working from the bottom up, will detoxify the body politic. The poetic procedure, the logic of rhyme, suggests otherwise: if the poison has seeped all the way down to the forge at Predappio, it may flow upward. And Allen "Upward"—"[']with a printing press by the Thames bank' / until I end my song / and shot himself'"—carries us back to London and Eliot and most poignantly registers Pound's dejection in *his* wasteland. Such moments in the *Cantos* convey emotional truths sounded by the medium itself.

Canto 71 ends with lines in Greek script, preceded by a passage on James Otis:

> Joseph Hawley, Otis, Sam Adams, Hancock
> add Jay, without knowing their actions
> you know not what made us our revolution
>   magis decora poeticis fabulis
> Otis wrote on greek prosody
>   I published what he wrote on the latin
> His daughter told me he had burnt all his papers
>   in melancholia
> may be from that swat on the pow
>   From '74 dates neutrality
> I begged Otis to print it (the greek prosody)
> He said there were no greek types in America
> and if there were, were no typesetters cd/ use 'em. (420)[19]

Partisan control of the newspapers, restricting the printing and distribution of historical documents, has been Adams's concern throughout the canto. Here we have a different kind of history and knowledge in danger of "blackout." The difficulty of printing nonpartisan writing and the impossibility of printing a treatise on Greek prosody "rhyme." Prosody is a technical matter, not a matter of poetic myth. Thus saving the historical and technical knowledge from "blackout" rhyme. And they rhyme in the person and "actions" of Otis. He is one of the "Saints," a founding father who also has a knowledge of Greek and Latin prosody. At once an active agent in history and a "man with an education," he bridges the political and poetic values.

His prominence here, however, owes just as much to the letters of his name, "Otis," as to the values he represents. "Otis" offers one instance of how sounds and letters also organize broad intercanto movements. It acoustically resonates or rhymes with Pound's "alias"—*Ou tis*, no man, which is Odysseus's alias. The link between Otis and Odysseus later becomes explicit:

> many men's mannirs videt et urbes πολῶμετιισ
> ce rusé personnage, Otis,   so Nausikaa
> took down the washing or at least went to see that the
> maids didn't slack. (78: 502)

OU TIS does a great deal of organizational, architectural, work in the poem, especially in linking the Pisan Cantos to the earlier cantos, where "no man" recurs regularly in various senses. As the poem that would "include history" gets included in history in the Pisan Cantos, Pound becomes "no man" with the loss of his voice. The audibility of "Ezra Pound," the constitutional right of the citizen, has been reft from him: "free speech without free radio speech is as zero" (74: 446). As his inscription of "Ezra" in "as zero" confirms, he has become a cypher, an 0 without a mouth; he has been silenced:

> and Rouse found they spoke of Elias
> in telling the tales of Odysseus   OY TIΣ
>   OY TIΣ
>
> "I am noman, my name is noman"
> but Wanjina is, shall we say, Ouan Jin
> or the man with an education
> and whose mouth was removed by his father
> because he made too many *things*
> whereby cluttered the bushman's baggage (446–47)

The passage weaves a series of metamorphoses. First, there is an oral tradition, where names change and characters blend into each other as different traditions come into contact and are assimilated. "Sagetrieb, or the / oral tradition" (89: 617) is metamorphic; it remembers and "forgets." As an example of Sagetrieb, "the reality of what is held in the general mind," Pound cites: "Dr Rouse found his Aegean sailors still telling yarns from the Odyssey though time had worn out Odysseus' name, down through O'ysseus, already latin Ulysses, to current Elias, identified with the prophet" (1970, 79). There are also changes brought about by writing—from Hebrew Elijah to Greek Elias in the New Testament. The prophet Elijah had authority or credit: "The word of the Lord," in Elijah's "mouth[,] is truth" (1 Kings 17:24); truth has to do with whose mouth speaks it. In the New Testament (Matt. 17:3; Luke 9:30, 33), there are stories of Elias talking to Christ on the Mount, the scene of the Transfiguration, and of Christ calling to Elias on the Cross (bystanders mishear his "Eli Eli").[20] But Odysseus's "OY TIΣ" is *a lie*, an *alias* used to trick Kyklops: "I was filled with laughter / to see how like a charm the name deceived them" (Homer 1998, 157). OY TIΣ, repeated in Pound's text, stands for the name of the writer (445, 446). The tradition, with its lies and mistakes, carries the truth, and the true "name" of the writer without a voice is "noman."

If we remember the *Cantos'* history and see and hear Itys, 'Tis, Ytis in "OY TIΣ," we can hear the silencing of the tongue and see how Pound rhymes his violation with other silenced figures. Hence the figure of Wanjina, who spoke and "created the named," for which his "mouth was removed by his father." Pound proceeds from Wanjina to Ouan Jin by letter affinity. With the conflation of the two figures ("Ouan Jin spoke and thereby created"), Pound presents the silencing of "the man with an education" into noman: "and so his mouth was removed / as you will find it removed in his pictures / in principio verbum." Ouan Jin's silencing rhymes with the crucifixion of the Word, as Wanjina's "pictures" lead directly to "in principio verbum." "In the beginning was the Word" (John 1:1), and "the word was God." The following line gives "verbum perfectum: sinceritas."[21] The verbum perfectum is also the "consummation" of Christ on the Cross: "Est Consummatum" (74: 452)—"It is finished." The Word is perfected, consummated, and silenced: he "gave up the ghost" (John 19:30).

This passage about silencing is surrounded by references to oral forms and traditions, tales and dialects in the "air." The prisoner quoted—"if we weren't dumb, we wouldn't be here"—speaks for the poet as well:

> the voiceless with bumm drum and banners,
>   and the ideogram of the guard roosts (74: 448)

The "4 giants at the 4 corners" (449) of the camp would make an ideogram that would look like 口, the sign for mouth (77: 496). On page 450, OY TIΣ gets an ideogram— 莫 —meaning "not to be." This is a silent sign, a picture we can't even attempt to voice; it marks silence. And Pound reads the ideogram pictorially, as representing the sun with vegetation above and below. He reads the vegetation under the sun as a man figure and comes up with: "a man on whom the sun has gone down." "Mouth, is the sun that is god's mouth" (77: 486), and the son is the god's word.[22] A man whose mouth has been removed is a man on whom the sun has gone down. He is a text in a dead language. He has "given up the ghost." And the Chinese ideogram confirms that silencing by its very silence.

In the Pisan Cantos, Pound turns to individuated voices and speech sounds:[23] word-of-mouth language in use, both remembered and heard in "the life of the D.T.C. passing OUTSIDE the scheme," organizes the textual movement.[24] He turns

to write dialog because there is
  no one to converse with (80: 519)[25]

Canto 81, for example, calls on memory, in an homage to what has carved a
trace in the mind and *ear*. This is a historical, literary, and personal memory
of sounds, voices, accents and inflections. The canto opens:

Zeus lies in Ceres' bosom
Taishan is attended of loves
    under Cythera, before sunrise
and he said: "Hay aqui mucho catolicismo—(sounded catoli*th*ismo)
  y muy poco reliHion"
and he said: "Y creo que los reyes desaparecen"
(Kings will, I think, disappear)
That was Padre José Elizondo
    in 1906 and in 1917
or about 1917
  and Dolores said: "Come pan, niño," eat bread, me lad (81: 537)

The speaker is borne back to 1906 by a word—one of his mantras, Cythera—
that activates the memory trace of a voice, marked by its distinctive pronunciation. When the voice gets a name, "Padre José Elizondo," that, too, makes
aural sense, because now our memory also holds "Zeus lies in Ceres' bosom."
Sound traces replace a plot and make for convincing *sequences* of lines.

  The personal and historical memories of Spain and the Spanish Civil War
that follow are organized by the word "said" and its variants—which is the case
in many Pisan cantos. After the initial two "and he said's," we have "and Dolores said"; "and later Bowers wrote"; "they said"; "Basil says"; "Possum observed"; "said old André Spire"; "said John Adams"; "as Jo Bard says"; "said
Henry Mencken"; Santayana "said"; "And George Horace said"; and "George
was a-tellin'." "Talking" and "speaking" also appear in the content of the "said"
material, and there are a number of quoted lines, implicitly "said" words,
though not introduced with "said"—the innkeeper's speech, the Spanish lines,
the words of "Mr Edwards," and so on. Up to the "libretto," no other verb is
repeated, and there are fewer verbs altogether—if we exclude the copulas—
than the number of "said's." What ties the passage together is not what people
say but that they say things—that they are in conversation.

  Language is the focus. The innkeeper's "We call *all* foreigners frenchies"
(538) prepares the way for a consideration of language and national character:

(To break the pentameter, that was the first heave).
or as Jo Bard says: they never speak to each other,
if it is baker and concierge visibly
  it is La Rouchefoucauld and de Maintenon audibly.
"Te cavero le budella"

> "La corata a te"
> In less than a geological epoch
>   said Henry Mencken
> "Some cook, some do not cook
>   some things cannot be altered" (538)

The pentameter has to go because some cook and some do not cook; people speak differently, in different rhythms. There are personal as well as language-specific differences. What cannot be altered are the sensibilities of individuals, languages, and languages within languages. So we immediately move back to Pisa, to "Mr. Edwards" who built Pound his writing table:

> What counts is the cultural level,
>   thank Benin for this table ex packing box
>   "doan yu tell no one I made it"
>   from a mask as fine as any in Frankfurt
> "It'll get you offn th' groun"
>   Light as the branch of Kuanon
> And at first disappointed with shoddy
> the bare ram-shackle quais, but then saw the
> high buggy wheels
>   and was reconciled,
> George Santayana arriving at the port of Boston
> and kept to the end of his life that faint *thethear*
> of the Spaniard
>   as a grace quasi imperceptible
> as did Muss the *v* for *u* of Romagna (539)

What enables the transition from Mr. Edwards to Santayana is individuating speech, and Santayana takes us back to the beginning of the canto and the Padre. The Padre, Mr. Edwards, Santayana, and "Muss" are linked not by what they "signify," some thought or value they hold in common, but by their distinguishing marks of speech. They share the "grace" of an audible, individuating difference of speech that carves a memory trace in the ear. And what makes Pound's text readable and often compelling is the way it keeps carving its sound trace in memory. The *Cantos* would not be readable if it did not establish some memory paths to replace the traditional means of coherence it gives up; it would not be a poem if its paths addressed only the faculties that handle subject rhymes.

Pound then remembers George Horace Lorimer's and his father's conversation—their American accents. Names continue to play into sounds and furnish literal links to get us to *George Horace Lori*mer from *Horace Cole* and *George* Santayana. While the American accents of George Horace and "my ole man" join the varieties of "languages" that justify breaking the pentameter, they work in a different emotional register. These voices that recall Pound's childhood are in his mother tongue, American.[26] And that particular memory calls forth the "AOI!":

> and my ole man went on hoein' corn
>   while George was a-tellin' him,
> come across a vacant lot
>   where you'd occasionally see a wild rabbit
> or mebbe only a loose one
>   AOI!
>   a leaf in the current (539)

The "AOI" is a poetic "swoon." A "word" of uncertain meaning, it is at once a personal cry of loss and pain, a generic Dionysian cry, and an allusion to *The Song of Roland*.[27] The sound of the lyric "I" is both Pound's and not Pound's. It sounds the birth of poetry in a Dionysian cry: an "I" is lost and found and lost again in "AOI," a breakdown of articulate language *and* the sound of the birth of the "I" in poetic language, which translates and transliterates that cry. "AOI" shatters and reinstitutes the histrion-poet and leads immediately to a restitution of poetic order and meter:

> Yet
> Ere the season died a-cold
> Borne upon a zephyr's shoulder
> I rose through the aureate sky

This stanza, with its dominant /z/ sounds, echoes the opening of the canto, but we now proceed to hear different poets' rhythms and charms, as distinct as the accents of different speakers. Yet the signature "Ezra Pound" is encrypted in both passages. Also remarkable is the inscription of "Pound" in the climactic passage, the lines that begin with "Pull down thy vanity." "Pull down," repeated ten times in twenty-one lines, has all the letters and phonemes of "Pound." Pound signs the imperative to "pull down" with his own name, both affirming humility and reaffirming his power; poems made of "mouthfuls of air" are not "vanity."

Pound's "I" is positioned at the intersection of different languages. "Io"—as "I" (Italian) and "hail" (Greek)—is a bilingual pun that recurs with regularity throughout the cantos. An "I" is one who "hails," who speaks and addresses; it is between two persons—an I and you—and between two languages. It is a marker of discourse taking place: hear me. The "I" is also the interface of sound and letter, pronunciation and script, oral and textual presence. In the play of Ytis-Itys, for example, the *Y* and *I* are interchangeable: *Ityn*; *Ytis*. In canto 47, on the most primal ground of fertility religions, Pound also plays with letter shapes and sexualizes them: "By prong have I entered these hills" (47: 238).

The prong,[28] "I," the "plow," the "wing-print," the "forked shadow" of the martin's wings, the "forked boughs" are all Y-shapes. With these "I" enter. The difference between *Y* and *I* is in their shape: I enter the hill as a written mark, a *Y*, and "score" my "light" "notch."[29] "I" go back. The phonetic value of *y* (ancestor of *U* and *V*) becomes that of *i* in the medieval period, and in the modern period *y* is used exclusively for the semivowel and *i* for the vowel. But since we are back in the time of Adonis, the *Y* does more work: a you and an I—a *u* and an *i*—are forked; we make one letter. The Greek *y* represents the sound of *u*: upsilon. The Roman tailless *y* or *v* also represents a *u* sound (see Muss's speech charm). "I" enters the text as the unstable differentiation of several letters and sounds and their historically changing and linguistically specific distributions.

"I" also enters the text through aliases equally fluid: Odysseus, Ulysses, Elijah, Elias, Elios/Helios,[30] OY TIΣ, Otis, OU TIS, Ytis, Iyts, it is, 'tis, Io, Hail, Y, J,[31] Aye, eye, "AOI."[32] All this flagrantly violates the standard of precise naming that Pound's political and economic agenda calls for: words must be clearly defined and the currency must be stable in the public sphere. But "poetry is a centaur,"[33] and the lyric poet knows that the Apollonian language of the epic project also comprises a variety of bodily produced and processed events. *The Cantos are* the war between the two languages—the two faces of language—waged over Ezra.

And this conflict saves Pound's text from its ideological burden. The muchvaunted epic polyvocality of Pound still serves ideological closure: different good/bad men keep telling the same truths/lies. Dante and Aristotle, the Bible and Mussolini, and Ezra Pound all condemn usury, for example. But "Azure hath a canker by usura" (45: 230) punctures the referential surface, as "Ez Po" deflates the didact's "EZthority" (1971, 272, 291), and allows a glimpse of the "azure" in canto 45, whose language partakes of the same oppressive practices it condemns. The "Ezra" encrypted in the "azure"-"usura" makes light of the didact's project and forces us to attend to the letters of the words, so that we see how "azure," the color of earthly paradise, is sickened by its near-anagram.[34] At another level, we also hear a history, the sickening of a poem—and a poet— that began with the "Gods float in the azure air" (3: 11) to succumb to the "murrain" of USURA.

Pound's anagrammatic signature also complicates his use of Latin. In canto 45, the personified economic practice that defers life, serves death, and sets corpses at banquet has a name in a dead language: "USURA." The crushing power and weight of the Latin word and the device of personification align with the deadly power of the economic institutions. The Latin word is also an abstraction, ruling over the concrete good things designated in words with Anglo-Saxon roots: house, stone, wool, bread, wheat, live, sell, and so on. The oppressive weight of a personified force over persons, of the past over the present, and of Latin over English "rhyme." The defender of Latin—"Latin is sacred, grain is sacred" (1975, 317)—may be conflicted, and if we register the ambivalence at this level, we would have to change absolutely the way we read the *Cantos* and its "foreign" languages, its allusions and quotations. They remember, but they also mortgage the present.

In a different way, the Chinese ideograms, for example, are both an authoritative and a silent language. Ideograms have an undeniable material presence, but for the Western reader, they also represent a principle alien to the materiality of spoken language. They represent a disembodied materiality. Ideograms represent "right naming," and the Ching Ming ideogram is, for Pound, a kind of generic ideogram of Adamic language. For the non-Chinese reader, however, it is a purely visual language. Assuming we were as good as Gaudier Breszka in reading what the ideograms signify, we still would have no audial and muscular relationship to these signs. They represent a language purged of sounds, cleansed of the body and its vicissitudes—"hygienic" (1968a, 21) but silent. "I *need* ideogram," Pound writes, "I mean I need it in and for my own job, but I also need sound and phonetics. . . . When it comes to the question of transmitting from the East to the West, a great part of the Chinese sound is no use at all. We don't hear parts of it, and much of the rest is a hiss or a mumble" (1971, 347). The ideograms are emblems of stability: right naming, sincerity, unwobbling pivot, equity, and all kinds of order—seasonal, political, social, economic—are recurrent themes represented by specific, recurrent ideograms. They are immune to the wanton play of sounds and letters, the lyric language that exceeds right naming and makes for an excess interest without regard to justice or equity.[35]

"OU TIS" reappears in canto 89 in an economic context. Jefferson is speaking of ratios of gold and silver coins:

> Mr Hamilton set 15 to one, 15 silver to one gold,
> when in Spain, Portugal it was sixteen,
>   From Natchez and N'Yoleans: doubloons
> and to suppose metal will stay with us when the exporter
> can gain one buck on every 15 carried out . . .
> doubloons, guineas, half-Joes
>   and, to depart from the great senator's most
>   courteous language,
> 6 suspensions till 1819,
>   exclusion of foreign coin part of the system:
> a currency (foreign coin was) for which they paid tribute to
>   no one."
>   OU TIS (613–14)

This most interesting juncture of economics and Pound's alias brings up the question of foreign currencies. The passage recapitulates the earlier lines:

Use of foreign coin until 1819.
    Exception Spanish milled dollars,
every dealer occupied in exporting them,   page 446
their exclusion an unconstitutional fraud . . .
a currency of intrinsic value FOR WHICH
They paid interest to NOBODY

                                        page 446
                                        column two

        ("Thirty Years," Benton)
Is suppressed in favour of fluctuation,
    this country a thoroughfare.
    OBEUNT 1826, July 4. (88: 602–3)

Pound's source for the passage is Thomas Hart Benton, who denounces the exclusion of all foreign coins except Spanish after 1819 as "a fraud . . . upon the people of the States. The States had surrendered their power over the coinage to Congress; they made the surrender in language which clearly implied that their currency of foreign coins was to be continued to them; yet that currency is suppressed; a currency of intrinsic value, for which they paid interest to nobody, is suppressed; and a currency without intrinsic value, a currency of paper subject to every fluctuation, and for the supply of which corporate bodies receive interest, is substituted in its place." Benton adds, "Since the law took effect the United States had only been a thoroughfare for foreign coins to pass through."[36] This unconstitutional act betrays the principles of Adams and Jefferson; hence the obituary notice for the two men, who died hours apart on the same day, July 4, 1826.

Hamilton fixed the gold-silver ratio at 15 to 1, while Europe and South America held to 16 to 1; as a result, gold was drained out of the States.[37] The exclusion of solid money, for which the people paid interest to no one, was meant to establish an American currency, for which people would pay interest to "no one" in an entirely different sense of anonymous "corporate bodies." Pound's reiteration of "no one" as OU TIS inscribes his alias into this context,[38] and implicates him both in the fraud and in the resulting transatlantic trade. The change from a literal no one to a figurative "no one" is analogous to the change from a solid to a fluctuating currency. Pound's textual war between right naming and all kinds of paronomasias is embodied in this "no one / OU TIS."

The trade that turns "this country" into "a thoroughfare for foreign coins to pass through" both profits from transposing tokens of value to another context/ market, and—insofar as Hamilton's ratio reduced the value of the coin beneath its value as metal—rights a wrong by establishing equity between the token-coin and intrinsic value. So that, in a sense, the trade both creates its *ex nihil* value and at the same time affirms real value.

This moment in the *Cantos* is a "truce" in the conflict between right naming and the generation of excess value in an instance of their coincidence in practice. But that coincidence also aligns Pound's textual practice with that of currency traders. Pound's anxieties about his transatlantic textual trade are not new: they are already articulated in just these terms of a trade triangle in an early poem, "Portrait d'une Femme" of 1912. This "lady," like "this country," is a "thoroughfare for foreign coins to pass through":

> Your mind and you are our Sargasso Sea,
> London has swept about you this score years
> And bright ships left you this or that in fee:
> Ideas, old gossip, oddments of all things,
> Strange spars of knowledge and dimmed wares of price.
> Great minds have sought you—lacking someone else.
> You have been second always. (1976, 184)

The "lady" is a repository of what "seafarers" leave her in fee, and she is a medium that hands down or passes on what she has received:

> And now you pay one. Yes, you richly pay.
> You are a person of some interest, one comes to you
> And takes strange gain away.

"A tale or two," "gaudy, wonderful old work," "rare inlays" and such "strange" things are her "riches," her "great store"; "and yet / For all this sea-hoard of deciduous things,"

> No! there is nothing! In the whole and all,
> Nothing that's quite your own.
>   Yet this is you. (185)

This satiric portrait oddly rhymes with Pound's depiction of ecstatic poetic possession in "Histrion" (1908) as a process of "dissociation," of "borrowing" a personality in order to be an "I" and pass on the tradition:

> No man hath dared to write this thing as yet,
> And yet I know, how that the souls of all men great
> At times pass through us,
> And we are melted into them, and are not
> Save reflexions of their souls. (1976, 71)

The "I" that is the "midmost us" is a sphere of "molten gold," and "great men" or the "Masters of the Soul" "pass through us" and leave their stamp on "us"; they mint their coin on "us." Then they leave, and the possessed poet, thus initiated into a cult, passes on what he has received.

The transaction of the tradition over the poet's "midmost" I and the trade of cultural capital over the woman's body clearly rhyme. The inmost "I" is a histrion; "Yet this is you." Pound's literary anxieties in "Portrait d'une Femme" are figured as gender anxieties:[39] he is "no man" (ou tis) but only a medium for great men to pass through, leaving him the labor of reproducing and "resusci-tating" them. His position as a translator-transmitter-"anthologizer" of "old" tales feminizes him. Hence the overtures to the American father, Whitman, for a trade "pact" (1913). "We" share more than "deciduous things"; we share "one sap and one root": "Let there be commerce between us."

Pound's early anxieties about his textual practice of using other poets' capital to generate his own interest ramify through the *Cantos*—and beyond. The commerce that aligns him with traders and middlemen, a class of people he does not look kindly upon (see canto 33, for one example) also breeds another class of middlemen of annotators, commentators, critics, and so on to maintain the formidable Pound industry. These middlemen redistribute what Pound redistributes (in canto 33, for example, Adams, Jefferson, Marx, et al.) and gain the value created in that trade. Pound's practice creates a demand: such texts that *require* annotation create a market where they can be traded, specu-lated on, and accrue interest. He is not only a medium for exchange of curren-cies; that very exchange he hosts also renders him a commodity for further trade. Hence the economic obsession *and* the concurrent obsession with the material medium that alone can resist the economy of exchange. Only Diony-sus can stop "stock fast" those who would trade on the God's body. And it is the Dionysian language, the song in the *Cantos* that redeems Pound's cant and currency, for the pleasure of the body of the text does not meet a demand in the marketplace of ideas and politics.

Pound invokes Horace: " 'Magna pars mei,' says Horace, speaking of his own futurity, 'that in me which is greatest shall escape dissolution.' " And he contin-ues: "The *accurate* artist seems to leave not only his greater self, but beside it, upon the films of his art, some living print of the circumvolving man, his taste, his temper and his foible—of the things about which he felt it never worth his while to bother other people by speaking, *the things he forgot for some major interest*. . . . We find these not so much in the words—which anyone may read—but in the subtle joints of the craft, in the crannies perceptible only to the craftsman" (1968a, 88; the first italic is Pound's).[40] The "forgotten" I is the forgetfulness of an I who is subject to another will and lives *on the page*, in the art-articulation of the sounded and written shapes of the language. And, in the case of "the *accurate* artist," that I "escapes dissolution" in the very dissolution of the meanings of words, in the material body of the word that can look back at the "greater self" that, for a poet, is ultimately at its mercy. And if Pound escapes "dissolution," he will do so as an "*accurate* artist," as what survives, in Eliot's words, "the complete extinction of interest in the issues with which the poet was passionately concerned" (1979, 6). For, ultimately, the artist as artist is accountable only to his words. And we are accountable for our choice to hear and voice them or not.

NOTES

The chapter subtitle is Pound's prescription (1971, 321). Elsewhere, he remarks on "how little Dante needs NOTES. The general lay reader has been hypnotized for centuries by the critical apparatus of the *Commedia*" and "never got through to the essential fact that it is really THERE ON THE PAGE" (1968a, 208). The epigraph is from "The Serious Artist" (51). The rest of the paragraph reads: "And 'this part of the work' is by now 'technique.' That 'dry, dull, pedantic' technique, that all bad artists rail against. It is only a part of technique, it is rhythm, cadence, and the arrangement of sounds."

1. *The Cantos of Ezra Pound* (1998, 5). Subsequent references will be cited in the text by canto number followed by page number.

2. Stevens 1954, 345.

3. Jakobson describes "interior speech" as composed not of sounds "but their acoustic and motor images" (1978, 37). Silent reading and reproduction of others' speech is the same.

4. Greek and Latin are also "quiet" and play up English and its sound textures, rhythms, and spoken movement.

5. Qtd. in Cookson 1985, xxi.

6. So-shu is most likely Pound's invention; the argument wouldn't change even if he were a real figure; since there hasn't been anything Eastern in the poem so far, this figure is not part of any thematic logic at this point. Moore links the line to Homer: "The ghost of Homer sings. His words have the sound of the sea and the cadence of actual speech. *And So-shu churned in the sea, So-shu also*" (1987, 268). Pound admired Homer's "Para thina poluphloisboio thalasses: the turn of the wave and the scutter of receding pebbles. Years' work to get that" (1971, 274).

7. "Our kinship to the ox we have constantly thrust upon us; but beneath this is our kinship to the vital universe, to the tree and the living rock"; the music of words links us to this "germinal universe of wood alive, of stone alive" (Pound 1968b, 92).

8. Such orders stop the metamorphic process, or they lead to "bad" metamorphoses, as in the Hell Cantos; the dissolution of names accompany both kinds of metamorphoses.

9. Peter Makin, in his good discussion of Pound's metamorphoses in canto 2, points out that things can become other things only when they are so absolutely individuated and the gradations between different things so finely calibrated. The complex of every object-space-time is utterly specific; we witness an eternal process of never-to-be-repeated perceptions, fortuitous creations of a certain angle of light, time of day or season, perspective, mood, and the resonances of the words (1992, 80–84): "Black azure and hyaline, / glass wave over Tyro . . . / Glass-glint of wave in the tide-rips against sunlight, / pallor of Hesperus, / Grey peak of the wave, / wave, colour of grape's pulp" (2: 10); everything is itself and nothing is its self.

The same holds for the metamorphoses of sounds: sound fluctuations and variations affect the relationships of the words so that their nuances are specific to time and place in the sound texture of a passage. The text presents an Apollonian individuation and clarity on Dionysian grounds; we see/hear a trembling appearance/disappearance.

10. Additionally, they may ground the "rhyme" of the Homeric compounds and Anglo-Saxon kennings of the first canto in a process of metamorphic perception.

11. Healey 1998, 201, 230. Cadmus also founded Thebes, and cities—Troy and Ecbatan—are among the canto's concerns.

12. Terrell translates Pindar's line as "Hymns that are lords of the lyre" and notes that it is about the "power of poetry and recorded words" (1980, 11).

13. See the "fur-hood," the "furred tail upon nothingness," the "lynx-purr," the "fur brushing my knee-skin," and so on. Canto 22 plays a different game with "fur." The audial memory calls a link to Dionysus, who is very much behind this canto on the unenforceability of laws: the words allow leeways—for better or for worse. The canto ends by invoking a thirteenth-century Florentine ban on fur:

> And the Judge says: Well, anyway, you're not allowed ermine.
> "Ermine?" the girl says, "Not ermine, that ain't,
> " 'At's lattittzo."
> And the judge says: And just what is a lattittzo?
> And the girl says:
>
> > "It'z a animal."
>
> Signori, *you* go and enforce it. (22: 106)

14. This is the same strategy used in canto 2, where the Ovidian passage seems to be called up to explain a naviform rock—a perception of a likeness. Does the perception of a likeness between the shape of a rock and a ship generate a story to "explain" it, or do we perceive a likeness because we have heard the story? Has the story written the landscape or the other way around? The same question can be asked about the wine-red algae. Language and landscape blur as the words focus observed phenomena, writing texts and landscape onto each other.

15. There is also a sense here of Pound swallowing up these languages and stories. Pound writes in a letter to Katue Kitasono: "English has conquered vast territories by absorbing other tongues, that is to say, it has poached most Latin roots and has variants on them handy for use where French and even Italian have shown less flexibility. It has taken in lashin's of Greek, swallowed Mediaeval French, while keeping its solid Anglo-Saxon basis. It then petrified in the tight little island, but American seems to be getting into Tokio. Question of whether you want to 'preserve' Japanese in test tubes or swallow the American vocabulary is for you to decide. _/_/" (1971, 347). In turn, American has to swallow the radio: "I was the last survivin' monolith who did not have a bloody radio in the 'ome. However, like the subjects of sacred painting as Mr. Cohen said: 'Vot I say iss, we got to svallow 'em, vot I say iss, ve got to swallow 'em.' Or be boa-constricted" (343).

16. Against this "primal" backdrop of bodily sounds, their emergence into words and measuring into verse, the living speech attributed to Circe is absolutely individuated and current. "Discuss this in bed said the lady": "Been to hell in a boat yet?" Or "I think you must be Odysseus. . . . / feel better when you have eaten. . . . / Always with your mind on the past. . . ." This sounds the siren call of American, sexier than all the dead languages. Also currently audible is "fucking" (Anglo-Saxon): its shock value marks a historical moment.

17. All sources cited are from Terrell 1980, vol. 1. Such decontextualizing quotation is the rule throughout the *Cantos*. In canto 33, for example, Pound's elliptical quoting practice—and ellipsis is the dominant punctuation mark in this canto that opens with ellipsis, yet actually denounces the evils of withholding information from the public—leaves the reader clueless, since Pound omits the subjects of the statements he quotes from Adams, Marx, Jefferson, et al. The punctuation marks the suppression of specific contexts so that certain issues are put on the agenda for the reader as issues that need to be rethought at present. So here ellipses keep the topics open for discussion—the topics of child labor, the inferior species of men capitalism breeds, aristocracy, despotism, etc. And these topics are put on the table by a series of related words: commissary, commiseration, commissar, commercial, commerce, and the subliminal echoes of "communism" and "community" that they conjure.

18. For the past is not a set of "anesthetized" data; the poet, like the archeologist Leo Frobenius whom Pound admires, "goes not only into the past and forgotten life, but points to tomorrow's water supply" (1970, 57). The needs of the present guide how past knowledge is to be distributed for use.

19. "Magis decora poeticis fabulis" (more suitable to poetic myths) is from Livy's histories: *Ab Urbe Condita* (*From the Founding of the City*) (Terrell 1980).

20. "And about the ninth hour, Jesus cried with a loud voice, saying, Eli, Eli, la' ma sa-baeh'tha-ni? that is to say, My God, my God, why hast thou forsaken me?" (Matt. 27:46). In Mark 15:34, he calls "Eloi, Eloi."

21. Also see 76: 474: "the word is made / perfect" is followed by the ideogram Pound translates as "sinceritas": "The precise definition of the word, pictorially the sun's lance coming to rest on the precise spot verbally" (Cookson 1985, 78). "Perfect or focus" is the definition he gives on p. 496 for the right half of the compound.

22. In canto 51, Pound has:

SHINES
in the mind of heaven God
who made it
more than the sun
in our eye. (51: 250)

God's mouth, the sun, speaks to our eye. Pound may be alluding to Psalm 19 in this figure:

The heavens declare the glory of God; and the firmament showeth his handiwork.
Day unto day uttereth speech, and night unto night showeth knowledge.
There is no speech nor language, where their voice is not heard. (Ps. 19:13)

Or he may have in mind an ideogrammic connection between the signs for dawn, mouth, and sun (see pp. 496, 486, 676).

The idea of the sun as god's mouth means the mouth is light, a body-spirit, a neoplatonic pneumatic spirit. "All things that are are lights" (74: 449). Fire is also associated with the mouth. Following "Est consummatum," we get a story:

but in Tangier I saw from dead straw ignition
    From a snake bite
  fire came to the straw

from the fakir blowing
foul straw and an arm-long snake
that bit the tongue of the fakir making small holes
   and from the blood of the holes
   came fire when he stuffed the straw into his mouth (74: 452)

And Dante's tongue of fire ("staria senza piu scosse") later invoked (455) recalls the fakir story.

23. and the very *very* aged Snow created considerable
   hilarity quoting the φαινε-τ-τ-τ-τττ-αι μοι
   in reply to *l'aer tremare*
     beauty is difficult
   But on the other hand the President of Magdalen
   (rhyming dawdlin') said there were
   too many words in "The Hound of Heaven"
     a modddun opohem he had read
   and there was no doubt that the dons lived well
           in the kawledg (464–65)

What possible interest could all this have except the words themselves that make Pound audible.

24. Qtd. in Cookson 1985, xx.

25. Throughout the Pisan Cantos, there is much reminiscing about conversation "and the idea that CONversation. . . . . . / should not utterly wither" (82: 544).

26. Pound specifies American as a distinct language (1971, 322).

27. The root of "ode" is the Greek "**aoi**de," song. The Indo-European root is "wed," to speak. This connection might be at work here, since Pound will directly proceed to his homage to the lyric tradition.

28. From ME: a forked instrument.

29. A notch is a V-shaped cut. See Graves on early alphabets.

30. See "ηλιοσ, αλιοσ, αλιοσ" [helios, alios, alios] (23: 107).

31. Pound's handwritten I is shaped like a J tilted left (see, for example, 1976, 317, 319). He also substitutes j for i, as in "jambic" (1971, 80). J, the shape of iota, sounded i and looked like an undotted i. In Roman, it represented the sound of i or y; capital I is used in Italica. Interestingly, the letter P, sounded p, was named pe, meaning mouth. The Phoenician and early Greek forms look like inverted J's (see the *American Heritage Dictionary*). Given his interest in Chinese writing, Pound would be sensitive to the shapes of the English letters that go back to the Phoenician alphabet and have names and shapes that often seem mimetic.

32. And Ouan Jin, Wanjina (74: 446); I Yin, Y Yin (85: 563, 566, 591); i jin (one man [89: 620]). In general, Pound takes great liberties with names, freely playing with their sounds and letters.

33. "Poetry is a centaur. The thinking word-arranging, clarifying faculty must move and leap with the energizing, sentient, musical faculties. It is precisely the difficulty of this amphibious existence that keeps down the census record of good poets" (1968a, 52).

34. Dante's usurers wear purses with colored emblems around their necks; azure ("azzuro"; "azzura") appears on two of these emblems (*Inferno*, 17: 59, 64). A note says

that the emblems on the purses are "coats of arms of families notorious for their usury" (348). Pound's source for the usura-azure might be Dante, who does not use "usura" in this passage. But the inscription of "Ezra" in these two words distinguishes Pound's play and suggests his ambivalence about his practice.

35. The visual elements in the *Cantos* signal silence and control; the frame containing John Adams, the ideograms, the layered imperial presence of the Japanese text in canto 49 (English transliteration over Japanese over Chinese) all signify silencing.

36. Quoted in Wilhelm 1977, 69–70.

37. This was part of Hamilton's plan. Terrell writes: "Benton showed Hamilton's plan was the eventual elimination of foreign coins which would be replaced by American currency. Since that didn't happen, and the law to exclude foreign coins didn't work, Congress suspended it for three years. Six further three-year suspensions became necessary and they didn't end until 1819" (1980, 519). The effect of the law was to reduce the value of Spanish coinage below its value as metal (506).

38. Terrell reiterates that OU TIS is "no one" and adds: "Used here as an intensive" (1980, 519). But surely a phrase that has gathered such wide-ranging associations throughout the *Cantos* is doing more work here. The fact that Terrell adds this note itself amounts to an admission that its appearance here needs explaining.

39. And Pound's name is inscripted into this title.

40. Moore, for one example, reads at this micro-level:

And there is discovery in the staccato sound of the conclusion to Canto XXX, in the patterning of the 'y' in 'thirty' on the 'i' in *mori*:

Il Papa Mori

Explicit canto
XXX
(1987, 275)

We could add that the X-Ex link seals the death both visually and audially—we would have to say "thirty," while we visually read Ex Ex Ex. Conversely, Il is relatively silenced because it looks numerical in this context.

Pound certainly read at the level of letters and syllables, as the most cursory glance over his writings on poetry and his letters to poets shows. See 1971, 326–27, for one example.

Chapter 8

※

ANNE SEXTON, "THE TYPO"

Who me? Sailing around like crazy in
LANGUAGE whatever it is and then brought up
short by reality (what is it, really?)
—*Anne Sexton*

I'm everything!!! Hysteric, manic, depressed,
schitz (spellomg spelling) etc.
—*Anne Sexton*

ANNE SEXTON WROTE "confessional" poems about "well, this human being [who] lived from 1928 to whenever, and . . . what she had to say about her life" (1985, 135). The relationship between the historically specific "human being," the maker of the poems, and the "I" in the poems is the question she keeps raising, and it is the question I want to pick up: who exactly is the "I" in the poem and how is it produced? This difficult question is additionally complicated in her case, for her psychological disorder, which was diagnosed as hysteria,[1] affects not only the life of the "human being" but the poetic configuration of the autobiographical subject, the subject in language, and the formally generated "I" of the lyric.

"When I was first sick I was thrilled (a language word translate, relieved) to get into the Nut House," Sexton writes about her initial hospitalization: "At first, of course, I was just scared and crying and very quiet (who me!) but then I found this girl (very crazy of course) (like me I guess) who talked language. What a relief! I mean, well . . . someone!" Then she finds that Doctor Orne, her psychiatrist, "talked language." Her husband, she writes, "has never once understood one word of language. . . . I don't know who else does. I don't use it with everyone" (1977, 244–45). "I *think* a different language than I must practice speaking" to the family and the children.[2] The mentally ill and the therapist "talk language." And, she later finds out, so did the poets in the workshop: in the writing class, as in the hospital, "I felt I belonged somewhere," Sexton says, felt "more real, sane" (1976, 403). Diane Middlebrook suggests that therapy and poetry are "language" because they work with metaphoric substitutions. The "talking cure" taught her, she writes, that "the symptoms of her mental illness were like metaphors" (DM, 64).

But was this the "language" she and the other crazy girl were talking? One association Sexton herself makes between what she calls "language" and poetry is that of rhyme. When she speaks of her "fear of psychotic," the doctor asks, "And this rhyming that you keep doing?" "I know it's silly," she answers, "And I keep laughing. I can't seem to feel anything but silly. I keep talking LAN-GUAGE." She writes of "a constant rhyming inside my head" and about talking to another patient: "We laugh for ten minutes at a group of rhymes" (DM, 225). "Language," she writes, "has nothing to do with rational thought. . . . I think language is beautiful. I even think insanity is beautiful (surely the root of language), except that it is painful" (1977, 245). Thorazine, she writes, "is supposed to make the rhymer go away" (DM, 226). And so would the talking cure. Both would "cure" the poet.

Thus there seem to be two kinds of "language," the language of illness and that of the cure. While rhyming language links to insanity, metaphoric language is the language of therapy, where words are "unreal" insofar as they "mean" something other than what they are in their materiality. Poetry comprises both languages, but at the level of the word, therapeutic discourse and poetic language are essentially at odds. The curative project would stabilize the subject and her story-history, while the poetic project works against reference and stability at the level of the signifier. Sexton's confessional work is shaped by the conflict between the therapeutic project of ego stabilization and the poetic practice that destabilizes an ego; her poetry registers the conflicting claims of the referential and material axes of language on the patient-poet.

What attracts Sexton to poetry initially is its rhyming language. When Dr. Orne suggests that she try writing about her therapy, Sexton could have chosen prose, which would have been more effective in terms of therapy. Later, in 1959, she reports "My psychiatrist wants me to write short stories as you have to use more ego in order to write them"; "I told him to get the hell out of my writing life!" (1977, 95, 97). Sexton chose poetry and began by following formal rules such as rhyme schemes. "I found some order there," as she later puts it (1981, 35). What draws her to poetry is its formality, not the motive of self-expression or self-understanding for ego stabilization but an impersonal order for patterning the surfaces, the nonsignifying components of the words. Hearing I. A. Richards describe various sonnet forms on TV, her repeated story goes, she decided she could write one. Poetic forms offer rules, based on the shape of the linguistic code, to shape the materials of the code. They both allow for the audibility of the materials of language and sanitize the metastases of the kinds of literal and phonemic substitutions and condensations that operate in the primary process of mental illness. She remarks "there are no guards in prose" (DM, 146). Unlike prose, poetry provides formal "guards" and thus can accommodate the rhymer "inside" her head.

The confessional "I" of the poems, the speaking subject of the "narrative" of "Anne Sexton," is the ego, which provides the rubric of a subject matter, a "conscious meaning," while the "unconscious" supplies the imagery.[3] But the confessional I who speaks in the poems can lie: "I've heard psychiatrists say, 'See, you've forgiven your father. There it is in your poem.' But I haven't forgiven my father. I just wrote that I did" (1974, 21–22). Similarly, the I in the office can also lie: she admits to producing stories for the doctor on the spot.[4] Sexton is clear about her situation: "I suspect that I have no self so I produce a different one for different people" (DM, 62). Both I's are histrionic I's, acting for different audiences on different stages, and in both cases, she is selling words, whether she is "selling poetry" or has "words for sale" for "you, Dr. Y.": "Words that have been hoarded up, / waiting for the pleasure act of coming out" (1981, 562).

And both productions aim for the doctor: "Now I see it!," she writes Dr. Orne, "I existed to mean something to you, to matter to you and then to belong to you. I made up a whole person, a poet, Anne Sexton, who would be worth something to you. . . . All those people who write to me and believe in me. God! I don't even exist" (DM, 201). Middlebrook comments on Sexton's understanding that "'poet' is an identity extrapolated from a published poem. The poem's 'I' is real because it has become visible in the medium of print and circulated among those who are positioned to recognize it. . . . Like other forms of currency, the first-person pronoun has a value established in a cultural marketplace" (DM, 82–83). She was good at stage managing this professional "I," "Anne Sexton," but was clear about its status: "Think I am a poet? false— someone else writes—I am a person selling poetry" (DM, 62). She is selling the figure of an "I." "I am an actress in my own autobiographical play," she says (1976, 422); I am acting out a text writing "me." And at the same time that Sexton was producing poems for Dr. Orne, she was reading up on psychiatric literature and producing a patient for him: "I had been with you only a week when I got all the books on psychiatry. I read them to try to find out what kind of patient to be" (DM, 53). If symptom production is a language, one can learn its rules and manipulate it to produce a patient, a self for the father-doctor, the "Father Inc."[5] And, in turn, poetic mentors can slip into the same position—of "Father Inc." She writes Snodgrass, "I've got you all mixed up in my mind with father-psychiatrist and god like folk" (1977, 74).

The rhymer "I," though, would seem to be distinct, outside this economy of "lies," more subject to language than a subject of stories that the ego produces. Sexton repeatedly speaks of the truth accessed through forms, and Maxine Kumin writes that Sexton believed "the hardest truths would come to light if they were made to fit a stanzaic pattern, a rhyme scheme, a prevailing meter" (1981, xxv). Middlebrook's alignment of rhymes, the markers of the formal order, with the work of the ego—"Another mode of ego was supplied by the end rhymes or half-rhymes . . . and the internal rhymes" (180)—misreads the work of rhyme. Sexton herself correctly aligns form with the superego: form "had worked as a kind of superego for me" (1976, 409).[6] Superego and the unconscious communicate, and the ego is not privy to that conversation.[7] In another interview, she says: "I like double rhyme. Driving once into Boston, I suddenly thought that 'cancer' rhymes with 'answer.' And so I wrote some lines. They are macabre, and yet it's an honest way of saying it. It makes it more real" (1974, 22). The I who operates in this way is not the ego, and form ensures that microrhetorical verbal and intraverbal processes are in play, so that this other, linguistic truth, which is the truth of verbal *surfaces*, may be audible. Such language is "more real" and "honest" because it is outside the referential economy. At this level words cannot lie because they cannot tell the "truth."

Sexton remarks that she would rather deal with the subject of madness in form than in free verse; in *Bedlam*, she points out, she felt she could "express" herself "better"—express, that is, the "experience of madness" better—in forms.[8] For forms sound another kind of "madness" that is not private, and they access another truth, which the hysteric and the poet both know: there is no core "I." At the same time that they provide "guards" for the rhymer "inside" her "head," forms also keep in view the linguistic and material construction of the "I" in the poems. The "I" that belongs to the code keeps belying the confessional I, the ego; the medium that makes the confessional I audible also makes audible what renders it a lie. The rhymer "I" feels more "real" because it is in touch with the truth of the subject, while the confessional I is a "fake," a "con." "The clang words are Mine," she insists, "and not from a textbook or a guess. fished them up out of my own machine even!" (DM, 225).

Rhymes, for Sexton, link to other kinds of wordplays such as homophones, puns, and anagrams, all devices that defy rational thought, metaphoric logic, and the control of the ego. She plays with these devices, and the "rat's star" palindrome that fascinated her, in a twelve-line uncollected poem titled "An Obsessive Combination of Ontological Inscape, Trickery and Love."[9] "Busy with an idea for a code," she threads her way from *write* to *right*, *routes*, *tiers*, *tries*, *rites*, *RATS*, which "amazingly and funnily become *STAR*," *stare*, and *store*, "as if it were a *star* / I touched and a miracle I really *wrote*" (emphases mine). And she defends to Dr. Orne the truths encrypted in anagrams, puns, and homophones: "If I write RATS and discover that rats reads STAR backwards, and amazingly STAR is wonderful and good because I found it in rats, then is the star untrue?" (DM, 82). What speaks to her and gives her hope is the power of the code to counter reference—the "anagrams," the "arts" that can right rats into star. And the star has to be "true"—or else, she is a rat, trapped in referential language and its rational norm. "Of course," she continues her letter to Dr. Orne: "I KNOW that words are just a counting game, I know this until the words start to arrange themselves and write something better than *I* would ever know" (DM, 82). When the words arrange themselves without her conscious control, they are more than counters. Their "I" is outside the economy that governs referential language and metaphoric thinking. It is outside the economy of the confessional poet on stage and the patient in the office, where one is paid for her words, and the other pays to be heard.[10]

"Said the Poet to the Analyst" defends the poet's literal, surface language—the language of the "real me"—against the metaphoric, interpretive language of analysis:

> My business is words. Words are like labels,
> or coins, or better, like swarming bees.
> I confess I am only broken by the sources of things;
> as if words were counted like dead bees in the attic,
> unbuckled from their yellow eyes and their dry wings.
> I must always forget how one word is able to pick
> out another, to manner another, until I have got
> something I might have said . . .
> but did not. (1981, 12)

The opening lines move words away from reference—from static "labels" with clear designations, to "coins" or counters in a currency, to "swarming bees." The poet's words are not to be "counted like dead bees" or as currency: they are moving, buzzing, communicating with each other by a different code in their hive. They have their own system, which poses a threat to the ego, as a swarm of bees would to the person. To the analyst, words are like money, symbols, and she gives him dreams and symbols and the money to "interpret" them. As she writes elsewhere, "Who listens to dreams? Only symbols for something— / like money for the analyst" (1981, 108). But the poet's words are not "symbols for something." Though necessarily once removed from the "swarm" of "bees," though they mean, they still have the feel of coins in the hand. In the second stanza, Sexton deploys a complex figural language to argue the material reality and physical affect of words. Poetic language works like the "lucky screen": you see three bells, but your hands feel "funny and ridiculous," "crowded" with real coins.[11]

The poet and the analyst have different relations to language. The analyst's interest is in sources and hidden meanings, how words may mean something other than what they say, or how memories might screen other memories. He is interested in uncovering sources, in substitutions along the paradigmatic-metaphoric axis, whereas the poet is "broken by the sources of things." Ultimately, the therapist's is a narrativizing project:

> I move my thin legs into your office
> and we work over the cadaver of my soul.
> We make a stage set out of my past
> and stuff painted puppets into it.
> We make a bridge toward my future
> and I cry to you: I will be steel! (1981, 567)

"We" construct a narrative subject, a "steel" bridge spanning the "past" and a "future," and such a project falls under the aegis of "Father Inc."—"that little

Freud shoveling dirt in the cellar, / that Mr. Man, Mr. Cellar Mann, brown as / old blood" (569). She is to comply, make up a story, invent "sources" and memories, and believe that that is who she is.

The lyric poet's procedure is the opposite: she knows but "must" forget the words' automatisms,[12] so that they might "pick out" and "manner" one another and yield something she might have said but did not—until she is said by the words that formulate what *she* "might" have said. Here words are prior to symbolic content, not the other way around: "All I am is the trick of words writing themselves" (DM, 82). The "real" me is a trick of words, audible when *my* meaning is drained away. "Manner" links this "trick" to form, but it still seems an odd word choice here, since it is not even a verb, until we see its "trick": it houses "anne." The poet's "trick" is a lyric procedure and "anne" is said by the words I, Anne Sexton, did not say. The "real me" lives in words, not in what words mean; it lives in what letters and words do and show, not in what they hide.[13]

Words in poetry are sounds, shapes, letters, feelings, sensations. While the analyst in therapy would establish the dominanace of the paradigmatic axis and deal with the relations of signifier-signified and vehicle-tenor, the poet also operates on the syntagmatic signifier-signifier axis. Here, the poet's activity aligns with symptom production—as opposed to the therapeutic, narrative project of "trauma production" to "explain" the symptoms—proceeding along phonemic and letteral linkages. Thus the "swarming bees"—a recurrent figure of the automatic programmed activity of language—is both the source of poetry and a dangerous "cave," accessing the "insanity." But they sound the "real me" on both counts.

Insofar as the poet aims to re-produce language—the currency—as physical sensation, insofar as words are also material, acoustic, and somatic events in poetic language, poetry is dangerous for one diagnosed with hysteria, which is, among other things, a disorder of proper symbolization of the body and thus the formulation of a coherent ego; "a leaky ego" is the Doctor's diagnosis (1976, 412). Bodily sounds and intraverbal play do not just threaten the symbolic order by standing for disorder, irrationality, or nonsense. In poetry, they insist on *another* order that crosses the "law" or "discipline" of referential logic and analogy. Sounds and letters are not anarchic; nor are they opposed to a norm of referential usage, which would render them dependent on representational logic. They institute a *different* order altogether and testify to a different, surface "unconscious" of the body of language. They anagram the "rat's star" (1981, 63). And while symbolic language would make for a coherent subject, the different systemic order of literal language threatens to dissolve rather than stabilizing the ego and the narrative subject, for the medium tends to dissolve rather than produce meaning.

"I don't really believe the poem, but the name is surely mine so I must belong to the poem. So I must be real," she writes (DM, 82). The coherence of her name and her words would make for psychic health and allay the anxieties of the confessional poet. But Sexton also knows that the name is *not* surely hers, that it is also a textual entity, the "real me" of language. Her name, in the intratextual order, is a crazy playground of "Anne": Anna (Dingley) or "Nana," her "twin," whose mental breakdown and accusation "You're not Anne!" (DM, 16) continue to haunt her; Anne (Wilder), another "twin," plus psychiatrist— though not Sexton's—plus lover; Anne of Rimbaud's elemental hunger (and even the *ane* Anne would flee on); Orphan Annie of Daddy Warbucks (1981, 543–44); and finally Anna O. of Breuer—the Anne of Dr. O.[14] Certainly, Sexton would be as sensitive to "Anna O." as she was to Rimbaud's Anne: "One day I was reading a quote from Rimbaud that said, 'Anne, Anne, flee on your donkey,' and I typed it out because it had my name in it and because I wanted to flee" (1976, 411). And the O is an important vowel as well; it is a nexus of Dr. O., the poet (an echoic effect of Apollo: "you gave me honor too soon Apollo. / . . . I wait / here in my wooden legs and O / my green green hands" [1981, 18]), the apostrophic O, signifying direct address, and the gaping cypher of the hysteric ("the washbasin / of my mouth, calling, 'Oh.' / I am empty" ["Oh," 303]). The proper name does not anchor the text to a person but itself enters a free play beyond reference, on lyric grounds of words "mannering" each other and the "real me." The letters ground the free substitutions of people for people, so that, in a sense, the "Nana-hex" that haunts her, the "Nana-song" that makes "a sonnet turn into a dirty joke," writes her in the first place (313). "Anna who was mad," she writes, "From the grave write me, Anna! / . . . / Write me" (312–13).

Powers that would stabilize her ego or "right" her I "watch" her. God watches her: she is a sinner, "evil," a possessed witch. And Doctor Orne watches her: she is crazy. Sexton articulates the collusion of these powers in a subliminal network of letters and images linked along letters. This is a material language of the oral zone: "I put bees in my mouth / to keep from eating" (1981, 315). We can enter this "swarm of bees" with, for example, Doctor Orne or Doctor O., whose "business is watching" her words. He modulates into "god of our block," a "third eye," "an oracular / eye" who watches her (3–4). In "You, Doctor Martin," his "third eye," the homophone of her one "I," is the mirror where the crazy I sees herself.[15] The hostility indirectly registered in the poem— "There are no knives / for cutting your throat" (3)—also becomes explicit in a literal aggression, as in the following passage: "What makes you think you know everything, Doc? You're a dog-god, a no good God damn dog or a Doc. All you do is sit there watching your precious little clock. . . . Hello little clock, Tickety-tockety-clockety. Who invented you anyhow? Freud, that fraud. Little clock, little clock what makes you stop? What you need is a sock, little clock . . . you little Doc Clock! . . . What you need very much more than a sock is a KNOCK. . . . A knock and a knock and a knock. . . . You're a locked up Doc!"[16]

Lacking "Sanity" and "God," she is prescribed a typewriter by both the doctor and the priest, who tells her "God is in your typewriter" (DM, 380). The type-writer amplifies her already difficult project of articulating a coherent ego in the disarticulative material medium of poetry by introducing an additional, mechanical articulation-disarticulation of her "I." The typewriter is certainly in collusion with the religious and social powers, and indeed it also watches her: "the forty-eight keys of the typewriter / each an eyeball that is never shut" (1981, 422). The typewriter is "my church / with an altar of keys always waiting" (449), and God is "in the swarm, the frenzy of the bees" (472): "I am, each day, / typing out the God / my typewriter believes in. / Very quick. Very intense, / like a wolf at a live heart," caught in a "frenzy, / like bees stinging the heart all morning" (466, 467). At the altar of the typewriter, she produces "Anne Sexton" out of the swarm of bees.[17] The discourses that offer salvation, sanity, and a coherent Anne Sexton are religion, therapy, and the printed script of "Anne Sexton," a commodity with a recognized value as public currency.

The typewriter effects the translation between "blabbing" and the printed commodity:

One learns not to blab about all this
except to yourself or the typewriter keys
who tell no one until they get brave
and crawl off onto the printed page. (1981, 548)

It transforms the woman into a text for public consumption, offering her audibility.[18] Yet the typewriter—"the frenzied sound of this machine" (1977, 247)—exacts its cost. The poet's job is to work the somatic materiality of language into the texture of her verse. The typewriter intervenes in this process, so that the materiality and the mechanisms of language appear elsewhere, in the medium of the typewriter and its separate mechanisms.[19] Sexton has much ambivalence about writing and a kind of paranoia about "the public voyeury eyes / of my typewriter keys" (1981, 550). In "The Room of My Life," the "sockets on the wall" that watch her, "waiting like a cave of bees," link to the typewriter keys' "eyeballs" that are "never shut" (422). In the mediation of the typewriter, the "swarming bees" (12)—her "name," her words, the "real me"—can turn hornets and see through her:[20]

Hornets have been sent.
They cluster like floral arrangements on the screen.
Hornets, dragging their thin stingers,
hover outside, all knowing,
hissing: *the hornet knows*.
I heard it as a child
but what was it that he meant?
The hornet knows!

. . . .

What did The Green Hornet mean, *he knows*? (98–99)

With the **horne**ts, of course, we circle back to Dr. Orne, the "god,"[21] "Father Inc.," who "knows." She is again seen through now by her very words:[22] "Father Inc." is also "Father Ink." The watching hornets are not benign, and in the later poem "Hornets," they are male figures threatening to mangle her body:

A red-hot needle
hangs out of him, he steers by it
as if it were a rudder, he
would get in the house any way he could

. . . .

Do not sleep for he wants to sew up your skin,
he wants to leap into your body like a hammer
with a nail, do not sleep he wants to get into
your nose and make a transplant . . . (1981, 499–500)

The mechanical mediation of the watching and knowing typewriter produces her as social currency for a public. The "twelve-fingered" witch of "Her Kind" (1981, 15), her hallmark poem, I would guess, sits at the typewriter. The keyboard requires twelve fingers; "forty eight keys," Sexton specifies (422)—twelve per line. Her deformity signals her transgression:[23] she is a poet writing herself on the typewriter as a "mad woman." Like yet another Anne, she would seem to be transgressing by speaking in public, now openly publicizing her specific, gendered, psychic and sexual experiences. Public audibility is the offense—and above all in her own eyes. "A woman came / with six fingers / and in the extra finger was fire." But the fire died out: "the bee went out of it" (461, 460).

Now the watching typewriter "knows" this. The typewriter that produces the I for a public also sees through this I—that it is a "fake," a "lie." For what kind of an I does she produce? Who is the I that has "cultural currency"? It is a witch, a mental case, and a hypersexual body. In other words, she plays into ready-made slots for "woman." "My typewriter writes" (1981, 169), *and* it types. The cultural "currency" of her I—which "has become visible in the medium of print" and has "a value established in a cultural marketplace" (DM, 82–83)—is also a mockery of the "real me" of the code, the one who submits to the code. Sexton knows all this, and she goes with it: she performs a "woman" of "her kind"—a certain type of woman, with cultural currency, the figure of poet-madwoman-sexpot-witch.

While "Her Kind" seems to say "I am a witch and mad and a poet," the typewriter types this I in another sense as well. For she is not "quite" an outsider as a witch or a psychotic would be, and she is not quite a transgressor. She is a woman at a machine, "fishing" up words out of her "own machine" (DM, 225) to market a transgressor. And the typewriter that converts her to currency also socializes her in an entirely different way: it quite literally mechanizes her body. "The Ballad of the Lonely Masturbator," for example, is a public marketing performance: "I horrify / those who stand by." The fingers work the typewriter and masturbate, hitting the letter keys and the key spots: "She's my workshop"; "I beat her like a bell" (1981, 198). I am Anne *Sexton*: I perform textually. And "I am fed"; the poems pay the bills, but more important, I eat myself, as the last stanza suggests, in masturbation/poems. In a letter she writes: "If 'an intellectual is someone whose mind watches itself' [Camus] the same could be said for masturbation or even better for suicide" (1977, 231). And yet better, it could be said about the person at the typewriter, watching the "words . . . fly out of the heart (via the fingers)" (159). That's why the fingers are "evil."

The first machine that was specifically gendered,[24] the typewriter defined the woman's job in the world outside the home, and it was certainly at home in the decor of the "mechanical bride," the fifties housewife, a role Sexton says she bought wholesale (1976, 400). Sylvia Plath's "An Appearance," for example, presents this mechanized domestic space, where the body is articulated to the mechanical rhythms of machinery—the icebox veins; the adding-machine lips; the washing-machine morals; the sewing-machine sex. The body is mechanized, and the "heart," "disorganized" with all this organization, articulates its disorganization on another machine—the typewriter: "ABC, her eyelids say" (1981, 189). Or, as Sexton "tip tap type[s] away," she notes: "My head is in the mixmaster" (1977, 57, 73).[25] This gender-specific mechanization of middle-class women in charge of the machinery at home, correlates only with the underclass of factory workers in the general population.[26] Sexton's accident of catching her arm in the washing machine—she speaks of this in the *Paris Review* interview and in "Cripples and Other Stories"—is a personal trauma and a public statement about women and the machines mangling them:

> I put it in the Easy Wringer.
> It came out nice and flat.
>
> I was an instant cripple
> from my finger to my shoulder.
>
> . . . .
>
> Though mother said a withered arm
> would put me in *Who's Who*. (1981, 161–62)

Machines exact a cost—though they may, in special cases, offer access to *Who's Who*. The death that "takes you and puts you thru the wringer, it's a man" (1977, 231). Something of all this makes a mockery of the one with the "demon within," the rhymer, the sexual body, the madwoman. Hence the tone of "Her Kind": her kind is the kind "typing out our lives like a Singer sewing sublimation" (1981, 588).[27]

But the typewriter is yet more complicated and turns the screw once again. Like the slot machine the poet works in "Said the Poet," which shows three

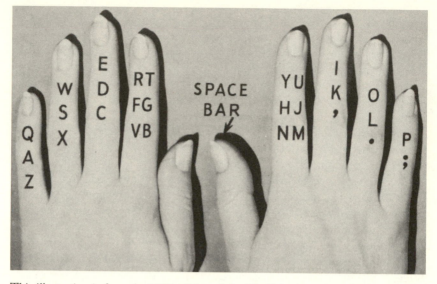

This illustration is from the 1967 edition of the *World Book Encyclopedia*. It is used by permission of Unisys Corporation.

bells and yields real coins, it both "lies" and tells the truth. For the machine that articulates a public "I" also disarticulates that "I." She gambles on the typewriter, for the generation of words—the machinery of the signifiers composing themselves on the typewriter, impressing themselves unto paper—is not entirely in her control. It "borrows" her (1981, 181). Unlike "Anne Sexton" the poet-personage or Anne Sexton the patient, the woman at the typewriter is an "anonymous woman / at that anonymous altar" (551). The "frenzied sound of this machine" (1977, 247) connects to the "frenzy of the bees" (1981, 472) on the surfaces of the signifier: the bees in her "mouth" (315) that keep her from eating and being eaten. But the mechanical mediation of the typewriter that protects from the bodily depths and stabilizes her I as a text for others, as currency, also annuls the possibility of a self-identical I. The typing cure is *not* the talking cure, which is about stitching up a subject. The typing subject can only fragment—separate a speaker and a writer, voice and text, the body and words, words and letters.[28] In this medium, in this mediation, the "I" she produces can only be a displacement, a symptom of the original split that allows its inscription.[29] The typewriter protects from bodily depths and keeps the dissociation in view: "I never write by hand," she says, it's "so ugly—like my adolescence" (1977, 305).[30]

Yet poems start out manually, first mapped out by hand. Middlebrook writes that, "[p]ouring over her rhyming dictionary, Sexton would work out elaborate sound patterns and rhyme schemes by hand and then, at her typewriter, fill them slowly to the brim with images, sentences, and phrases that finally turned into poems" (DM, 74); she would fit her images within the boundaries of the pattern of end rhymes (DM, 75). A manuscript page Middlebrook reproduces shows the visual shape of the poem pencilled in on a grid. The visual shape and the sound grid are worked by hand; the content is literally "filled in" by the typewriter. "Sexton never wrote out poems by hand" (DM, 48). There is a division of labor between the hand that immediately maps out the sound shape of the poem and the mechanical mediation of the typewriter that fills the content with the "images" and "symbols" from the "unconscious" (Sexton 1974, 22).

And she speaks of form in tactile terms: "I can see a poem, even my long ones, as something you could hold, like a piece of something." She thinks of the poem—its form and sound—"as something you can hold. I think of it with my hands to begin with" (1985, 79). Once the hands draw the "object"-poem, the words "tear their way out of my soul and onto the typewriter keys" (1977, 270), a process that involves many revisions on the typewriter: "I will fool around on the typewriter. It might take me ten pages of nothing, of terrible writing, and then I'll get a line, and I'll think, 'That's what I mean!' What you're doing is hunting for what you mean, what you're trying to say. You don't know when you start. . . . For one lyric poem I rewrote about three hundred typewritten pages" (1985, 73). Thus if poetry "milks the unconscious" (1976, 401), it does so through the agency of this machine and the obsession with the letter (the three hundred pages). For the typewriter in effect composes not only the literal words but what she wants to say—that is, the images that are supposed to come from the unconscious, the poems that are supposed to be torn out of the soul.

As a machine that protects against and sanitizes the "ugly" adolescence, the typewriter links to rational thought.[31] But "I get so horribly furious and disturbed with rational thought. Language is the opposite of the way a machine works" (1977, 245). Language is to work emotionally; "a book should serve as the ax for the frozen sea within us," she cites Kafka as epigraph to *All My Pretty Ones*. How can a language articulated on a machine do this, if, as Nietzsche wrote on *his* typewriter, "Our writing instruments contribute to our thoughts"?[32] This writing instrument severs the link between the body and the script: unlike writing with a pen, a noise and a ribbon intervene; unlike cursive writing, words shatter into letters arbitrarily placed on a keyboard that one must mechanically master.

Or rather, agree to be mastered by. For not only is the body mechanized, but the psyche is prescribed or shaped by the machine that "milks" it. Kittler cites a physiologist's "test-person" typing, in 1904, into his "test-diary": "Today, I found myself not infrequently striking letters before I was conscious of seeing them. They seem to have perfected themselves just below the level of consciousness"; Kittler adds: "typing, in other words, is automatic writing, and its psychology, the unconscious. . . . From 1881 on, the glory of typing coincides with the enigmatic and meaningless letter itself" (1990, 196). This is the historical demise of the "word." The machine that shatters the word can access only an "unconscious" it had already shaped by the fingers' learned behavior of hitting the letters on the QWERTY keyboard. The "depths," the "frozen sea within us," that it accesses is its own arbitrary mechanisms. The unconscious and the "soul" are being redefined here as residual effects of the material medium training the body to its tune. The problem, then, is no longer one of the "demon within"; the problem is that there is no "demon within"— which the hysteric already knows. There is no "frozen sea within us" that the typewriter can access.[33]

The trauma inflicted on the word by the technology of the typewriter is an uncanny return of the initial trauma of the word, and it historically spells the end of phallogocentrism. The economic empowerment of women at the typewriter is a symptom of the empowerment of the signifier, the economic loss of power, in the marketplace of ideas, of the phallogocentric Word, the Truth, the depths. Nietzsche knew, Kittler argues, that he was feminized at his typewriter (1990, 198); at that point truth is no longer phallogocentric. Marianne Moore's use of the typewriter's resources works precisely to the effect of dismantling "Truth." Writing instruments affect discursive practices, and this one castrates the Word.

Sexton's "That Day" is one poem that testifies to the typewriter's letter power, which dismantles the story of the "ego," the narrative of phallus worship, and its referential language-logic:[34] "That day" "only your body sat before me," she writes; "That was the day I followed the king's rules" (1981, 180). But "That was yesterday, that day," and "today," it is "the typewriter that sits before me" and "bears" "the ghost of you." Her "bearing" in letters is a "burial" of the story, and it reburies the "monument," the "tower" that the story celebrates:

> A multitude should gather for an edifice.
> Surely The Press is here looking for headlines.
> Surely someone should carry a *banner* on the sidewalk
>
> . . . .
>
> If a phenomenon arrives shouldn't the Magi come *bearing* gifts?
> Yesterday was the day I *bore* gifts for your gift (emphases mine)

"Today," however, the "I" is "borrowed" and follows the queen's rules, the bee's, as the king dreams and "mumbles" himself into letters on her typewriter: " 'Sh. We're driving to Cape Cod. We're heading for the *Bourne* / Bridge. We're circling around the *Bourne* Circle.' *Bourne!*" (emhases mine). Dr. *Orne* is in this poem too, also born in the "household" of the "I," borne on her banner. A banner, a headline spanning the width of a newspaper page, gets her from "The Press" to the carrying or bearing a banner. "B*anner*," both a public proclamation and a prohibition, bans the "I" that is "*anne*," just as "bourn[e]"—a boundary between two properties—locates the bearings of "Anne," and her "little household." This

Anne would not seem to be a woman of "her kind." She is the "laughing bee" now and may even be a real "twelve-fingered" witch after all. "My voice alarms / my throat. 'Name of father—none.' I hold / you and name you bastard in my arms": "Go child, who is my sin and nothing more" (1981, 25).

In the light of the lies and truths of the typewriter—of its blind insight,[35] so to speak—Sexton's notorious carelessness not just with spelling but with typing has a logic.[36] She lets typos stand in her letters, and sometimes she will comment on them, presumably spending at least as much time as it would take her to strike out and correct. Her excuses vary: the typewriter doesn't type right today; I'm tired; it's late; I'm in a hurry; I'm doped up; I'm feeling crazy; the typewriter won't spell; "my fingers won't obey" (1977, 277), and so on. And the "damn electric typewriter" (283) compounds the problem with a second mind of its own: "This typewriter likes to write k and g every so often so don't mind them as they appear" (284). "Perhaps my next book should be titled THE TYPO," she writes (277). This would have been a good title. She is both typist and the typo-error she produces[37]—both an agent and the mangling of the agent on the typewriter, which tells the lie/truth that she/we? *want* to hear:

ACTUALLY THE TYPEWRITER DOESN'T
know everything (278)

POSTSCRIPT: HYSTEROLOGY

> Hysterology[1]: hysteron protoron. (from Greek usteron proteron, the latter (put as) the former). Gram. and Rhet. A figure of speech in which the word or phrase that should properly come last is put first.
>
> > 1623: Cockeram, *Historologie*, an altering of the order of speech, by placing that after that should be before.
> >
> > 1589 Puttenham *Eng. Poesie* "Another manner of disordered speech . . . we call it in English prouerbe, the cart before the horse, the Greeks call it *Histeron proteron*, we name it the preposterous . . . as he . . . said: 'my dame that bred me vp and bare me in her wombe.' Whereas the bearing is before the bringing up."
> >
> > —OED

By definition, hysteria is a gendered condition; the word comes from Greek "hustera," womb. It was thought to be a case of a "traveling" uterus, displacing uterine troubles onto other organs, before it became a case of a "traveling" libido, a displacement of psychosexual troubles onto bodily organs. A source trouble changes discourses, so to speak, and comes up elsewhere in such a way that defies the natural—physiological, neurological—order of cause and effect. For the travels of the psyche follow linguistic paths of figural and literal substitutions and transcribe psychic troubles onto a body that can only be understood as a representation of a body, a text, for such transposition to be possible. The focus on the signifier, its elements and their combinatorial and substitutive processes, protects from the bodily depths, for hysteria, with its oral zone fixation, attests to a too-intimate link between the body and language and poses the threat that the body might absorb surfaces, that referential language may regress into bodily sounds and noises, physiological and alimentary events.

But in this very defense, language confronts its own emptiness, as it risks dissolution into the material elements and mechanisms of the code. The typewriter was there before Lacan, spelling out that very dissolution. Now it is the word that travels, and it not only comes after the letters, but it comes up elsewhere than the keys one hits. This spatial displacement distinguishes it from handwriting, where the word comes up in the same place as the letters that compose it, on the same surface that the hand is in contact with, which is the writing surface. But the typed word is reconstituted *after* its dissolution into its meaningless components, after the disarticulation of word-concept into letters on a keyboard, and it is reconstituted elsewhere. The typed word is a symptom that formulates, on paper, the disarticulation of the subject and the word. The muscular movements of hitting the keys and the sounds the hit keys produce have no history of established, intimate, somatic pathways to language. A word so constituted is an effect not of the word-concept but of the typing activity. The typewriter's displacement, then, effects a preposterous reversal, a hysterology. Hysterology or hysteron proteron is a figure of displacement, an anastrope: the word comes not where it should but elsewhere; its syntactic travels upset beginnings and ends, befores and afters. This preposterous figure of "disordered speech" threatens natural and logical order, "placing the conclusion before the premises," "particulars before universals," "effects before causes."[38] It is an anagramming.

Thus, the typewriter shares the gender of hysteria. The body and the mechanisms of the code equally threaten the priority and authority of the word; the phallogocentric truth, order, logic, the Logos, dissipate in hysterological displacements, anagramming into sounds and letters. The word is only ventriloquized, an effect, and it emerges elsewhere—if not from the belly, then from QWERTY.

These displacements challenge the priority of the word without the reciprocity of the intimate connection between sounds and sense otherwise ensured in poetry. Poetic language, organized according to the material properties of the signifiers, internally threatens its own sense. It threatens referential stability, as arrangements of sounds and letters question the priority of sense. But its generic metaleptic logic establishes reversibility: sounds and sense are at once causes and effects of each other. In poetry, language is at once more intimate and more estranged than language confined to referential use. This intimate otherness, I have argued, constitutes the lyric "I." The hysteric, especially the hysteric at her typewriter, continually risks losing this precarious "I" to histrionic effects.

NOTES

1. She exhibited characteristic symptoms—dissociation, trances, amnesias, and eating disorders among them.

2. Qtd. in Diane Wood Middlebrook (1992, 73). Subsequent references will be cited in the text as DM, followed by page number.

3. "Images come from the unconscious," she writes; hence "Any poem is therapy. The art of writing is therapy" (1974, 22, 21).

4. She tells a story, for example, of being molested by an older man, a family friend, knowing it is a lie: "I'm a story-maker, a—doesn't it strike him as odd that this 'story' is too pat???? . . . [I]t was funny to have thought up this nice theory for my symptoms—I am acting the part of a nice case history" (DM, 62).

5. It is hard to know what, if any, traumatic event might have led to the formation of her hysterical symptoms, for the stories change all the time. She tries out various traumas to fit her symptoms. Yet the scenarios she produces still fit Freud's "thesis that at bottom of every case of hysteria there are *one or more occurrences of premature sexual experience*" (1989, 103)—whether actual or fantasized.

6. In an interview, she says: "I found that the more difficult the subject, then the easier it was to do in some difficult form. . . . I'd begin, say, with rhyme, and then I'd count it out syllabically, maybe, and then I was stuck with it, and then I often broke it and cheated, . . . because what I was trying to get out was the honest, the truth. . . . It took over the superego function" (1985, 140–41). "I think all form is a trick in order to get at the truth. Sometimes in my hardest poems, the ones that are difficult to write, I might make an impossible scheme, a syllabic count that is so involved, that it then allows me to be truthful. It works as a kind of superego. It says, 'You may now face it, because it will be impossible ever to get out' " (80).

7. In "The Ego and the Id," Freud writes that the super-ego "appears as the representative of the id": it "displays its independence of the conscious ego and its intimate relations with the unconscious id"—its sources in the id, in "things heard" (1989, 658, 654). In Sexton's scheme, the super-ego lays out the formal plan and organizes the unconscious impulses at work on the auditory material, the body of the signifier.

8. 1976, 409. "I've noticed that Robert Lowell felt freer to write about madness in free verse," she adds, "whereas it was the opposite for me." Only after setting up elaborate formal structures did she feel "free to allow myself to express what had really happened." Forms, for her, are not necessarily conventional forms: "For me each poem has its own sound or its own voice or its own form, whatever you want to call it" (1985, 42). "My conventions are my own" (116).

9. Cited as epigraph to *No Evil Star* and in DM, 124. She has published the palin-dromic "Rats Live on No Evil Star" (1981, 359). In her *New York Quarterly* interview she says: "Conrad Aiken once saw a palindrome on the side of a barn: Rats Live On No Evil Star (and I want that to be on my gravestone, because I see myself as a rat, but I live on no evil star). Rats and star: I wrote a list of all the words I could make out of those letters. Then I sat down with the words and made up a poem" (1974, 21).

10. She links the economies of therapy and a certain kind of poetry in "January 1st." Her parents, "in the end," had used up "All that pale green dough":

> The rest I spent on doctors
> Who took it like gigolos.
>
> . . . .
>
> I will not speculate today
> with poems that think they're money. (1981, 593)

And her "complaint" to Dr. Y. plays with the same link:

> Everything I say to you is awfully serious.
> I don't make puns.
> I have no slips of tongue.
> I pay in cold hard cash. (570)

11. This indexical—not symbolic—language is associated with gambling, chance, luck and with something "funny"—both here and in "An Obsessive Combination." It beats the odds; it allows chance into play; it is "language"—irrational, funny. And it is intimate, sounding "the wild bee farms / of your nerves" (1981, 25). The poem may also have the reader in mind: her words are not to be read as symptoms of illness or symbols of a "real" meaning: "I admit nothing." Poems either work as poems and have an affect or they are dead—mere currency.

12. "Must" makes most sense when read as a supposition indicating probability rather than an imperative indicating obligation, unless she is referring to her position in the doctor's office. The phrase would suggest that she forgets whether she for-gets, and thus accesses a different, audial memory and self, other than the self in the doctor's office.

13. The analyst might say A is not A but B; he's a decoder of metaphoric logic. She says A is A—the poem, words picking and mannering each other. But because she deals in words, of course, A is also not A; it is also B. Coins are both signifiers of exchange value and objects, and coins won when the poet gambles and hits the jackpot exceed the exchange system altogether in a "weird abundance" (1981, 89).

14. She was likely aware of this case by 1958, Middlebrook speculates (55). Sexton, initially diagnosed with depression, started reading psychiatric literature when Dr. Orne became her therapist. She says she wanted to produce a good patient for him, and a hysteric is a more interesting patient. But Dr. Orne's statement suggests that the hyster-ical symptoms of amnesias, trances, and dissociation preceded their acquaintance (DM, 39).

15. She says that she needs her therapist "to tell me who I am" (1976, 412). Her letters make clear her dependency on Dr. Orne. She comes apart when he decides to move to Philadelphia: he is her "love," her "life," her "mother-dad-Nana" (1977, 240)—the full transference thing. He in effect made a person out of a "nothing . . . really

nothing" (229). But "[s]till, I wish there were some nonguilty escape from the self . . . psychiatry is a dirty mirror" (121).

16. 1977, 250–51. This is a scene from her play "Mercy Street"; the words accompany Daisy's smashing the doctor's desk clock. Surely, "fury" against "the cocks" is audible in this passage.

17. Her personal history is encoded in the "bees": Middlebrook writes that James Wright called Sexton " 'Blessing' (sometimes 'Bee' or 'B')" (DM, 130). This "name," though, predates Wright. In "You, Doctor Martin," she has "And I am queen of this summer hotel / or the laughing bee on a stalk // of death" (1981, 3). The name is part the letter B, as on a typewriter key, and part queen bee who rules the buzzing swarm.

18. Friedrich Kittler points out that the typewriter "interconnected for the first time the two hitherto separated acts of literary composition and publication" (1990, 195). W. H. Auden writes: "Much as I loathe the typewriter, I must admit that it is a help in self-criticism. Typescript is so impersonal and hideous to look at that, if I type out a poem, I immediately see defects which I missed when I looked through it in manuscript" (1989, 17). Typescript distances, offers an outsider's view on the text. "If you are not only retyping a manuscript but actually composing on the typewriter," Richard Polt writes, "this has a more dramatic effect on the character of your writing. Reporters and policemen traditionally love typewriters because the activity of writing on them has a special quality, the quality of public reportage" (1996, 3).

19. Thus the typewriter that articulates her also "silences" her. She epigraphs "The Silence," quoting C. K. Williams: "The more I write, the more the silence seems to be eating away at me" (1981, 318). And she presents this silence as a speechless mouth that eats her mouth:

> I am zinging words out into the air
> and they come back like squash balls.
> Yet there is silence.
> Always silence.
> Like an enormous baby mouth.
>
> The silence is death.
> It comes each day with its shock
> to sit on my shoulder, a white bird,
> and peck at the black eyes
> and the vibrating red muscle
> of my mouth. (319)

"Demon" uses similar imagery about her "demon within," "standing like a carrion, / wanting to eat me, / starting at the lips and tongue" (551).

20. The typewriter and hornets are also associated (1981, 548–49).

21. Her "seamstress" speaks of her son, who decides to "take the cloth": "Christ was a hornet inside his head" (1981, 79).

22. Fear of shopping was one of her symptoms: "I hate to go to the market because it's full of making up your mind, it's full of decisions and crowds of people. . . . Somebody sees me, *and I see myself through them*. Then it's all gone, the whole world falls apart" (DM, 138).

23. Witches came with something extra—like an extra nipple to suckle their familiars. Six fingers are common extras.

24. Kittler, writing about Nietzsche's typewriter, proposes that the typewriter, which allowed women into the field of writing as secretaries of professors, ended the male monopoly of the universities and the "homosexual" dissemination of truth (1990, 195). Historically, women's "tremendous capacity for 'degrading themselves into writing machines' "—(Jenny Schwabe, 1902)—increased the economic value of their "useless piano fingers": from 1881 on more women worked at typing than anything else. Their "so-called 'emancipation' " (Schwabe) is due to "Remington, Underwood, IBM, and their many successors" (Kittler 1990, 196).

25. Also see "Self in 1958" and its "synthetic doll": "Someone plays with me, / plants me in the all-electric kitchen" (1981, 155). The typographically interesting line "*Am I* approximately an I. Magnin transplant?" implicates letters in the condition of the synthetic doll (emphasis mine).

26. Explaining why she "dare not fire" her "cleaning woman," Sexton also levels the two women: "While she irons, I type" (1977, 304). Also see:

I'm an empress.
I wear an apron.
My typewriter writes. (1981, 169)

27. "Like bees caught in the wrong hive, / we are the circle of the crazy ladies," she writes in "Ringing the Bells" (1981, 28). This "marketplace" is another wrong hive, and it is one that "ladies" are likelier to get "caught in." But in Sexton's case, her mind is another wrong hive: "I am in my own mind. / I am locked in the wrong house" (133).

28. "You, Doctor Martin" enacts this process of articulating a speaker by disarticulating her, pitting the poet against the patient. Following a "breakdown," the speaker articulates herself, chronicling an institutionalized patient's day. But the text that puts her together also breaks her apart in another way, elsewhere. The rhyme scheme (abcabca) articulates the stanzas, but the typographical indentations of the rhymed lines and the centering of the poem also disarticulate the stanzas; starting at the left margin would have stabilized the shape of the poem. The number of strong caesurae, with short sentences ending mid-lines (eighteen of the twenty-three sentences of the forty-two-line poem end mid-line), insist on the disarticulation of the line units and the syntactic units. The writing of the poem is partly a cure, like "counting this row and that row of moccasins / waiting on the silent shelf," and partly a derangement of the imposed "tunnels," "rows" and "lines" of the hospital routine that silences her. She invokes a poetic order and deranges it so that a speaker may be heard in her difference. Hence "Each angry finger . . . demands / I mend what another will break // tomorrow" (1981, 3).

29. Laurence Rickels speaks of the typewriter in a Freudian figure, as a "Mystic Writing Pad or Wunderblock which, with its styluslike keys, rips into one surface—the typewriter ribbon or unconscious memory—so that another surface can be printed upon. This Wunde-block leaves a wound that blocks the emergence of one inscription so that imprinted text can emerge in some other place" (1990, 150). The typewriter produces a "symptom" via the inked strip; it produces the subject, in the case of Sexton, as a script—a symptom.

This is an apt figure also for the hysterical transference of memory onto the body through the mediation of language. For Freud, "Hysterics suffer mainly from reminiscences" and "hysterical symptoms can only arise with the cooperation of memories"

(Breuer and Freud 1955, 7; Freud 1989, 102). And this cooperation of symptoms and memories occurs at the site of language—the memory traces of "things heard." The signifier hits one surface—the memory slate—to imprint another surface—the body. It is a typewriterly conversion, and the machine might have something to do with the formulation of Freud's theory itself.

30. She writes Tillie Olsen: "Your letters look like poems and here I am typing on this paper that looks like I run a business or that, at least, I knew who I was. . . . I must look like a rather stout man who sits by a very respectible black typewriter" (1977, 127).

31. And to neat life stories. "The life story or better named, the case history, is only a machine, a Kafka machine" (1977, 271). I assume she is referring to "The Penal Colony," where a kind of typewriter kills the body in inscribing its life sentence upon it.

32. Cited in Kittler 1990, 195.

33. The medium shapes the unconscious it can access. The "talking cure" also does just that, but typewriting calls for a different figuration of the unconscious, shifting the terms from words and metaphors to letters and syllables. This shift also traces the history of psychoanalytic theory.

34. Here she taps into a generic connection: narratives and the phallogocentric word are coenablers.

35. The first typewriters were designed for the blind. They were understroke machines that typed on the bottom of the paper; their script was not visible. Nietzsche had one of these.

36. The editors of her letters unfortunately corrected her "erratic typing and myriad misspellings," keeping only "the misspellings of which Anne was aware." Their reason is that the letters were "difficult to read" (Sexton 1977, ix), and there are passages marked "[illegible]" in the published letters.

37. She signs one letter:

    & haste
In chaos——df453679c;!./'¢#!!!!
    Anne

38. All from OED. Lanham defines hysteron proteron as a figure of syntax or sense out of normal logical or temporal order; same as "Anastrophe" (Greek: turning back); "Reversio"; "Perversio" (inversion) (1969). It undoes causal sequencing.

Coda

THE HAUNTED HOUSE OF "ANNA"

Was Saussure mistaken? Did he allow himself to be fascinated by a mirage? Do his anagrams resemble the faces one
can read in ink-blots?

Is this the vertigo of error? It is also the discovery of the
simple truth that language is an infinite resource, and that
behind each phrase lies hidden the multiple clamor from
which it has detached itself to appear before us in its isolated
individuality.

—*Jean Starobinski*

[M]any languages in use today can only render the German
expression "an *unheimliches* house" by "a *haunted* house."

—*Sigmund Freud*

"ANNA" SNARES FREUD HIMSELF in a return of the repressed surfaces of
the body of language. Early in his essay on the uncanny, Freud considers
E. Jentsch's idea that the uncanny may involve a sense of "automatic, mechanical processes" at work (1963b, 31). The uncanny is an event experienced as
more than a chance accident and less than willed; it entails a sense of "fate,"
and "weird," a synonym of "uncanny," retains this association with fate. But
Freud does not pursue Jentsch's idea and goes on to define the uncanny as a
return of the repressed, more primitive animistic and narcissistic thought systems that have been surmounted in cultural and personal history. And in his
discussion of the Hoffman story "The Sand Man," he overlooks the mechanisms of the linguistic code that are clearly at work and beg to be engaged.
Freud resists reading that which returns as "something fateful and inescapable"
(43)—as "something long known to us, once very familiar" (20)—in terms of
the mechanisms of the code, a revenant that not only refuses to stay buried in
the symbolic but refuses to be *reinterred* by the symbolic. For this revenant code
attests to "automatic, mechanical processes at work" and jeopardizes theories of
psychic depths and buried histories that would shore up the symbolic.

Jean Baudrillard argues that Freud had to abandon hysteria to formulate
psychiatry as a science; he had to "repress" the hysteric, as it were, because
there is no depth or unconscious to the hysteric (1990, 56). Hysteria has to do
with the seduction of surfaces:

Seduction takes from discourse its sense and turns it from its truth. It is, therefore, contrary to the psychoanalytic distinction between manifest and latent discourses. For the latent discourse turns the manifest discourse not *from* its truth, but *towards* its truth. It makes the manifest discourse say what it does not want to say; it causes determinations and profound indeterminations to show through in the manifest discourse. . . . The manifest discourse has the status of an appearance, a laboured appearance, traversed by the emergence of meaning. . . .

In seduction, by contrast, it is the manifest discourse—discourse at its most superficial—that turns back on the deeper order (whether conscious or unconscious) in order to invalidate it, substituting the charm and illusion of appearances[,] . . . the seduction of the signs themselves being more important than the emergence of any truth. . . . This is why interpretation is what, *par excellence*, is opposed to seduction. . . . What truly displaces discourse, "seduces" it in its literal sense, and renders it seductive, is its very appearance, its inflections, its nuances, the circulation (whether aleatory and senseless, or ritualized and meticulous) of signs at its surface. . . . *All meaningful discourse seeks to end appearances*: this is its attraction, and its imposture. (53–54)

What Freud abandons is the superficial abyss—the superficial sublime— that is the very "ground" of poetry. Poetic language yields to the seduction of surfaces, and it will elude interpretation on the Freudian—or any other symbolic—model based on a hierarchy of surfaces and depths. Lyric poetry might seduce with an illusion of depth but ultimately refuses any depth other than the "Dionysian" abyss of the signifier, the dissolution of meaning into the elements of the linguistic code. This knowledge, again, is one the hysteric also possesses and even acts out.

Jean-Michel Oughourlian, who reads hysteria in terms of René Girard's triangular model of mimetic desire, argues that the social order has a stake in concealing that the self is constituted by the desire of an other or the cultural Other, because this is a source of rivalry, conflict, and violence (1991, 149). Hence the long history of hysteria, a series of cultural inventions of "other" others—sequestered within, internal to the self—to safeguard the illusion of an autonomous individual self. What causes hysterical symptoms and puts in question the self's autonomy and control is first explained to be the body— flesh or sex (the uterus, from which "hysteria" derives), which has a mind of its own—then possession by the Devil, and then, when the Devil can no longer do the job, the Freudian unconscious (151).

But insofar as the "other" other, in Freud, depends on the signifier—is constituted by the elements of the signifier—it is in a sense a social Other; the code itself is the Other. The desire of the Other would now be the desire of the signifier, which "my" desire imitates. What is the desire of the signifier but to disseminate its code, its surfaces? In the signifier itself, Freud comes up against the limits of interpretation and the limit of *his* discourse, itself structured as a liminal discourse of the threshold of the semiotic and the symbolic—a discourse that would harness the body of the signifier to symbolic, discursive work.

This limit of interpretation might be named "Anna," and I want to conclude by reading "Anna" as the uncanny return of the irrepressible. Anna O., "the founding patient of psychoanalysis," and Breuer engender psychoanalysis; Freud credited Breuer "more than once" for "originating psychoanalysis."[1] Freud was most interested in what we could call this "parental" case history and pressed Breuer for "intimate clinical details" concerning the case,[2] but his own work proceeds by abandoning hysteria. The "classic dream of psychoanalysis" (Freud 1989, xxxv) is Freud's Irma dream (July 1895), and its interpretation, Freud sees fit to add in a note in 1914, is the "first" such interpretation. "Irma" stands for Anna Hammerschlag, the patient at the origin of Freud's work on dreams. In the dream, Irma is conflated with Freud's wife on the basis of her "paleness"; Irma's pallor does not fit Freud's patient's usual rosy appearance but fits that of his wife, who was at the time pregnant with the Freuds' sixth and last child, to be born December 1895. Anna Freud, who will continue her father's work, is named after Anna Hammerschlag, the woman represented by Irma. Anna H. was the daughter of Samuel Hammerschlag, Freud's religion teacher at the gymnasium, to whom he was very close. Anna was also the name of Freud's first sister, and a second, literal path links Freud's wife, Martha Bernays, to "Anna": Freud's sister Anna married Eli Bernays, becoming Anna Bernays.

Irma is also conflated with two other women in the dream. One is a friend of Irma's, and Freud writes, "I had often played with the idea that she too might ask me to relieve her symptoms"; she suffered, not like the real Anna H. but like the Irma of the dream, from "hysterical choking." The second woman Irma is conflated with was a patient who brings up what Freud calls "a tragic event in my practice": he had "repeatedly" prescribed "what was at that time regarded as a harmless remedy (suphonal)," and the patient had "succumbed to the poison" (1989, 135). This patient had the same name as Freud's eldest daughter, Mathilde, named after Breuer's wife.

Freud explains the conflation of the first threesome on the basis of a shared "recalcitrance to treatment" by him—imaginary except in the case of Irma (1989, 134). The second threesome is not treated as such, but the relationship between Irma-Anna and the two Mathildes is established on two counts. The first link is "poison": Freud relates the dream to the previous day, and the event of the opening a bottle of ananas liqueur that smelled like "poison," with this note: "I must add that the sound of the word 'Ananas' bears a remarkable resemblance to that of my patient Irma's family name." Actually, it bears a "remarkable resemblance" to her first name, "Anna," but the statement is not inaccurate, for Anna is, in a sense, her "family name." The second link is through a detail of the dream, which is about a throat examination, that reminds Freud of his eldest daughter's diphtheria "and the fright I had had in those anxious days." The association of the two Mathildes in the dream—his daughter and his patient—makes him think: "It had never occurred to me before, but it struck me now almost like an act of retribution on the part of destiny. It was as though the replacement of one person by another was to be confirmed in another sense: this Mathilde for that Mathilde, an eye for an eye and a tooth for a tooth. It seemed as if I had been collecting all the occasions I could bring up against myself as evidence of lack of medical conscientiousness" (135).

This is an extravagant reading of a divine plan into an accident of shared names. Freud does not engage his procedure and he names the name: Mathilde. The name is not suppressed because less is at stake here; even though medical competence and conscientiousness are serious concerns in the dream, the "Mathilde" episode is a decoy for an even more serious concern with what threatens all such attribution of meanings and designs to literal accidents. Psychoanalytic theory, apart from medical practice, is at stake.

While Freud reprimands those who are not "amenable" patients, those who do not "yield" to his treatment (1989, 134), he also exhibits anxieties that he might be overlooking physiological disorders in treating his patients' pains. In Irma's case, these are pains in the stomach and complaints of nausea and disgust, represented in the dream as pains in the throat and abdomen and constriction of the throat (133), which would affect her speech. Freud is concerned with the patient's "recalcitrance"; in the dream, Irma does not *open her mouth properly* for her examination, and Freud's interpretation is that he felt she might have told him more than she did (134). Overlapping this concern is Freud's anxiety about the legitimacy of his psychoanalytic practice. Hence it is significant that he stops short of thinking through the conflation of these figures, *and* he calls attention to that fact: "I had a feeling that the interpretation of this part of the dream was not carried far enough to make it possible to follow the whole of its concealed meaning. If I had pursued my comparison between the three women, it would have taken me far afield.— There's at least one spot in every dream at which it is unplumbable—a navel, as it were, that is its point of contact with the unknown" (134). Many have noted that Freud is silent on the clearly sexual elements of the dream in his interpretation, but these, as we know, are plumbable depths, and his silence is likely due to discretion.

Freud's phrasing is surprising. The "unplumbable" is not the unknowable depths but the "navel" that links what is interpretable to what is not. He backs off from his analysis at the point when the unplumbable threatens to be revealed as the surface of the signifier—which would indeed take him "far afield" of what he is trying to establish as a *discursive* field. But the pervasive and systematically repressed sexual aggression in the dream correctly identifies the source of what eludes analysis—the signifier that is represented by the proper name "Anna." Anna links the patient who is reluctant to be *analyzed* to his wife, the mother with a fetus connected to her by a navel cord. "Anna" is the "navel" that dissolves the depth of the dream, and it is the unspoken, silenced name "Anna" that links the personal and professional threads of the dream. It is the "navel" of "Sigmund Freud."

To plumb this unanalyzable navel and the unanalyzed aggression, we might go to Freud's short piece "The Theme of the Three Caskets" (1913). Written eighteen years after the dream, this essay strangely resonates with the Irma dream and its "navel."[3] Although Anna is not named in the paper—just as "Anna" is not named in the dream—Peter Gay writes that "we have Freud's private word that one central motive for writing the paper was his growing awareness that his daughter Anna, his third and last daughter, was not only intellectually remarkable but also emotionally very special to him" (Freud 1989, 514).

The essay links two scenes in Shakespeare. First is the suitors' choice among the three caskets in *The Merchant of Venice*. Symbolically, Freud writes, the "caskets are also women"; thus the "*man's choice [is] between three women*" (1989, 515). Since caskets are not only symbolic wombs but also literal coffins, the choice is for the right woman-coffin. And Bassanio chooses the lead casket over the gold and silver caskets; his remark "Thy paleness moves me more than eloquence" links paleness and silence as what motivate his choice. Freud then moves to the second scene of a choice, King Lear's choice among his daughters: "An old man cannot very well choose between three women in any other way. Thus they become his daughters" (516). Freud refers to Cordelia's silence: "psycho-analysis will tell us that in dreams dumbness is a common representation of death"—as are pallor and concealment (517). Lear makes the wrong choice: "the doomed man is not willing to renounce the love of women; he insists on hearing how much he's loved. Let us now recall the moving final scene":

> Lear carries Cordelia's dead body on to the stage. *Cordelia is Death*. If we reverse the situation it becomes intelligible and familiar to us. She is the Death-goddess who, like the Valkyrie in German mythology, carries away the dead hero from the battlefield. Eternal wisdom, clothed in the primae-val myth, bids the old man renounce love, choose death and make friends with the necessity of dying. . . . We might argue that what is represented here are the three inevitable relations that a man has with a woman—the woman who bears him, the woman who is his mate and the woman who destroys him; or that they are the three forms taken by the figure of the mother in the course of a man's life—the mother herself, the beloved

one who is chosen after her pattern, and lastly the Mother Earth who receives him once more. But it is in vain that an old man yearns for the love of woman as he had it first from his mother; the third of the Fates alone, the silent Goddess of Death, will take him into her arms. (522; emphasis mine)

"The third of the Fates" is called "Atropos, the inexorable" (518), immovable, unturnable.

If we return to the dream with this figure of the three women, it turns out that the concealed, silent "Anna" names all three women, both professionally (Anna O.; Anna Hammerschlag; Anna Freud) and personally, since Anna H.-Irma is conflated with the mother-wife-fetus. Unlike Anna O., which substitutes for the real name of an "amenable" patient who talked and in fact gave us the term "talking cure," Freud's "Anna" is a real but silent name that absorbs the three women who are reluctant to talk. "Anna"—the mother, the substitutable woman/women loved, and the daughter—is death. The link between Anna and Cordelia, who is "death," can also be read backwards in a Saussurian fashion. Freud was the son of Amalia Nathansohn and Jacob Freud; "Amalia" provides the end rhyme with Cordelia, and "Jacob Freud" provides the initial phonemes to complete the full name. **Cordelia** is the navel linking the mother/daughter/death to the son. The mother is death; or, **Nathansohn** is **Thanatos**.

The abysmal surface of the signifier resists interpretation and meaning. It writes the personal and professional limits of the analyzer, and it generates the activity of the substitution of referents, the desires that constitute the subject, but is itself immune to substitution. It is the "motive for metaphor," to borrow Stevens's phrase, but it only turns in on itself, as in the palindrome *Anna*; it is the "recalcitrance" of Atropos to *anal*ysis, to being turned. Her only turn is her return to look back at us in the signifier. The "A B C of being" (Stevens 1954, 288) draws the limits of analytic discourse yet allows those limits to substitute for the limits of "real" life and death, which do not exist otherwise or elsewhere.

NOTES

1. Peter Gay in Freud 1989, 61.

2. Gay writes: "The case had its embarrassing aspects, notably Anna O.'s infatuation with her physician (Freud would later call this a case of 'transference love'), but precisely these interested Freud, and he pressed Breuer again and again for more details" (Freud 1989, 60).

3. Patrick Mahoney makes this connection and notes: "Anna is Thanatos" (1988, 66).

WORKS CITED

Abraham, Nicolas. 1995. *Rhythms: On the Work, Translation, and Psychoanalysis.* Trans. Benjamin Thigpen and Nicholas T. Rand. Stanford: Stanford University Press.

Abse, Wilfred. 1966. *Hysteria and Related Mental Disorders.* Bristol: John Wright and Sons Ltd.

Adorno, Theodor W. 1991. *Notes to Literature.* Vol. 1. Trans. Shierry Weber Nicholson. New York: Columbia University Press.

Agamben, Giorgio. 1991. *Language and Death: The Place of Negativity.* Trans. Karen E. Pinkus, with Michael Hardt. Minneapolis: University of Minnesota Press.

———. 1993. *Infancy and History: Essays on the Destruction of Experience.* Trans. Liz Heron. London: Verso.

———. 1995. *The Idea of Prose.* Trans. Michael Sullivan and Sam Whitsitt. Albany: SUNY Press.

———. 1999. *The End of the Poem: Studies in Poetics.* Trans. Daniel Heller-Roazen. Stanford: Stanford University Press.

Allen, Gay Wilson. 1961. *Walt Whitman.* New York: Grove.

Aristotle. 1984. *The Rhetoric and the Poetics of Aristotle.* Trans. Ingram Bywater. New York: Random.

Ashbery, John. 1977. *Houseboat Days.* New York: Penguin.

———. 1983. "The Art of Poetry XXXIII." Interview with Peter Stitt. *The Paris Review* 90:30–59.

Auden, W. H. 1989. *The Dyer's Hand.* New York: Vintage.

Auer, Peter, Elizabeth Couper-Kuhlen, and Frank Muller. 1999. *Language in Time: The Rhythm and Tempo of Spoken Interaction.* New York: Oxford University Press.

Aviram, Amittai F. 1994. *Telling Rhythm: Body and Meaning in Poetry.* Ann Arbor: University of Michigan Press.

Barilli, Renato. 1989. *Rhetoric.* Trans. Giuliana Menozzi. Minneapolis: University of Minnesota Press.

———. 1993. *A Course on Aesthetics.* Trans. Karen E. Pinkus. Minneapolis: University of Minnesota Press.

Bataille, Georges. 1988. *Inner Experience.* Trans. Leslie Anne Boldt. Albany: SUNY Press.

Baudrillard, Jean. 1990. *Seduction.* Trans. Brian Singer. New York: St. Martin's Press.

Bellamy, Joe David. 1984. *American Poetry Observed: Poets on Their Work.* Urbana: University of Illinois Press.

Benjamin, Walter. 1969. *Illuminations.* Trans. Harry Zohn. New York: Shocken.

Bishop, Elizabeth. 1979. *The Complete Poems 1927–1979.* New York: Farrar.

Boomsliter, Paul C., and Warren Creel. 1977. "The Secret Springs: Housman's Outline on Metrical Rhythm and Language." *Language and Style* 10, no. 4 (Fall): 296–323.

Breuer, Josef. 1955. "Fräulein Anna O." In Breuer and Freud 1955, 21–48.

Breuer, Josef, and Sigmund Freud. 1955. *Studies on Hysteria.* Trans. and ed. James Strachey. New York: Basic Books, [1957]. Reprint of vol. 2 of the *Standard Edition of the Complete Psychological Works of Sigmund Freud.* London: Hogarth Press.

Brogan, T.V.F. 1993. "Rhythm." In Preminger and Brogan, *New Princeton Encyclopedia of Poetry and Poetics*.

Burke, Sean. 1997. "The Ethics of Signature." In *Language and the Subject*, ed. Karl Simms, 237–43. Amsterdam: Editions Rodopi B. V.

Bush, Ronald. 1983. *T. S. Eliot: A Study in Character and Style*. New York: Oxford University Press.

Calinescu, Matei. 1987. *Five Faces of Modernity*. Durham: Duke University Press.

Carson, Anne. 1998. *Eros the Bittersweet*. Normal, IL: Dalkey Archive Press.

Caruth, Cathy, ed. 1995. *Trauma: Explorations in Memory*. Baltimore: Johns Hopkins University Press.

Cookson, William. 1985. *A Guide to the Cantos of Ezra Pound*. New York: Persea.

Cowley, Malcolm, ed. 1959. *Walt Whitman's Leaves of Grass: His Original Edition*. New York: Viking.

Culler, Jonathan. 1975. *Structuralist Poetics*. Ithaca: Cornell University Press.

———. 1988a. "The Call of the Phoneme: Introduction." In Culler, *On Puns*, 1–16.

———., ed. 1988b. *On Puns: The Foundation of Letters*. Oxford: Basil Blackwell.

Dann, Kevin T. 1998. *Bright Colors Falsely Seen: Synaesthesia and the Search for Transcendental Knowledge*. New Haven: Yale University Press.

Dante, Alighieri. 1982. *Inferno*. Vol. 1, *The Divine Comedy of Dante Alighieri*. Trans. Allen Mandelbaum. New York: Bantam.

David-Menard, Monique. 1989. *Hysteria from Freud to Lacan: Body and Language in Psychoanalysis*. Trans. Catherine Porter. Ithaca: Cornell University Press.

Deacon, Terrence W. 1997. *The Symbolic Species: The Co-evolution of Language and the Brain*. New York: Norton.

Deleuze, Gilles. 1990. *The Logic of Sense*. Ed. Constantine V. Boundas. Trans. Mark Lester, with Charles Stivale. New York: Columbia University Press.

Deleuze, Gilles, and Félix Guattari. 1987. *A Thousand Plateaus: Capitalism and Schizophrenia*. Trans. Brian Massumi. Minneapolis: University of Minnesota Press.

De Man, Paul. 1983. *Blindness and Insight: Essays in the Rhetoric of Contemporary Criticism*. Minneapolis: University of Minnesota Press.

———. 1989. *The Resistance to Theory*. Minneapolis: University of Minnesota Press.

Dickinson, Emily. 1960. *The Complete Poems of Emily Dickinson*. Ed. Thomas H. Johnson. Boston: Little, Brown.

Dissanayake, Ellen. 1999. "Antecedents of Musical Meaning in the Mother-Infant Dyad." In *Biopoetics: Evolutionary Explorations in the Arts*, ed. Brett Cooke and Frederick Turner. Lexington, KY: International Conference on the Unity of the Sciences.

Donoghue, Denis. 1993. "On 'Burnt Norton.'" In Lobb, *Words in Time*, 1–19.

Dore, John. 1994. "Feeling, Form, and Intention in the Baby's Transition to Language." In *The Women and Language Debate*, ed. Camille Roman, Suzanne Juhasz, and Christanne Miller, 234–53. New Brunswick, NJ: Rutgers University Press.

Dove, Rita. 1993. *Selected Poems*, New York: Vintage.

Ducrot, Oswald, and Tzvetan Todorov. 1987. *Encyclopedic Dictionary of the Sciences of Language*. Trans. Catherine Porter. Baltimore: John Hopkins University Press.

Eliot, T. S. 1932. *Selected Essays, 1917–1932*. New York: Harcourt.

———. 1970. *Collected Poems*. New York: Harcourt.

———. 1979. *On Poetry and Poets*. New York: Farrar.

————. 1986. *The Use of Poetry and the Use of Criticism.* Cambridge: Harvard University Press.

Emerson, Ralph Waldo. 1904. *The Complete Works of Ralph Waldo Emerson.* 12 vols. Ed. Edward Waldo Emerson. Boston: Houghton Mifflin.

Engstrom, Alfred Garwin. 1965. "Synaesthesia." In *Princeton Encyclopedia of Poetry and Poetics,* ed. Alex Preminger, 839–40. Princeton: Princeton University Press.

Felstiner, John. 1975. *Paul Celan: Poet, Survivor, Jew.* New Haven: Yale University Press.

Foucault, Michel. 1972. *The Archaeology of Knowledge and the Discourse on Language.* Trans. A. M. Sheridan Smith. New York: Pantheon.

Freud, Sigmund. 1963a. *Character and Culture.* Ed. Philip Rieff. New York: Macmillan.

————. 1963b. *Studies in Parapsychology.* New York: Collier.

————. 1975. *Three Essays on the Theory of Sexuality.* Trans. James Strachey. New York: Basic Books.

————. 1989. *The Freud Reader.* Ed. Peter Gay. New York: Norton.

Frost, Robert. 1968. *Selected Prose of Robert Frost.* Ed. Hyde Cox and Edward Connery Lathem. New York: Collier.

————. 1979. *The Poetry of Robert Frost.* Ed. Edward Connery Lathem. New York: Henry Holt.

Frye, Northrop. 1957. *Anatomy of Criticism.* Princeton: Princeton University Press.

Gelpi, Albert, ed. 1985. *Wallace Stevens: The Poetics of Modernism.* Cambridge: Cambridge University Press.

Gioia, Dana, David Mason, and Meg Schoerke, eds. 2004. *Twentieth-Century American Poetics: Poets on the Art of Poetry.* Boston: McGraw Hill.

Godzich, Wlad. 1983. Forward to de Man, *Blindness and Insight.*

Graves, Robert. 1980. *The White Goddess: A Historical Grammar of Poetic Myth.* New York: Farrar.

Griswold, Charles. 2004. "Plato on Rhetoric and Poetry." In *The Stanford Encyclopedia of Philosophy (Spring 2004 Edition),* ed. Edward N. Zalta. http://plato.stanford.edu/archives/spr2004/entries/plato-rhetoric/.

Hanson, Kristin, and Paul Kiparsky. 1997. "The Nature of Verse and its Consequences for the Mixed Form." In *Prosimetrum: Crosscultural Perspectives on Narrative in Prose and Verse,* ed. Joseph Harris and Karl Reichl, 17–44. Cambridge, UK: D. S. Brewer.

Healey, John F. 1998. "The Early Alphabet." In *Reading the Past: Ancient Writing from the Cuneiform to the Alphabet,* intro. J. T. Hooker, 197–258. New York: Barnes and Noble.

Heaney, Seamus. 1980. *Preoccupations: Selected Prose 1968–1978.* New York: Farrar.

————. 1990. *Selected Poems 1966–1987.* New York: Farrar.

Hegel, G.W.F. 1967. *The Phenomenology of Mind.* Trans. J. B. Baillie. New York: Harper.

Hollander, John. 1975. *Vision and Resonance: Two Senses of Poetic Form.* New York: Oxford University Press.

————. 1981. *The Figure of Echo: A Mode of Allusion in Milton and After.* Berkeley: University of California Press.

Homer. 1998. *The Odyssey.* Trans. Robert Fitzgerald. New York: Farrar.

Jakobson, Roman. 1978. *Six Lectures on Sound and Meaning.* Trans. John Mepham. Cambridge: MIT Press.

Jakobson, Roman. 1985. *Verbal Art, Verbal Sign, Verbal Time*. Ed. Krystyna Pomorska and Stephen Rudy. Minneapolis: University of Minnesota Press.

———. 1987. *Language in Literature*. Ed. Krystyna Pomorska and Stephen Rudy. Cambridge: Harvard University Press.

Johnson, Barbara. 2003. *Mother Tongues: Sexuality, Trials, Motherhood, Translation*. Cambridge: Harvard University Press.

Johnson, James William. 1965. "Lyric." In *Princeton Encyclopedia of Poetry and Poetics*, ed. Alex Preminger, 460–70. Princeton: Princeton University Press.

Johnson, W. R. 1982. *The Idea of Lyric: Lyric Modes in Ancient and Modern Poetry*. Berkeley: University of California Press.

Kittler, Friedrich. 1990. "The Mechanized Philosopher." In *Looking After Nietzsche*, ed. Laurence A. Rickels, 195–208. Albany: SUNY Press.

Kristeva, Julia. 1984. *Revolution in Poetic Language*. Trans. Leon S. Roudiez. New York: Columbia University Press.

Kumin, Maxine. 1981. Forward to Sexton, *Complete Poems*.

Lacan, Jacques. 1977. *Ecrits: A Selection*. Trans. Alan Sheridan. New York: Norton.

Lacoue-Labarthe, Philippe. 1988. *Typography: Mimesis, Philosophy, Politics*. Trans. Christopher Fynsk. Stanford: Stanford University Press.

Lanham, Richard A. 1969. *A Handlist of Rhetorical Terms*. Berkeley: University of California Press.

Leclaire, Serge. 1998. *Psychoanalyzing: On the Order of the Unconscious and the Practice of the Letter*. Trans. Peggy Kamuf. Stanford: Stanford University Press.

Lobb, Edward, ed. 1993. *Words in Time: New Essays on Eliot's "Four Quartets."* Ann Arbor: University of Michigan Press.

Longenbach, James. 1991. *Wallace Stevens: The Plain Sense of Things*. New York: Oxford University Press.

Mahoney, Patrick. 1988. "Play, Work, and Beyond." In *The Ear of the Other: Otobiography, Transference, Translation*, ed. Christie McDonald. Lincoln: University of Nebraska Press.

Makin, Peter. 1992. *Pound's Cantos*. Baltimore: Johns Hopkins University Press.

Merrill, James. 1986. *Recitative*. Ed. J. D. McClatchy. San Francisco: North Point.

Middlebrook, Diane Wood. 1992. *Anne Sexton: A Biography*. New York: Random.

Miner, Earl. 1990. *Comparative Poetics*. Princeton: Princeton University Press.

Moore, Marianne. 1982. *The Complete Poems of Marianne Moore*. New York: Penguin.

———. 1987. *The Complete Prose of Marianne Moore*. Ed. Patricia Willis. New York: Penguin.

Nietzsche, Friedrich. [1917?]. *Beyond Good and Evil*. Trans Helen Zimmern. New York: Modern Library.

———. 1956. *The Birth of Tragedy and the Genealogy of Morals*. Trans. Francis Golffing. New York: Doubleday.

———. 1979. *Twilight of the Idols and The Anti-Christ*. Trans. R. J. Hollingsdale. New York: Penguin.

Oughourlian, Jean-Michel. 1991. *The Puppet of Desire: The Psychology of Hysteria, Possession, and Hypnosis*. Trans. Eugene Webb. Stanford: Stanford University Press.

Packard, William, ed. 1974. *The Craft of Poetry: Interviews from the "New York Quarterly."* New York: Doubleday.

Perloff, Marjorie. 1985a. *The Dance of the Intellect*. Cambridge: Cambridge University Press.

———. 1985b. "The Supreme Fiction and the Impasse of Modernist Lyric." In Gelpi, *Wallace Stevens*, 41–64.

Piaget, Jean. 1962. *Play, Dreams and Imitation in Childhood*. Trans. C. Gattegno and F. M. Hodgson. New York: Norton.

———. 1971. *The Child's Conception of Time*. Trans. A. J. Pomerans. New York: Ballantine.

Pindar. *The Odes of Pindar*. 1947. Trans. Richmond Lattimore. Chicago: University of Chicago Press.

Plath, Sylvia. 1981. *The Collected Poems*. Ed. Ted Hughes. New York: Harper.

Plato. 1974. "From the *Republic*." In *Classical and Medieval Literary Criticism*, ed. Alex Preminger, Leon Golden, O. B. Harrison Jr., and Kevin Kerrane, 49–89. New York: Frederick Ungar.

Plimpton, George, ed. 1976. *Writers at Work: "The Paris Review" Interviews*. 4th series. New York: Viking.

Polt, Richard. 1996. "Typology: A Phenomenology of Early Typewriters." *Classic Typewriter Page*. http://staff.xu.edu/~polt/typewriters/typology.html.

Pound, Ezra. 1960. *ABC of Reading*. New York: New Directions.

———. 1968a. *Literary Essays*. Ed. T. S. Eliot. New York: New Directions.

———. 1968b. *The Spirit of Romance*. New York: New Directions.

———. 1970. *Guide to Kulchur*. New York: New Directions.

———. 1971. *Selected Letters 1907–1941*. Ed. D. D. Paige. New York: New Directions.

———. 1975. *Selected Prose, 1909–1965*. Ed. William Cookson. New York: New Directions.

———. 1976. *Collected Early Poems of Ezra Pound*. New York: New Directions.

———. 1998. *The Cantos of Ezra Pound*. New York: New Directions.

———. 1990. *Personae: The Shorter Poems*. Ed. Lea Baechler and A. Walton Litz. New York: New Directions.

Preminger, Alex, and T.V.F. Brogan, eds. 1993. *The New Princeton Encyclopedia of Poetry and Poetics*. New York: MJF Books.

Ransom, John Crowe. 1949. "Poetry: A Note on Ontology." In *Critiques and Essays in Criticism 1920–1948*. ed. Robert Wooster Stallman, 30–46. New York: Ronald Press.

Richards, I. A. 1949. "The Bridle of Pegasus." In *Critiques and Essays in Criticism: 1920–1948*, ed. Robert Wooster Stallman, 289–315. New York: Ronald Press.

Rickels, Laurence. 1990. "Friedrich Nichte." In *Looking After Nietzsche*, ed. Laurence A. Rickels, 137–58. Albany: SUNY Press.

Rolleston, James L. 1989. "The Politics of Quotation: Walter Benjamin's Arcades Project," *PMLA* 104, no. 1 (January).

Saussure, Ferdinand de. *See* Starobinski, Jean.

Sayre, Henry M. 1983. *The Visual Text of William Carlos Williams*. Urbana: University of Illinois Press.

Schwartz, Lloyd, and Sybil Estess, eds. 1983. *Elizabeth Bishop and Her Art*. Ann Arbor: University of Michigan Press.

Sexton, Anne. 1974. Interview with *New York Quarterly*. In *The Craft of Poetry: Interviews from the "New York Quarterly,"* ed. William Packard. New York: Doubleday.

———. 1976. Interview with Barbara Kevles. In Plimpton, *Writers at Work*.

Sexton, Anne. 1977. *Anne Sexton: A Self-Portrait in Letters*. Ed. Linda Gray Sexton and Lois Ames. Boston: Houghton Mifflin.

———. 1981. *The Complete Poems*. Foreword by Maxine Kumin. Boston: Houghton Mifflin.

———. 1985. *No Evil Star: Selected Essays, Interviews, and Prose*. Ed. Steven E. Colburn. Ann Arbor: University of Michigan Press.

Shell, Marc. 1978. *The Economy of Literature*. Baltimore: Johns Hopkins University Press.

Sidney, Sir Philip. 1948. "An Apologie for Poetrie." In *Criticism: The Foundations of Modern Literary Judgment*, ed. Mark Schorer, Josephine Miles, and Gordon McKenzie, 407–31. New York: Harcourt.

Solomon, Maynard, ed. 1979. *Marxism and Art: Essays Classic and Contemporary*. Detroit: Wayne State University Press.

Starobinski, Jean. 1979. *Words Upon Words: The Anagrams of Ferdinand de Saussure*. Trans. Olivia Emmet. New Haven: Yale University Press.

Stern, Daniel N. 1994. "The Sense of a Verbal Self" from *The Interpersonal World of the Infant: A View from Psychoanalysis and Developmental Psychology* (1985). In *The Women and Language Debate*, ed. Camille Roman, Suzanne Juhasz, and Christanne Miller, 199–215. New Brunswick, NJ: Rutgers University Press.

Stevens, Wallace. 1951. *The Necessary Angel*. New York: Vintage.

———. 1954. *The Collected Poems*. New York: Knopf.

———. 1966. *Letters of Wallace Stevens*. Ed. Holly Stevens. Berkeley: University of California Press.

———. 1982. *Opus Posthumous*. Ed. Samuel French Morse. New York: Vintage.

Stewart, Susan. 2002. *Poetry and the Fate of the Senses*. Chicago: University of Chicago Press.

Terrell, Carroll F. 1980. *A Companion to the Cantos of Ezra Pound*. 2 vols. Berkeley: University of California Press.

Todorov, Tzvetan. 1984. *Theories of the Symbol*. Trans. Catherine Porter. Ithaca: Cornell University Press.

Trevarthen, Colwyn. 1994. "Communication and Cooperation in Early Infancy: A Description of Primary Intersubjectivity." In *The Women and Language Debate*, ed. Camille Roman, Suzanne Juhasz, and Christanne Miller, 216–33. New Brunswick, NJ: Rutgers University Press.

Tsur, Reuven. 1992. *What Makes Sound Patterns Expressive? The Poetic Mode of Speech Perception*. Durham: Duke University Press.

Upanishads. 1957. Trans. Swami Prabhavananda and Frederick Manchester. New York: New American Library.

Valéry, Paul. 1961. *The Art of Poetry*. Trans. Denise Folliot. New York: Random.

Waugh, Linda R. 1985. "The Poetic Function and the Nature of Language." In Jakobson 1985, 143–69.

Whitman, Walt. 1973. *Leaves of Grass*. Ed. Sculley Bradley and Harold W. Blodgett. New York: Norton.

Wilhelm, James J. 1977. *The Later Cantos of Ezra Pound*. New York: Walker and Company.

Williams, William Carlos. 1957. *The Selected Letters of William Carlos Williams*. Ed. John C. Thirlwall. New York: New Directions.

———. 1988. *The Collected Poems*. Vol. 2, 1939–1962. Ed. Christopher MacGowan. New York: New Directions.

Wordsworth, William. 1979. *The Prelude: 1799, 1805, 1850*. Ed. Jonathan Wordsworth, M. H. Abrams, and Stephen Gill. New York: Norton.

———. 1981. *The Poems*. 2 vol. Ed. John O. Hayden. New Haven: Yale University Press.

Wright, Charles. 1981. *The Southern Cross*. New York: Random.

Yeats, William Butler. 1989. *The Collected Works of W. B. Yeats*. Ed. Richard J. Finneran. New York: Macmillan.

INDEX